European Yearbook of International Economic Law

Editors
Christoph Herrmann
Jörg Philipp Terhechte

Marc Bungenberg • Jörn Griebel •
Steffen Hindelang
Editors

International Investment Law and EU Law

Springer

Editors
Professor Dr. Marc Bungenberg, L.L.M.
University of Siegen
Economics and Economic Law
Hölderlinstr. 3
57068 Siegen
Germany
marc.bungenberg@gmx.de

Professor Dr. Jörn Griebel, D.E.S.
University of Cologne
International Investment Law
Centre Cologne
Albertus Magnus Platz
50935 Köln
Germany
joern.griebel@uni-koeln.de

Dr. Steffen Hindelang, L.L.M.
Humboldt-University of Berlin
Juristische Fakultät, WHI
Unter den Linden 6
10099 Berlin
Germany
st.hi@gmx.de

ISBN 978-3-642-14854-5 e-ISBN 978-3-642-14855-2
DOI 10.1007/978-3-642-14855-2
Springer Heidelberg Dordrecht London New York

Cover design: WMXDesign GmbH, Heidelberg, Germany

Printed on acid-free paper

Springer is part of Springer Science+Business Media (www.springer.com)

Preface

The entry into force of the Lisbon Treaty entails sweeping changes with respect to foreign investment regulation. Most prominently, the Treaty on the Functioning of the European Union (TFEU) now contains in its Article 207 an explicit competence on the regulation of foreign direct investment as part of the Common Commercial Policy (CCP).

With its new competence the EU will become a new actor in the field of international investment policy and law. Although the Lisbon Treaty solves problems of the past in some policy fields, the new empowerment in the field of international investment law prompts a multitude of questions. *Karel de Gucht* was asked in his parliamentary hearings before being appointed Commissioner for External Trade on his position on the "investment topic". He stated:

> Investment is a completely new competence for DG Trade. . . . We will have to address a lot of issues in this respect, and I suggest that some time soon we should have a follow-up discussion on this matter on the basis of a communication on how the European Commission is going to address it. There are existing investment agreements, by which I mean agreements for protecting investments. . . . First of all we will preserve legal certainty, then we will look closely at what initiatives we should take, and towards which countries. Within our prerogatives with respect to investment, legal certainty for investments in third countries is a main topic that we should certainly address very soon because, for example, it has a lot to do also with energy security. . . .

As this statement of Commissioner *van Gucht* only gave slight indications of what the answers to many of the key questions arising following the shift of competence are, it is the purpose of this volume to analyse in depth the new "post-Lisbon situation" in the area of investment policy, provoke further discussion and offer new approaches. The *"Tübingen Workshop on International Investment Law and EU Law"* of 18 September 2009 – just a little more than 2 months before the entry into force of the Lisbon Treaty – dealt with the most prominent problems resulting from the transfer of competences to the European level. This conference formed the basis of this publication.

The analysis starts off with a contribution by *Steffen Hindelang* und *Niklas Maydell* which does not only reflect on the Union's new explicit competences on foreign investment in a historic perspective, but places it in their broader context, i. e. the interrelations with the fundamental freedoms and other Treaty provisions. Following this, *August Reinisch* and *Marc Bungenberg* discuss the division of competences between the EU and its Member States after the entry into force of the new treaty. *Jörg Philipp Terhechte* und *Markus Burgstaller* proceed with analysing the impact of the shift of competences on the existing net of bilateral investment treaties of the Member States. In this context *Jörg Philipp Terhechte* also deals with the Lisbon decision of the German Constitutional Court in regard to EU and German investment policy.

The possible future of a European investment policy is addressed by *Tillmann R. Braun* und *Carsten Nowak*, who discuss the possible options for a future agreement/future agreements. In his comment *Jörn Griebel* proposes the adoption of a multilateral/plurilateral investment platform as the probably most efficient solution to the problem. Finally, *Lars Markert* and *André von Walter* discuss one of the key questions of a future investment system, the question of how to balance investors' rights with regulatory interests of the host state.

As organizers of the Tübingen Workshop and editors of this volume, we would like to thank Martin Nettesheim and his chair from the University of Tübingen for their kind support in organizing the conference at Tübingen University. Thanks are also due to Gleiss Lutz, Stuttgart, for interest in the topic and the kind financial support. *Albert Alexander Link* from the chair of *Christoph Herrmann* at the University of Passau took care of language editing and the layout of the manuscript of this volume – special thanks to him for this substantial help. We are equally grateful to *Christoph Herrmann* and *Jörg Philipp Terhechte* as well as *Brigitte Reschke* from *Springer* for considering this topic as one of the current "hot topics" in international economic law and accepting it as the first "Special Issue" of the *European Yearbook of International Economic Law*.

Marc Bungenberg
Jörn Griebel
Steffen Hindelang

Contents

Contributors

Tillmann Rudolf Braun currently serves in the Coordination Unit of the Federal Foreign Office, Berlin, Germany. He was Deputy Head, Directorate-General for External Economic Policy, Federal Ministry of Economics and Technology, Berlin, where his professional responsibilities included inter alia negotiating bilateral investment treaties (BITs) on behalf of the German Government. He was a global fellow of practice and government and visiting scholar at New York University School of Law. He studied law in Munich and holds an MPA from Harvard University, Kennedy School of Government, Cambridge, Massachusetts. He has published and lectured on international investment law and on Germany's BITs in German, English and Chinese and is on the scientific board of the International Investment Law Centre Cologne, Germany.

Marc Bungenberg is Professor of Public Law, European Law, Public International Law and International Economic Law at the University of Siegen, Germany. He studied law in Hanover and Lausanne (LL.M. 1995). Marc received a doctorate in law from the University of Hanover, Germany, and his *Habilitation* from the University of Jena, Germany. His main fields of research are European and international economic law (especially the EU Common Commercial Policy , state aid, procurement and international investment law). Marc is Academic Advisor at the International Investment Law Centre Cologne, Germany.

Markus Burgstaller is a Senior Associate in Hogan Lovells' international arbitration practice area in London. He has significant experience in advising both investors and states in international disputes, including arbitrations under ICSID, ICC, LCIA and UNCITRAL rules. He also advises investors on structuring investments worldwide. Before joining Hogan Lovells in 2007, Markus worked as International Legal Advisor to the Austrian Chancellor. Previously, he worked as Assistant Professor at the University of Vienna's Institute of Public International Law and at international law firms in Vienna and Paris. Markus is the author of numerous publications on public international law and European law. He also frequently speaks on his areas of interest at international conferences. In 2008 the Austrian Government nominated Markus to the ICSID Panel of Conciliators. Markus holds an LL.M. degree from New York University, a master's degree in both law and philosophy and a Ph.D. degree in public international law from the University of Vienna. He is qualified as an attorney and counsellor at law in New York and as a solicitor in England and Wales.

Jörn Griebel is Assistant Professor of Public Law, International Law and International Investment Law at the International Investment Law Centre Cologne (University of Cologne). He studied at the University of Cologne and University College London. He gained the qualification *diplôme d'études supérieures* (D.E.S.) from the Institut Universitaire de Hautes Études Internationales (Geneva) and holds a Ph.D. (Dr. jur.) degree from the University of Cologne. Jörn has published in various fields of law, in particular international law and international investment law. His practical experience includes inter alia investment proceedings.

Steffen Hindelang is a Senior Research Associate and Lecturer at Humboldt University Berlin, Germany, Faculty of Law, Walter Hallstein Institute of European Constitutional Law. He is also an academic adviser to the International Investment Law Centre Cologne. Previously, Steffen worked as a Research Associate and lecturer at the Eberhard Karls University Tübingen. He studied law and economics at the universities of Bayreuth, Sheffield and Marburg and holds an LL.M. degree from the University of Sheffield and a Ph.D. degree in law (Dr. iur.) from Eberhard Karls University Tübingen. His research interests and advisory experiences comprise constitutional law; European Union law, especially fundamental freedoms; public international and international economic law, especially international investment law, international arbitration and dispute settlement; and comparative public law. Steffen is a frequent speaker at conferences and seminars on European and public international law. He has authored several publications in English, German and Russian.

Niklas Maydell is an Associate in Cleary Gottlieb's Brussels office. He specializes in EU law and public international law, in particular investment arbitration. Previously, he worked as an Assistant Professor at the Vienna University of Economics and Business, Institute of European and Public International Law and at the European Commission's Directorate-General for External Trade, where he was closely involved in the European Commission's reform of its investment law regime. Niklas is the author of numerous publications on EU and public international law. He also frequently speaks on his areas of interest at international conferences. Niklas holds an LL.M. degree from Columbia University, a Ph.D. (Dr. iur.) degree in public international law from the University of Vienna (Prof. A. Reinisch) and a master's degree in law (Mag. iur.) from the University of Vienna. He also studied law at the University of Urbino in Italy.

Lars Markert is an Associate in the Stuttgart office of Gleiss Lutz. He specializes in international commercial and investment arbitration, cross-border transactions and litigation. He is an academic advisor at the International Investment Law Centre Cologne and frequently publishes on issues of international investment law and arbitration. Lars studied law at the universities of Würzburg and Cologne (Dr. iur). He has also obtained degrees from both the University of Aix-en-Provence (*maîtrise en droit*) and Georgetown University Law Center (LL.M.). He has been admitted to the German and New York bars and is a lecturer on international arbitration and investment law at the University of Speyer.

Carsten Nowak is Professor of Public Law, especially European Union law, at the Europe University Viadrina Frankfurt (Oder), Director of the new Frankfurt Institute for the Law of the European Union (FIREU) and Lecturer at the University of Hamburg/Europa-Kolleg Hamburg (Postgraduate Programme Master of European and European Legal Studies). He studied law at the University of Hamburg, from which he received a doctorate in law and his *Habilitation*. His main fields of research are German and international public law and European law (especially European economic law, fundamental freedoms, competition law, judicial protection and fundamental rights).

August Reinisch is Professor of International and European Law at the University of Vienna and Adjunct Professor at the Bologna Center/SAIS of Johns Hopkins University. He holds master's degrees in philosophy (1990) and in law (1988) as well as a doctorate in law (1991) from the University of Vienna and an LL.M. degree (1989) from NYU Law School. He has widely published on international law, with a recent focus on investment law and the law of international organizations. He currently serves as an arbitrator on the In Rem Restitution Panel according to the Austrian General Settlement Fund Law 2001, dealing with Holocaust-related property claims, and as an arbitrator and expert in a number of investment disputes.

Jörg Philipp Terhechte is Acting Professor for Public Law, European Law and International Economic Law at Leuphana University Lüneburg, Adjunct Professor at Europa-Kolleg Hamburg, Bielefeld University, the State University of Mongolia and the China–Europe School of Law, Beijing, and Visiting Lecturer at the University of the Saarland. He studied law, economics and philosophy and holds a doctoral degree from Bielefeld University. In 2005 and 2006, he was a visiting professor at the US Federal Trade Commission, Washington, DC, and a visiting scholar at the George Washington University Law School as well as at Georgetown Law Center, Institute for International Economic Law, Washington, DC. He is a consultant to the OECD, GTZ, the European Commission, the Hungarian Competition Authority and the Mongolian Competition Authority in Ulaan Bator (Mongolia). His main fields of research are EU law, competition law and international economic law.

André von Walter is a Political Advisor and Negotiator for International Investment and Corporate Social Responsibility at the Ministry of Foreign and European Affairs,

Paris. Previously, he was a Lecturer of public international law and international economic law at the University Paris I Panthéon-Sorbonne (2008–2009) and a Senior Research Fellow at the Institute for Public International Law of the University of Bonn (2003–2008). He holds an LL.M. degree (Université Paris I Panthéon-Sorbonne/University of Cologne) and an MPA from the École Nationale d'Administration, Paris–Strasbourg, France. André has authored numerous publications on international law and international economic law, with an emphasis on international investment law. He is also an academic advisor to the International Investment Law Centre Cologne, a former advisor to the OECD and the IMF and a member of the International Law Association and the European Society of International Law.

The EU's Common Investment Policy – Connecting the Dots

Steffen Hindelang and Niklas Maydell

Introduction

The entry into force of the Treaty of Lisbon has shed light on an area that has widely lacked public attention in recent years: the treatment of investment from non-EU Member State countries, i.e. third countries, under EU law. By explicitly expanding the EU's external competence under the Common Commercial Policy to "foreign direct investment", the Lisbon Treaty has posed two questions which, as we argue in this paper, warrant a holistic view, so far apparently not propagated in the literature.

The Lisbon Treaty revives the question of, first, what is the predetermining framework in which the EU's competences to regulate access and treatment of third-country investment will have to be exercised and, second, what are in fact the EU's internal and external competences with respect to third-country investment. To this end, the present paper combines in its effort to provide a holistic view on what we term the Common Investment Policy (CIP), first, an analysis of the framework preconditioning the exercise of the competence, i.e. primarily the provisions on free movement of capital, and, second, turning to the competences, we will focus on the EU's external competences under Art. 207 of the Treaty on the Functioning of the European Union (TFEU) and its implied external powers based on the case law of the Court of Justice of the European Union (ECJ). Key value is added by putting the Lisbon Treaty's provisions not just in the perspective of the previous EU constitutional order but also by showing how the analytical outcome is indeed determined by the pre-Lisbon legal framework. This historic-systematic approach will ultimately allow us to comprehensively understand the EU's powers

S. Hindelang
Chair of Public, International and European Law, Walter Hallstein Institute of European Constitutional Law, Humboldt University, Berlin, Germany
e-mail: st.hi@gmx.de

N. Maydell
Cleary Gottlieb Steen & Hamilton LLP, Brussels, Belgium
e-mail: nmaydell@cgsh.com

M. Bungenberg et al. (eds.), *International Investment Law and EU Law*,
DOI 10.1007/978-3-642-14855-2_1, © Springer-Verlag Berlin Heidelberg 2011

with respect to third-country investment in all its central aspects and provide the groundwork for those authors and studies focusing on what and how to deal with the EU's "newly old" competence inventory.

Competence and Fundamental Freedom

At first glance one might wonder what the provisions on free movement of capital and those on the CIP have to do with each other, aside from a certain terminological overlap.[1] A closer look reveals, however, that the scope of Art. 63 (1) TFEU (ex-Art. 56 (1) EC) significantly predetermines the basis on which a CIP will operate.

Art. 63 (1) TFEU (ex-Art. 56 (1) EC) contains the freedom of capital movement, which extends in its scope also to third countries. It reads "[. . .] all restrictions on the movement of capital between the Member States and between Member States and third countries shall be prohibited". Although one might think that this wording leaves hardly any room for ambiguity – the scope of the freedom in intra-EU and third-country context being, in principle, the same – the interpretation of this provision in a third-country context can hardly be described as settled in ECJ jurisprudence.[2] Also, views in the legal literature are divided on the scope of free movement of capital in respect of third countries.[3] As there is no agreement on the interpretation of the freedom of capital movement in relation to third countries, the basis on which a currently developing CIP will operate is, hence, burdened with uncertainties: If Art. 63 (1) TFEU (ex-Art. 56 (1) EC) is read as a mere programmatic statement which endeavours to achieve the objective of free movement of capital between the Member States and third countries, the opening up of the EU market to third countries must then be essentially achieved by means of secondary (autonomous) legislation and the conclusion of international treaties, which emblematize the notion of reciprocity. If, however, the scope of Art. 63 (1) TFEU (ex-Art. 56 (1) EC) goes beyond a mere programmatic statement and the freedom transfers subjective rights to a third-country investor similar to those of an intra-EU investor, then the EU would have committed itself not to interfere with – neither to discriminate[4] nor to hinder[5] – the access and operation of investments originating from third countries. The same seems to apply mutatis mutandis for outbound investment.

[1]The jurisprudence and writing in the area of free movement of capital offers valuable guidance on the interpretation of such notions as "direct investment" now also found in Art. 206 et seq. TFEU.

[2]For an overview, see Hindelang, Gestufte Freiheitsverbürgung? – Art. 63 Abs. 1 AEUV (ex-Art. 56 Abs. 1 EG) im Drittstaatenkontext, IStR (2010), pp. 443 et seq.

[3]Summarized and discussed in Hindelang, *The Free Movement of Capital and Foreign Direct Investment: The Scope of Protection in EU Law*, 2009.

[4]Cf., e.g. ECJ, *Test Claimants in the FII Group Litigation/Commissioners of Inland Revenue*, C-446/04, [2006] ECR I, p. 11753.

[5]Cf., in respect of an intra-EU context, for the first time in ECJ, C-367/98, *Commission of the European Communities/Portuguese Republic*, [2002] ECR I, p. 4731 (para. 45).

In this case the EU market would have "automatically" been liberalized unilaterally towards third countries and a CIP would basically be limited to secure market access and favourable treatment standards for EU investments in third countries.

But what would be the appropriate reading of Art. 63 (1) TFEU (ex-Art. 56 (1) EC)? Providing a clear and precise answer to this question faces several challenges. There is, to start with, no clarity on the delineation of free movement of capital and the freedom of establishment with respect to direct investment, an economic activity potentially covered by both freedoms. Uncertainty also exists in regard to the issue of whether the same teleological considerations apply to the interpretation of the freedom's prohibition of any restriction on free capital movement in an intra-EU and a third-country context. Last but not least, a clear picture has yet to emerge on the principles governing the justification of restrictions on the freedom in a third-country context. All these interpretive challenges shall now be addressed in turn.

The Relationship between Free Movement of Capital and the Freedom of Establishment

The relationship between the free movement of capital and the freedom of establishment in respect of direct investment is still a matter of debate. Although direct investment is not mentioned explicitly within Art. 63 (1) TFEU (ex-Art. 56 (1) EC), it is generally accepted that it forms a subcategory of capital movement. Owing to the fact that the notions of establishment and direct investment are not mutually exclusive but overlap to a great extent,[6] the economic activity of direct investment falls generally also within the scope of Art. 49 AEUV (ex-Art. 43 EC)[7]. The follow ing discusses the judicial and literary treatments of this "double topical relevance".

The ECJ's Jurisprudence

What the ECJ today describes as "settled case law" on the relationship of the two freedoms originated from two strands of case law. One strand comprised situations in which the ECJ is ignorant of whether there is, in addition to capital movements, an element of definite control over an undertaking in existence (or vice versa), either because the facts of the case did not hint at such or because the parties concerned simply did not refer to the freedom of establishment or free movement of capital,

[6]Ohler, *Europäische Kapital- und Zahlungsverkehrsfreiheit*, 2002, Art. 56 EC, mn. 120 et seq.; Somewhat more cautious: Tiedje and Troberg, in: *von der Groeben/Schwarze (eds.)*, Art. 43 EC, mn 26 (2003); in respect of shareholdings: J. Lübke, *Der Erwerb von Gesellschaftsanteilen zwischen Kapitalverkehrs- und Niederlassungsfreiheit*, 2006, pp. 210 et seq.

[7]Hindelang, *The Free Movement of Capital and Foreign Direct Investment: The Scope of Protection in EU Law*, 2009, pp. 82 et seq.

respectively. The second strand of judgements implicitly proceeded from the assumption that both freedoms are to be applied in parallel in respect of direct investment.[8]

In more recent decisions, however, the ECJ shifted towards a "centre of gravity" approach which under certain conditions grants, in respect to direct investment, priority to the freedom of establishment over the free movement of capital. Although this is without any significant consequence in terms of protection granted to a market participant in an intra-EU context, in a third-country context, the scope of protection potentially offered by the TFEU is nullified.

The situations in which the freedom of establishment would supersede free movement of capital have yet to be spelled out by the ECJ. There are cases such as *FII Group Litigation,*[9] *Thin Cap Group Litigation,*[10] *Holböck*[11] and – more recently – *Glaxo Welcome*[12] which suggest that the "purpose of the national legislation" – which refers to the intended regulatory ambit or scope of application of the national rule – determines predominantly the applicable freedom, not the actual economic activity pursued by the market participant. If the national measure at issue applies only to those market participants who are in the position to exercise definite influence over their holdings, then the national measure is only measured against the background of the freedom of establishment. As this freedom does not extend to third-country economic activities, a third-country direct investment would be without protection. In contrast, if the national measure applies independently of the size of the holding, both freedoms apply.

Other cases, though, point in a different direction. In *Burda,*[13] *Société de Gestion Industrielle SA,*[14] *Commission v. Italien*[15] and – albeit less clear – in the joined case *Belgische Staat v. KBC Bank NV and Beleggen, Risicokapitaal, Beheer NV v. Belgische Staat*[16] the ECJ focused on the actual economic activity

---

[8]See Hindelang, The EC Treaty's Freedom of Capital Movement as an Instrument of International Investment Law? in: Reinisch/Knahr (eds.), *International Investment Law in Context*, 2008, pp. 43 et seq. with further references.

[9]ECJ, C-446/04, *Test Claimants in the FII Group Litigation/Commissioners of Inland Revenue*, [2006] ECR I, p. 11753 (paras. 36 et seq.).

[10]ECJ, C-524/04, *Test Claimants in the Thin Cap Group Litigation/Commissioners of Inland Revenue*, [2007] ECR I, p. 2107 (para. 27 et seq.); See also ECJ, Case C-492/04, *Lasertec Gesellschaft für Stanzformen mbH/Finanzamt Emmendingen*, [2007] ECR I, p. 3775 (paras. 19 et seq.).

[11]ECJ, Case C-157/05, *Winfried L. Holböck/Finanzamt Salzburg-Land*, [2007] ECR I, p. 4051 (para. 23).

[12]ECJ, C-182/08, *Glaxo Wellcome GmbH & Co./Finanzamt München II*, [2009] ECR I, n.y.p. (paras. 40, 47 et seq.).

[13]ECJ, C-284/06, *Finanzamt Hamburg-Am Tierpark/Burda GmbH*, [2008] ECR I, p. 4571 (paras. 68–73).

[14]ECJ, C-311/08, *Société de Gestion Industrielle (SGI)/Belgian State*, [2010] ECR I, n.y.p. (paras. 23–36).

[15]ECJ, C-531/06, *Commission of the European Communities/Italian Republic*, [2009] ECR I, n.y.p. (paras. 40–42).

[16]ECJ, Joined Cases C-439/07 and C-499/07, [2009] ECR I, n.y.p. (paras. 68–73).

pursued and the degree of influence which a market participant can in fact exercise over its holding.

Aside from the objections in principle which the ECJ's "centre of gravity" approach faces,[17] the present uncertainties in respect of the relationship of two fundamental freedoms – a key area of EU law – leaves behind a vacuum which is filled by national measures that most likely do not carry the most liberal notion. The effectiveness of the freedom is, hence, not only diminished by a doubtful delineation test of free movement of capital and the freedom of establishment but also by its still missing contours.

The Views in the Literature

The literature presents itself in a fragmented state. Two main broad tendencies can be identified: one favouring exclusivity of the freedom of establishment in respect of direct investment[18] and the other pleading parallel applicability of the free movement of capital and the freedom of establishment.[19]

Those views which favour exclusivity encounter, to begin with, one fundamental criticism. Each freedom uniquely covers and protects an aspect of a certain economic activity. Especially, in respect to cross-section economic activities which cannot be detangled into single components,[20] preventing the application of one of the freedoms would mean blending out the uniquely covered economic aspect and potentially exposing it to unjustified discrimination or hindrance. Only the consolidation of the freedoms can prevent such a result and furthers the effectiveness of EU law.[21]

In the event the freedom of capital movements were to become secondary to the freedom of establishment, third-country direct investments would be without any protection, as already explained. Accepting such a result would be contrary to the words and intent of the treaty,[22] which explicitly provides in Art. 63 (1) (ex-Art. 56

---

[17] See Hindelang, *The Free Movement of Capital and Foreign Direct Investment: The Scope of Protection in EU Law*, 2009, pp. 96 et seq.; Hindelang, Gestufte Freiheitsverbürgung? – Art. 63 Abs. 1 AEUV (ex-Art. 56 Abs. 1 EG) im Drittstaatenkontext, IStR (2010), pp. 443 et seq, with further references.

[18] E.g. Schön, Europäische Kapitalverkehrsfreiheit und nationales Steuerrecht, in: Schön (ed.), *Gedächtnisschrift für Brigitte Knobbe-Keuk*, 1997, pp. 743 et seq. (750 et seq.).

[19] E.g. Hindelang, *The Free Movement of Capital and Foreign Direct Investment: The Scope of Protection in EU Law*, 2009, pp. 81 et seq.

[20] Weber, Kapitalverkehr und Kapitalmärkte im Vertrag über die Europäische Union, EuZW (1992), pp. 561 et seq.

[21] See also Hindelang, in: Reinisch/Knahr (eds.), *International Investment Law in Context*, 2008, pp. 43 et seq.

[22] It would go beyond the scope and subject of this paper to set out the economic effects of liberalized capital movements and their benefits for the attainment of the treaty aims in detail. For

(1) EC) for unilateral liberalization of capital movements *erga omnes* without any "cavities" from the scope of application in respect of certain categories of capital movements.[23] The expansion of the protective scope of the provision introduced with the Treaty of Maastricht would be nullified for economic cross-section activities, such as direct investment and, thus, the effectiveness of the fundamental freedom would be clearly limited. Ultimately, it would lead to the odd result that *the protection enjoyed by an investor would be inversely proportionate to the size of his holdings*.[24]

Moreover, the opinions which favour strict exclusivity are difficult to reconcile with the words of the treaty, which confirm in Art. 64 TFEU (ex-Art. 57 EC) that direct investment – largely, as regards the content of the term, overlapping with the notion of establishment found in Art. 49 TFEU (ex-Art. 43 EC) – constitutes a (sub)-category of "capital movement".[25] Also, the nomenclature of the EC Capital Movements Directive,[26] having indicative character under "post-Maastricht law", expressly refers to direct investment as a (sub-)category of capital movement.[27]

Apart from that, the suggested "distinguishing criteria" are largely unfeasible. To delineate the two freedoms by the way of a "centre of gravity" approach is of little practical value but rather helps to create the illusion of resolving delineation problems on a rational basis. This view basically encounters the pitfall of failing to determine clearly what constitutes a direct or indirect impairment with a given freedom when it comes to cross-section activities. The problem of delineation is not resolved but is just "relocated".[28]

It appears, therefore, that the more convincing arguments speak in favour of a parallel application of Art. 49 TFEU (ex-Art. 43 EC) and Art. 63 (1) TFEU (ex-Art. 56 (1) EC) in respect of direct investment.

---

an in depth discussion, see Hindelang, *The Free Movement of Capital and Foreign Direct Investment: The Scope of Protection in EU Law*, 2009, pp. 18 et seq.

[23]Haferkamp, *Die Kapitalverkehrsfreiheit im System der Grundfreiheiten des EG-Vertrages*, 2003, pp. 196 et seq.

[24]Case C-251/98 (Opinion of A.G. Alber), [2000] ECR I, p. 2787 (para. 50).

[25]Rohde, *Freier Kapitalverkehr in der Europäischen Gemeinschaft*, 1999, p. 97; Müller, *Kapitalverkehrsfreiheit in der Europäischen Union*, 2000, p. 193; Haferkamp, *Die Kapitalverkehrsfreiheit im System der Grundfreiheiten des EG-Vertrages*, 2003, p. 195.

[26]Annex I, Heading I of Directive 88/361/EEC.

[27]Ibid., at Annex I (I); See also, e.g. Kiemel, in: von der Groeben/ Schwarze (eds.), *EUV/EGV*, 2003, Art. 56 EC mn. 21.

[28]Ohler, *Europäische Kapital- und Zahlungsverkehrsfreiheit*, 2002, Art. 56 EC mn. 117; Weber, Kapitalverkehr und Kapitalmärkte im Vertrag über die Europäische Union, EuZW 3 (1992), pp. 561 et seq. (564); Case C-452/04 (Opinion of A.G. Stix-Hackl), [2006] ECR I, p. 9521 (para. 62).

The Scope of Prohibition of Restriction – Equal Treatment and Market Access

Jurisprudence

Although free movement of capital takes part in the broader context of converging tendencies of construction among the fundamental freedoms – i.e. Art. 63 (1) TFEU (ex-Art. 56 (1) EC) contains, besides a prohibition of discrimination, also one of hindrance[29] – the ECJ has failed so far to put forward a coherent doctrinal construction of Art. 63 (1) TFEU's (ex-Art. 56 (1) EC) scope of prohibition of restriction in a third-country context.

In more recent decisions the ECJ, in a rather formulaic fashion, has reiterated with respect to the prohibition of discrimination in a third-country context that one has to take into account *the fact that movement of capital to or from third countries takes place in a different legal context from that which occurs within the European Community. Accordingly, because of the degree of legal integration that exists between Community Member States*[30] intra-EU economic activities and such activities involving relations between Member States and third countries are not always comparable. Precise criteria for determining the comparability of third-country and intra-EU capital movements remain in the dark.

Doctrinal Construction of Art. 63 (1) TFEU (ex-Art. 56 (1) EC)

If one seeks to describe the scope of prohibition of Art. 63 (1) TFEU (ex-Art. 56 (1) EC) in a third-country context, the wording of the provision can serve as a starting point. Art. 63 (1) TFEU (Art. 56 (1) EC) provides unambiguously just one rule for both intra-EU and third-country capital movement, speaking in favour of an understanding in a third-country context that does not deviate from the one valid for intra-EU capital movement.

Teleological and systematic arguments advanced by commentators[31] who would like to interpret the scope of prohibition of Art. 63 (1) TFEU (Art 56(1) EC) more narrowly in a third-country context are ultimately not compelling. In particular, the proposition that certain preconditions are still lacking, which, only if they were

---

[29]See Hindelang, *The Free Movement of Capital and Foreign Direct Investment: The Scope of Protection in EU Law*, 2009, pp. 115 et seq.

[30]ECJ, Joined Cases C-439/07 and C-499/07, [2009] ECR I, n.y.p. (para. 72).

[31]E.g. Schön, Der Kapitalverkehr mit Drittstaaten und das internationale Steuerrecht, in: Gocke/ et al. (eds.), *Festschrift für Franz Wassermeyer*, 2005, pp. 489 et seq.; Ståhl, Free movement of capital between Member States and third countries, EC Tax Review 13 (2004) 2, pp. 47 et seq.

fulfilled would justify interpreting the scope of prohibition similarly in an intra-EU and a third-country context,[32] cannot be upheld:

The unilateral liberalization of capital movements between the EU and third countries would not only be justified if the EU wanted to make an "altruistic" contribution to the advancement of a liberalized world capital market at large – although there is evidence in the TFEU that the EU indeed could have wanted this – but the EU itself benefits. Liberalized capital movement with third countries, for example, furthers economic growth within the EU by intensified competition, increased freedom of choice, especially for European capital recipients, and pressure on the Member States to maintain fiscal and tariff discipline. Liberalized capital movement *erga omnes* is also necessary to build up and maintain trust in the common currency, which is intended to live up to it being a global investment, financing, trade and reserve currency. The *erga omnes* principle can be seen as one of the clearest affirmations of the EU's commitment to a non-protectionist, open market economy, disproving any notion of a "Fortress Europe". Therefore, the unilateral liberalization of capital movements *erga omnes* advances those treaty aims that are directed at the development of the Internal Market.[33]

Moreover, liberalizing capital movements in third-country relations, economically speaking, requires – in the sense of a *conditio sine qua non* – neither the harmonization of third-country and Internal Market rules nor the coordination of monetary and economic policies between the EU and third countries. However, aiming at some degree of harmonization or coordination is desirable. It is also ultimately not convincing to argue that the bargaining powers of the EU vis-à-vis third countries are not sufficient to press for reciprocal market access and equal treatment of EU capital in third-country markets. Thus, the configuration of the EU competences (especially Art. 64 (2) TFEU (ex-Art. 57(2) EC), Art. 66 TFEU (ex-Art. 59 EC), Art. 75 TFEU (ex-Art. 60 EC), Art. 113, 114, 115 and 352 TFEU (ex-Art. 93 EC, and 94 EC together with Arts. 95 (2) EC and 308 EC) as well as Art. 207 (2) TFEU) are not of such a kind as to describe the EU as not sufficiently equipped to defend its and its Member States' interests. Protecting EU and Member State interests, therefore, does not require making liberalization of third-county capital movement subject to reciprocity.

Moreover, restricting third-country capital movement would not meaningfully prevent the access of third-country investors to the Internal Market, but the circumvention of restrictive access regimes in some Member States is caused by the so-called channel phenomenon. The "channel phenomenon", i.e. more-liberal-minded Member States functioning as "access channels" to the Internal Market for third-country capital movements that less-liberal-minded Member States wished to have

[32]Schön, Der Kapitalverkehr mit Drittstaaten und das internationale Steuerrecht, in: Gocke/et al. (eds.), *Festschrift für Franz Wassermeyer*, 2005, pp. 489 et seq. (502 et seq.); Mohamed, *European Community Law on the Free Movement of Capital and the EMU*, 1999, pp. 217 et seq.

[33]Hindelang, *The Free Movement of Capital and Foreign Direct Investment: The Scope of Protection in EU Law*, 2009, pp. 173 et seq.

excluded or otherwise restricted, is caused by the way in which the other fundamental freedoms operate.[34]

Concerning the non-discrimination test, a distinction has to be made between case-specific considerations and those that we have termed "value-based decisions stipulated by the EU legal order". The former can always lead to a negation of the comparability of domestic/intra-EU and third-country direct investments. With respect to the latter, however, we cannot identify "value-based decisions" that would suggest incomparability per se. Arguments based on existing differences between a Member State and a third country on the level of taxation, social contributions, labour costs, etc. or the existence of intra-EU harmonization cannot form the basis for "value-based decisions" and are, thus, unsuitable to justify the negation of "comparability". Consequences springing from the unilateral opening of the EU capital market to the world have to be borne in the same way as in an intra-EU context.[35]

This interpretation leaves us with the following picture: the access, exit and transit of third-country capital must, in principle, be free of any restrictions. Once a third country investment has been made within the Internal Market (inbound) or an investment originating from a Member State has been established in a third-country market (outbound), the Member States are not allowed to treat that investment less favourably than a comparable domestic investment or an investment from another Member State. Hence, the scope of prohibition of Art. 63 (1) TFEU (ex-Art 56(1) EC) in a third-country context should be interpreted along the same lines as that developed for intra-EU capital movement.

Exceptions to the Freedom

The exceptions to the freedom of capital movement split in two groups: those exceptions which apply to intra-EU and third-country capital movements alike, and those that exclusively relate to third-country capital movement.

Art. 65 (1) lit. b. TFEU (ex-Art 58(1) lit. b EC) forms the only written exception applicable to intra-EU and third-country situations within the treaty chapter on free movement of capital. Supported by the wording and the existence of specific exceptions to third-country capital movements by which the treaty drafters expressly indicated those situations in which they wished to make a distinction between intra-EU and third-country capital movement, Art. 65 (1) lit. b. TFEU (ex-Art. 58(1) lit. b EC) must, in principle, be interpreted in the same way irrespective of whether intra-EU or third-country capital movements are involved. The lack of persuasiveness of teleological and systematic considerations, such as the purported

[34] Hindelang, *The Free Movement of Capital and Foreign Direct Investment: The Scope of Protection in EU Law*, 2009, pp. 181 et seq.

[35] Ibid. 183 et seq.

"limited purpose" pursued by the liberalization of third-country capital movements or missing harmonization with third countries, prohibits an across-the-board treatment of such capital movements within the ambit of this provision. In particular, third-country capital movement does not constitute a general danger of infringement of national rules and regulations. Furthermore, the economic activity of direct investment in a third-country context does not per se constitute a threat to public policy or public security. The economic sectors in which public security concerns were recognized by the ECJ as legitimate are identical in an intra-EU and a third-country context.[36]

Possible differences between intra-EU and third-country capital movements are best considered in the balancing process taking place within the proportionality test. However, under the given conditions it is unclear why the ECJ should significantly deviate from the guidelines informing the application of the proportionality test developed in an intra-EU context. Concerning effective fiscal supervision, the Member States must resort first to international treaties concluded between the respective Member State and a third country to gain the information needed before restricting the freedom. Even if the means available under international law prove insufficient in the individual case, the market participant should first be given the opportunity to provide the information itself before recourse is taken to additional national restrictive measures.[37]

National measures that restrict foreign direct investment on the basis of the *ordre public* exception must fulfil the same high standards in terms of predictability, transparency and due process as are applicable in an intra-EU context. This is because, in principle, the threat posed does not differ depending on the origin or destination of the capital movement.

The "rule of reason" also applies in a third-country context. Its interpretation does not vary depending on whether the capital movement relates to another Member State or to a third country, but may follow in a third-country context the same lines that have been drawn by the ECJ for intra-EU capital movement. In particular, no across-the-board judgements penalizing third-country capital movements shall be applied, but the mandatory requirement pursued with a national measure and the freedom of capital movements have to be balanced carefully on a case-by-case basis. Sufficient argumentative support for the view which suggested interpreting accepted mandatory requirements, such as "fiscal cohesion", differently depending on the geographical mapping cannot be identified as missing reciprocity in a third-country context is not a valid argument. On the basis of the *telos* and systematic of the treaty, the unilateral liberalization of free movement of capital *erga omnes* is to be perceived as unconditional. Ultimately, missing reciprocity is not an argument for a restriction of third-country capital movement,

[36]Hindelang, *The Free Movement of Capital and Foreign Direct Investment: The Scope of Protection in EU Law*, 2009, pp. 216 et seq., 236 et seq.

[37]Hindelang, *The Free Movement of Capital and Foreign Direct Investment: The Scope of Protection in EU Law*, 2009, pp. 242 et seq.; different view: ECJ, Case C-101/05, *Skatteverket*, [2007] ECR I, p. 11531, para. 63.

but the very consequence of this unilateral act. Thus, the introduction of mandatory requirements pursuing budgetary purposes also based on "lacking reciprocity" in a third-country context must be rejected. Closely related to the "lacking reciprocity" argument is that of "lacking harmonization" in a third-country context, which also cannot form a valid plea to restrict third-country capital movement.[38]

Evaluation

If one is prepared to accept that Art. 63 (1) TFEU (ex-Art. 56 (1) EU) unilaterally liberalizes capital movements between the EU and third countries basically on the same terms as within the EU, then a CIP is limited essentially to secure market access and favourable treatment standards for EU investments in third countries. Secondary legislation liberalizing market access which exists, for example, in the area of free movement of goods[39] would not be necessary in the ambit of free movement of capital. Meaningful harmonization is conceivable in respect of Member State legislation on market access of third-country investment which is currently rather heterogeneous. Also useful could be a regulation roughly modelled on the "Trade Barriers Regulation",[40] which could offer some means of defence against third-country access restrictions on investment from the EU. Moreover, an empowerment of the European (Commission) to unilaterally restrict third-country investment into the EU on a temporary basis could increase the bargaining power of the EU towards third countries in the course of pushing for market access rights.

However, if one takes the current "sovereignty-oriented jurisprudence" of the ECJ in respect of third-country capital movements as a basis, then the function of secondary legislation and international agreements shifts basically from accompanying to allowing for liberalization. Although the "sovereignty-oriented jurisprudence" of the ECJ affects primarily the "initial situation" in the area of direct investments owing to the ECJ's doubtful delineation of free movement of capital and the freedom of establishment, third-country portfolio investments are also struck – albeit to a lesser extent – by the ECJ's restrictive understanding of the scope of application of the freedom of capital movement and the expanding reading of applicable exceptions to the freedom in a third-country context.

On a factual basis, Member States in the Council are "re-empowered" to decide on the level of openness of the EU Internal Market in respect of foreign direct investment; a situation which by and large existed prior to the entry into force of the Maastricht Treaty.

---

[38]Hindelang, The EC Treaty's Freedom of Capital Movement as an Instrument of International Investment Law?, in: Reinisch/Knahr (eds.), *International Investment Law in Context*, 2008, pp. 43 et seq. (255 et seq.).

[39]Regulation (EC) No. 260/2009 of 26.02.2009, OJ L 84 of 31.3.2009, p. 1; Regulation (EC) No. 1061/2009 of 19.10.2009, OJ L 291 of 07.11.2009, p. 1.

[40]Regulation (EC) No. 3286/94 of 22.12.1994, OJ L 349 of 31.12.1994, p. 71.

The EU's External Competences in the Area of International Investment Law

The EU's Investment Competences pre-Lisbon as the Key to its post-Lisbon Competence Conglomerate

The EU's competence for conclusion of international agreements on investment before the entry into force of the Lisbon Treaty is not only of interest from a historical perspective, but is equally relevant today after entry into force of the Lisbon Treaty.[41] Indeed, one can only fully understand today's reach of EU competences in the area of international investment regulation if one properly grasps the concepts of implied shared external EU competence established before the entry into force of the Lisbon Treaty. This is particularly true for the EU's external, i.e. treaty-making powers, as opposed to its internal (autonomous) competence, which is not discussed in this paper.[42]

In the context of EU investment competences, it seems commonly accepted in the literature that the EU has – after the entry into force of the Lisbon Treaty – (explicit) exclusive competence to conclude international agreements on foreign direct investment. This is enshrined in Art. 207 TFEU (ex-Art. 133 EC).[43] Dispute remains, however, in how far, if at all, this EU competence also includes portfolio investments, the other major type of investment next to direct investment. This question is of particular importance as almost all bilateral investment treaties

---

[41]For an analysis of the EU's competences before the entry into force of the Lisbon Treaty, see Maydell, *The European Community's Competence to Conclude International Agreements on Investment - Revealing the Inconvenient Truth*, Vienna 2008, available at the Austrian National Library Vienna (Österreichischen Nationalbibliothek Wien) and the University Library of the Vienna University School of Law (Universitätsbibliothek der Rechtswissenschaftlichen Fakultät Wien).

[42]For a discussion of the EU's internal competences regarding foreign investment, see Hindelang/Maydell, Die Gemeinsame Europäische Investitionspolitik – Alter Wein in neuen Schläuchen? in: Bungenberg/Griebel/Hindelang (eds.), *Internationaler Investitionsschutz und Europarecht*, 2010, pp. 11 et seq., pp 71 et seq.

[43]Art. 207 (1) TFEU under Title II *Common Commercial Policy* reads: *The common commercial policy shall be based on uniform principles, particularly with regard to changes in tariff rates, the conclusion of tariff and trade agreements relating to trade in goods and services, and the commercial aspects of intellectual property, foreign direct investment, the achievement of uniformity in measures of liberalisation, export policy and measures to protect trade such as those to be taken in the event of dumping or subsidies. The common commercial policy shall be conducted in the context of the principles and objectives of the Union's external action.* Emphasis added. Art. 3 (1) (e) confers exclusivity on the EU's investment competence: *The Union shall have exclusive competence in the following areas: (...) (e) common commercial policy.* On views in the literature regarding the EU's investment competence under Art. 207 TFEU, see, for instance, Tietje, *Die Außenwirtschaftsverfassung der EU nach dem Vertrag von Lissabon*, Beiträge zum Transnationalen Wirtschaftsrecht, Heft 83, January 2009, p. 13; Eilmansberger, Bilateral Investment Treaties and EU Law, CMLR 46 (2009), pp. 383 et seq. (394).

(BITs) currently in force between EU Member States and third countries embrace both direct and portfolio investment. In other words, if the EU only had competence to conclude international agreements on foreign direct investment, it would not be capable of concluding agreements according to the commonly accepted international standard. Indeed, any new agreement concluded by the EU, unless concluded together with the Member States (mixed agreement), could and would necessarily lag behind the level of investment protection afforded by BITs today.

As will be argued in this paper, the EU continues to have implied non-exclusive, i.e. shared, competence[44] to conclude international agreements relating not just to foreign direct investment, but also to portfolio investment. Therefore, the EU will be competent, based on its explicit exclusive competence in Art. 207 TFEU for foreign direct investment and its implied shared competence for portfolio investment, to conclude international agreements providing for the standard commonly seen in today's BITs without any Member States' involvement.[45] For such a conclusion to be reached, the following analytical sequence shall be followed. First, it shall be discussed whether implied external competences still exist after the entry into force of the Lisbon Treaty and, if so, under which standard allowing for their exercise. Second, the conditions for exercising implied shared competences shall be more closely studied in light of most recent case law and, third, a comprehensive understanding of how implied shared EU competences cover portfolio investment commonly found in today's EU Member States' BITs shall be developed.

Implied Competences – The Quest for Their Existence After the Entry into Force of the Lisbon Treaty

According to the ECJ's long-standing case law and as the name already implies, the central characteristic of implied competences is that this type of competences is, or at least was, not explicitly laid down in EU primary law. This competence has only been developed by case law, in regard to both its existence as well as its requirements for exercise.[46] We will, thus, analyse in the first place whether or not, and if so, in how far, this changed owing to the Lisbon Treaty. As a starting point, we should look at the two key provisions newly introduced by the Lisbon Treaty in this regard. Both Art. 3 (2) TFEU and Art. 216 (1) TFEU did not exist in the Treaty establishing the European Community, the predecessor treaty of the TFEU, and

---

[44]Art. 2 (2) TFEU now defines the EU's non-exclusive competence as "shared competence": *When the Treaties confer on the Union a competence shared with the Member States in a specific area, the Union and the Member States may legislate and adopt legally binding acts in that area. The Member States shall exercise their competence to the extent that the Union has not exercised its competence. The Member States shall again exercise their competence to the extent that the Union has decided to cease exercising its competence.* Emphasis added.

[45]Whether this is politically desirable and/or feasible is not part of the legal assessment undertaken in this paper.

[46]Schmalenbach, in: Calliess/Ruffert (eds.), *EUV/EGV*, (3. ed.) 2007, Art. 300, mn. 19.

both provisions deal with implied competences. These two provisions are key to understanding the concept of implied competences after the entry into force of the Lisbon Treaty. Art. 3 (2) TFEU reads: *The Union shall also have exclusive competence for the conclusion of an international agreement when its conclusion is provided for in a legislative act of the Union or is necessary to enable the Union to exercise its internal competence, or in so far as its conclusion may affect common rules or alter their scope.* Art. 216 (1) TFEU almost identically states that: *The Union may conclude an agreement with one or more third countries or international organizations where the Treaties so provide or where the conclusion of an agreement is necessary in order to achieve, within the framework of the Union's policies, one of the objectives referred to in the Treaties, or is provided for in a legally binding Union act or is likely to affect common rules or alter their scope.* The interplay between these two provisions raises a multitude of questions, in particular in how far Art. 216 (1) TFEU goes beyond Art. 3 (2) TFEU in terms of competence reach and why Art. 216 (1) TFEU is partly identical with Art. 3 (2) TFEU and partly very similarly phrased, most likely leading to the same result. *In so far as its conclusion may affect common rules or alter their scope* (Art. 3 (2) TFEU) most likely has the same meaning as the subsentence of Art. 216 (1) TFEU, which reads as follows: *is likely to affect common rules or alter their scope.* And other, very narrow parts of Art. 216 (1) TFEU have a roughly similar phrasing but with most likely a different outcome: *is necessary to enable the Union to exercise its internal competence* (Art. 3 (2) TFEU) most likely has a meaning different from that of *is necessary in order to achieve, within the framework of the Union's policies, one of the objectives referred to in the Treaties* (Art. 216 (1) TFEU).

Despite these and other unclear points in the relationship between these two articles, this paper follows the apparently prevailing doctrine that Art. 216 (1) TFEU gives the EU external competence without defining its nature and only becomes exclusive when the requirements of Art. 3 (2) TFEU are fulfilled. The nature of Art. 216 (1) TFEU, thus, becomes only clear in the interplay with Art. 3 (2) TFEU, namely that Art. 216 (1) TFEU always provides the EU with exclusive external competence if its wording is identical with that of or has the same meaning as Art. 3 (2) TFEU. This in turn means that Art. 216 (1) TFEU generally establishes exclusive competence, as the meaning of Art. 216 (1) TFEU and that of Art. 3 (2) TFEU are almost identical or are the same. External competence is only non-exclusive, i.e. shared, *where the conclusion of an agreement is necessary in order to achieve, within the framework of the Union's policies, one of the objectives referred to in the Treaties.* Most likely, this represents the only part of Art. 216 (1) TFEU which is not covered by Art. 3 (2) TFEU as Art. 216 (1) speaks of *objectives referred to in the Treaties*, whereas Art. 3 (2) TFEU refers to *internal competences*, two different legal terms in the TFEU.

On the basis of this diagnosis, one can assume that Art. 216 (1) TFEU together with Art. 3 (2) TFEU confers exclusive as well as shared external competences on the EU. This, in turn, leads to the crucial question of this paper, namely in how far these two newly included provisions in EU primary law affect, i.e. codify, and, thus, alter or terminate, the existence of implied external competences as developed by the ECJ over the course of the four past decades. To answer this question, we will take a brief look at implied exclusive competences first and subsequently undertake a more thorough analysis of implied shared competences and the impact of Art. 216 (1) TFEU and Art. 3 (2) TFEU on these two categories of implied competences.

This paper will conclude that Art. 216 (1) TFEU in connection with Art. 3 (2) TFEU codifies the ECJ's case law with respect to implied exclusive competences but does not codify or otherwise affect implied shared competences. As will be shown below, this follows from an ECJ case law analysis and the understanding of the only shared competence under Art. 216 (1) TFEU, namely the conferral of explicit shared competence on the EU *where the conclusion of an agreement is necessary in order to achieve, within the framework of the Union's policies, one of the objectives referred to in the Treaties*. This provision represents nothing more than, in accordance with the rephrasing under the Lisbon Treaty of Art. 352 TFEU (ex-Art. 308 EC), the extension of the competence sweeping clause of ex-Art. 308 EC from internal to external matters.[47] And, importantly, this clause already existed when the ECJ developed and refined its implied competence doctrine and has continuously existed since then.

Implied Exclusive Competence After the Entry into Force of the Lisbon Treaty

As already indicated, Art. 216 (1) TFEU together with Art. 3(2) TFEU clearly codifies what has been developed by the ECJ and is commonly known in the literature as implied exclusive competence. This is the case as Art. 216 (1) TFEU together with Art. 3(2) TFEU contains the same language and substance and stipulates the same conditions for when exclusive competence exists as was developed by the ECJ. The ECJ-developed *acquis communautaire* on the EU's implied *exclusive* competence before the entry into force of the Lisbon Treaty can be summarized as follows:

[47]With respect to the concept of the competence sweeping clause, see Winkler, in: Grabitz/Hilf (eds.), *Kommentar zum EGV*, (EL 34 January) 2008, Art. 308 EGV, para. 11. Art. 352 (1) TFEU reads: *If action by the Union should prove necessary, within the framework of the policies defined in the Treaties, to attain one of the objectives set out in the Treaties, and the Treaties have not provided the necessary powers, the Council, acting unanimously on a proposal from the Commission and after obtaining the consent of the European Parliament, shall adopt the appropriate measures*. Emphasis added. Ex-Art. 308 EC was limiting the competence sweeping clause to the EU's internal sphere (compare emphasis): *If action by the Community should prove necessary to attain, in the course of the operation of the common market, one of the objectives of the Community, and this Treaty has not provided the necessary powers, the Council shall, acting unanimously on a proposal from the Commission and after consulting the European Parliament, take the appropriate measures*.

1. First, the EU has implied exclusive competences if and as far as the EU has already adopted internal rules in a certain field.[48] Also, the conclusion of international agreements constitutes internal rules in that sense through the necessary internal act of adoption. Regularly, this is the case with internal (full) harmonization measures.[49] They automatically render an internal competence exclusive and do not require any affecting test. As far as only minimum standard legislation is concerned, it appears to be necessary to assess whether the international agreement at stake could indeed affect and, thus, render less effective these internal rules.[50]
2. Second, even though an internal legislation does not fully cover a certain subject area of the treaty, the EU can nevertheless claim implied exclusive competence if that subject area is largely (and not necessarily entirely) covered by EU rules with a perspective of additional internal harmonization in the future. It remains unclear how exactly "largely covered" is to be interpreted and to what extent the adoption of future legislation must be certain. As regards the ECJ's case law, this competence category has been applied within Opinion 2/91-ILO.[51]
3. Third, the EU has exclusive competence if this is explicitly enshrined in EU secondary legislation. This is the case where internal legislation provides for the conclusion of international agreements in that field and/or which includes provisions on the treatment of third-state nationals, be they natural or legal persons.[52]
4. Fourth, the EU has implied exclusive external competence in a certain subject area when and insofar that this is necessary to make effective use of the respective internal competence.[53] This requires that the internal competence must cover the same field as the external one and that the use of the implied

---

[48]ECJ, Opinion 2/92, OECD, [1995] ECR I, p. 521: *(...) the Member States, whether acting individually or collectively, only lose their right to enter into obligations with non-member countries as and when there are common rules which could be affected by such obligations.*

[49]Gilsdorf, Die Außenkompetenzen der EG im Wandel, EuR (1996), p. 149.

[50]Louis, La Cour et les Relations extérieures de la Communauté, CDE 42 (2006), pp. 285 et seq. (287).

[51]ILO Opinion, mn. 25: *While there is no contradiction between these provisions of the Convention and those of the directives mentioned, it must nevertheless be accepted that Part III of Convention No 170 is concerned with an area which is already covered to a large extent by Community rules progressively adopted since 1967 with a view to achieving an ever greater degree of harmonization (...).*

[52]ECJ, Opinion 1/94, WTO, [1994] ECR I, p. 5267, para. 95; and ECJ, Opinion 2/92, OECD, [1995] ECR I, p. 521, para. 33.

[53]ECJ, Opinion 1/76,. [1977] ECR, p. 741, para. 4; ECJ, Opinion 1/94, WTO, [1994] ECR I, p. 5267, para. 87; Open Skies, paras. 56 et seq. For a summary, see ECJ, Opinion 2/92, OECD, [1995] ECR I, p. 521: *It is true that, as the Court stated in Opinion 1/76, the external competence based on the Community's internal powers may be exercised, and thus become exclusive, without any internal legislation having first been adopted. However, this relates to a situation where the conclusion of an international agreement is necessary in order to achieve Treaty objectives which cannot be attained by the adoption of autonomous rules.*

external competence must serve one of the objectives underlying the respective internal provision. In addition, the implied external competence can only be established if the effective exercise of the corresponding internal competence cannot be guaranteed by "concerted action" of the Member States or by autonomous internal EU legislation.[54]

From the above case law analysis one can clearly see that Art. 216 (1) TFEU together with Art. 3 (2) TFEU indeed codify the ECJ's case law on implied *exclusive* competences. The first and second implied competence categories – possible impact on already existing secondary legislation – is now covered in Art. 216 (1) TFEU by stating *is likely to affect common rules or alter their scope* and by Art. 3 (2) TFEU by stating *in so far as its conclusion may affect common rules or alter their scope*. Art. 3 (2) TFEU's part *when its conclusion is provided for in a legislative act of the Union* and Art. 216 (1) TFEU's part *is provided for in a legally binding Union act* correspond to above third category of case law. The fourth category is enshrined in Art. 3 (2) TFEU's *is necessary to enable the Union to exercise its internal competence*. To conclude, Art. 3 (2) TFEU and partially Art. 216 (1) TFEU codify the ECJ's case law on implied exclusive external competences. They do not go beyond what has been developed by the ECJ and the ECJ's case law, thus, will also in the future continue to be a helpful and legitimate guide when interpreting Art. 3 (2) TFEU and Art. 216 (1) TFEU.

Existence and Requirements for the Exercise of Implied Shared Competences Before the Entry into Force of the Lisbon Treaty

Although there has been a lot of discussion in the past on whether implied shared external EU competences exist at all, this seems to be undisputedly answered in the positive, at least since the ECJ's Lugano Opinion.[55] The Lugano Opinion was the ECJ's answer to a request as to the "exclusive or shared" competence of the EU to conclude the Convention on Jurisdiction and the Recognition and Enforcement of Judgements in Civil and Commercial Matters, in short, the Lugano Convention.[56] It, therefore, had been explicitly asked to speak out also on shared (read

[54]Koutrakos, *EU International Relations Law*, 2006, pp. 113 and 125. Since no internal legislation must have been released before, this competence category is the only quasi-parallel within implied exclusive competences. It is only quasi-parallel since the necessity test applies. See, for instance, Lenaerts/Van Nuffel, *Constitutional Law of the European Union*, 2005, p. 858.

[55]For an extensive discussion on this competence category's proof of existence, also in addition to the Lugano Opinion, and a related discussion in literature, see Maydell, The European Community's Minimum Platform on Investment or the Trojan Horse of Investment Competence, in: Reinisch/Knahr (eds.), *International Investment Law in Context*, 2008, p. 84.

[56]Opinion 1/03, Lugano Convention, [2006] ECR I, p. 1145, para. 134: *The request for an opinion does not concern the actual existence of competence of the Community to conclude the agreement envisaged, but whether that competence is exclusive or shared.*

"non-exclusive") competences, in decisive contrast to earlier cases, such as the WTO Opinion or the Open Skies case law.[57] The relevant paragraphs are worth quoting in full:

> The competence of the Community to conclude international agreements may arise not only from an express conferment by the Treaty but may equally flow implicitly from other provisions of the Treaty and from measures adopted, within the framework of those provisions, by the Community institutions (see ERTA, paragraph 16). The Court has also held that whenever Community law created for those institutions powers within its internal system for the purpose of attaining a specific objective, the Community had authority to undertake international commitments necessary for the attainment of that objective even in the absence of an express provision to that effect (Opinion 1/76, paragraph 3, and Opinion 2/91, paragraph 7).
>
> <u>That competence of the Community may be exclusive or shared with the Member States.</u> As regards exclusive competence, the Court has held that the situation envisaged in Opinion 1/76 is that in which internal competence may be effectively exercised only at the same time as external competence (see Opinion 1/76, paragraphs 4 and 7, and Opinion 1/94, paragraph 85), the conclusion of the international agreement being thus necessary in order to attain objectives of the Treaty that cannot be attained by establishing autonomous rules (see, in particular, Commission v Denmark, paragraph 57).[58]

That competence in the first line of the second paragraph must be understood to refer only to implied competences since it is them the ECJ discussed in the preceding paragraph. Thus, there is an unambiguous statement on the existence of implied shared competences.[59] The remainder of the second paragraph, and of the judgement as a whole, is concerned with exclusive powers and finds the EU alone competent for concluding the Lugano Convention.[60] There was, consequently, no need and occasion for the ECJ to declare further on shared competences, especially on the requirements for the exercise of this competence type.

In theory, two alternative assumptions may possibly be made. First, the EU has an implied shared external competence whenever and wherever it has an internal shared competence to act. This goes under the term "parallelism" or *in foro interno, in foro externo*.[61] This alternative has been dismissed by the ECJ. Indeed, contrary

---

[57]Opinion 1/94, WTO, [1994] ECR I, p. 5267, para. 1, and Case C-467/98, *Commission/Denmark (Open Skies)*, [2002] ECR I, p. 9519, para. 1.

[58]Opinion 1/03, Lugano Convention, [2006] ECR I, p. 1145, paras. 114 and 115. Emphasis added.

[59]This has also been noted by Cremona, *External Relations of the EU and the Member States: Competence, Mixed Agreements, International Responsibility and Effects of International Law*, 2006, p. 2, and not mentioned by Lavranos, Annotation to Opinion 1/03, CML Rev. 43 (2006), pp. 1087 et seq.

[60]See Opinion 1/03, Lugano Convention, [2006] ECR I, p. 1145, para. 173. The ambiguity observed regarding the Opinions 1/94 and 2/91 as to the result (mixity) proclaimed by the ECJ mentioned above, therefore, did not arise here.

[61]Without elaboration, see Tridimas, The WTO and OECD Opinions, in: Dashwood/Hillion (eds), *The General Law of EC External Relations*, 2000, pp. 48–60 at p. 57; Schmalenbach, in: Callies/Ruffert (eds), *EUV/EGV*, 2007, (3rd edn) Art. 300 para. 15. This also seems to be the opinion of Eeckhout, *External Relations of the European Union*, 2004, pp. 90–91, who has submitted that Opinion 1/76 *did not establish exclusive external competence, but simply confirmed general*

to misleading wording in earlier case law,[62] the Lugano Opinion clarifies that the EU may not enter into international agreements absent of some enabling criterion.[63] Second, shared competence must be conditional on some enabling criterion, which logically must constitute a minus compared with criteria for establishing implied exclusive external competence. According to this theory, which has been called the principle of complementarity,[64] the EU does not automatically have an external competence when it has a competence to enact directives or regulations such as under Art. 114 TFEU (ex-Art. 95 EC).

The pertinent requirement for implied shared competences thus has to be attached to the nature of an internal competence in the sense of the Opinion 1/76 line of jurisprudence. Since the EU is exclusively competent for the conclusion of an international agreement if it is the only way an EU objective can be attained, it is to be argued that the competence is shared when the participation merely facilitates the exercise of an internal competence. An implied shared competence, according to this theory, requires that the entering into obligations by the EU vis-à-vis third states furthers the attainment of one or several of its internal competences.[65] This test of facilitation is to be derived from the necessity element to establish exclusive external competence as introduced by the ECJ in Opinion 1/76. Facilitation, thus, constitutes a second, lower-threshold test under a "double standard" of necessity established as a principle of law by case law cited above.[66] To put it differently, fulfilling the requirements of the necessity test prompts EU exclusivity, as has been

parallelism between internal and external powers and that *it is only the exercise of competence which creates its exclusive character*. See also Heliskoski, *Mixed Agreements as Technique for Organizing the International Relations of the European Community and its Member States*, 2001, p. 44, and the joined opinion by A.G.Tizzano in the *Open Skies Cases*, [2002] ECR I, p. 9427, paras 49 et seq. cf. also the account of the diverging doctrine by Holdgaard, *The European Community's Implied External Competence after the Open Skies Cases*, 2003, pp. 372–373.

[62]Opinion 1/94, WTO, [1994] ECR I, p. 5267, para. 85: *It is understandable, therefore, that external powers may be exercised, and thus become exclusive, without any internal legislation having first been adopted.* See also Opinion 2/92, ILO, [1993] ECR I, p. 1061, para. 4.

[63]In somewhat reluctant agreement, see Cremona, *External Relations of the EU and the Member States: Competence, Mixed Agreements, International Responsibility and Effects of International Law*, 2006, p. 3.

[64]Dashwood, The Attribution of External Relations Competence, in: Dashwood/Hillion (eds), *The General Law of EC External Relations*, 2000, pp. 127–136.

[65]See Dashwood and Heliskoski, The Classic Authorities Revisited, in: Dashwood/Hillion (eds), *The General Law of EC External Relations*, 2000, pp. 3–19 at pp. 16–18. They, however, seem to read the (early) case law only as providing for the "lower" standard of necessity to establish an implied shared competence. See, in contrast, Dashwood, *The Attribution of External Relations Competence, in: The General Law of EC External Relations*, 2000, pp. 132–134: *implied external competence arises, where this will help ensure the optimal exercise of the expressly conferred internal competence.*

[66]Griller and Gamharter, External Trade: Is There a Path Through the Maze of Competences?, in: Griller/Weidel (eds), *External Economic Relations and Foreign Policy in the European Union*, 2002, pp. 79–80.

codified in the Lisbon Treaty, whereas a positive test of facilitation elicits shared EU competence.

This view finds support in the Lugano Opinion, as explained above. Comparison with proportionality pursuant to Art. 5(3) EC is misguided,[67] since this principle weighs upon EU acts against alternative measures in the sense of a test of appropriateness and indispensability.[68] Moreover, contrary to the application of the proportionality principle,[69] review by the ECJ of the necessity test is objective, ex post facto and might replace the assessment of the authorities.[70] Apprehension of a *Kompetenz-Kompetenz* of the EU is, thus, not warranted.[71] Unresolved is the question of the exact standard of facilitation to be required for establishing implied shared competence.

Necessity, we know, has been understood as requiring an inextricable link leaving no other choice than for the EU to act externally to fulfil its tasks internally.[72] As a consequence of this high threshold, application of the necessity test has, but in a single case, always resulted in denial of exclusive competence of the EU.[73] Assuming a double standard, "necessity" to generate shared competence must, thus, presuppose some lesser connection to the realization of EU Treaty goals. This, conversely, is not to say that the criterion should not be as objective as the necessity test for exclusive competences, or that it need not embody more than pure political expediency.

Two thoughts, we submit, can instruct us on this. First, the term "necessary" implies that there must still be a close, though not indispensable, link to the internal competence. Second, the ECJ has never rationalized its award of exclusive external competence in the 1/76 constellation that has been deplored in the doctrine.[74] Justification cannot be to preserve the unity and consistency of EU law such as with the AETR line of case law.[75] It is submitted that the test of necessity and more so the test of facilitation are rather guided by the principle of effectiveness.[76] Both

[67]But see Schütze, *Parallel External Powers in the European Community: From "Cubist" Perspectives Towards "Naturalist" Constitutional Principles?* 2004, p. 239.

[68]Lenaerts and Van Nuffel, *Constitutional Law of the European Union*, 2005, pp. 109–115.

[69]Lenaerts and Van Nuffel, *Constitutional Law of the European Union*, 2005, p. 111.

[70]See Koutrakos, *EU International Relations Law*, 2006, p. 124. But see A.G. Tizzano, *Open Skies Cases*, [2002] ECR I, p. 9427, para. 51.

[71]Eeckhout, *External Relations of the European Union*, 2004, pp. 89 and 97. See also Dörr, *Die Entwicklungen der ungeschriebenen Außenkompetenzen der EG*, 1996, p. 41.

[72]But see Cremona, *External Relations of the EU and the Member States: Competence, Mixed Agreements, International Responsibility and Effects of International Law*, 2006, p. 3, who suggests that in Opinion 1/03 this test has been relaxed again by the ECJ.

[73]Lenaerts and Van Nuffel, *Constitutional Law of the European Union*, 2005, p. 858.

[74]Eeckhout, *External Relations of the European Union*, 2004, p. 99; Koutrakos, *EU International Relations Law*, 2006, p. 113.

[75]Louis, Editorial: La Cour et les Relations extérieures des la Communauté, CDE (2007), pp. 285 et seq. (289).

[76]Kovar, Les compétences implicites: jurisprudence de la Cour et pratique communautaire, in: Demaret (ed), *Relations extérieures de la Communauté européenne et marché intérieur: aspects juridiques et fonctionnels*, 1986, pp. 15 et seq. (20–21).

are rooted in the *effet utile* of the internal power that requires external action in order to be effectively exercised. This suggests that there must be an actual, reasoned assessment of whether the internal competence would be furthered by external action of the EU. Account must be taken of both the international agreement and the internal competence concerned before affirming facilitation and, thus, the right of the EU to act.

Continued Existence of Implied Shared Competences After the Entry into Force of the Lisbon Treaty

On the basis of the above explanations with respect to existence and requirements of exercise of implied shared competences, it is clear that the only part of Art. 216 (1) TFEU which does not establish exclusive competence together with Art. 3 (2) TFEU, namely *where the conclusion of an agreement is necessary in order to achieve, within the framework of the Union's policies, one of the objectives referred to in the Treaties*, does not represent a codification of the ECJ's case law with respect to implied *shared* competences. Put simply, the EU has a shared competence according to Art. 216 (1) TFEU whenever this is necessary for the achievement of one of the treaties' objectives. The EU (only) has implied shared competence, according to the ECJ's case law if the conclusion of an international agreement would facilitate the exercise of an internal *competence*. Art. 216 (1) TFEU and implied shared competences according to the ECJ's case law thus differ within both categories of competence exercise, namely objective versus competence and necessity versus facilitation.[77]

Even though the part of Art. 216 (1) TFEU discussed does not represent a codification of the ECJ's case law, the question remains whether from the mere existence of Art. 216 (1) TFEU it could follow that implied shared competences founded on the ECJ's case law would no longer be valid, even if it does not represent a codification. As far as can be seen, both opinions, for the continued existence of implied shared competences after the entry into force of the Lisbon

[77]Note that the facilitation test is considerably easier to fulfill than the encessity test of Art. 216 (1) TFEU. The necessity standard represents a legal and factual condition sine qua non. while the facilitation standard is already met when the exercise of internal EU competence is being facilitated through external EU treaty making. Therefrom also follows the significantly increased attractiveness of implied external competences as compared to Art. 216 (1) TFEU, in particular for inclusion of portfolio investment in future EU treaties. Judging the inclusion of portfolio investment merely on the basis of Art. 216 (1) TFEU would not allow the EU to include this type of investment in an international treaty, as the EU could simply conclude a mixed agreement together with Member States in order to cover protfolio investment. Such a possiblity frustrates the necessity requirement, as EU external action is not necessary, i.e., the only alternative, to achieve one of the objectives referred to in the Treaties.

Treaty and against it, are expressed in the literature.[78] This paper sees more convincing arguments for a continued existence of implied shared competences on the basis of the requirements for exercise of this competence as developed by the ECJ also after the entry into force of the Lisbon Treaty. This view is based, first, on the fact that no provision to the contrary is contained in the TFEU or the TEU, not even in the general competence foundations section in Art. 2–6 TFEU. It is therefore unlikely that, without an explicit provision to the contrary in the treaties, a commonly accepted principle of international law and many national constitutions, which has been (explicitly) accepted by the ECJ in an elaborated and long-standing case law, would suddenly no longer be a part of EU law. Second, the ECJ has explicitly acknowledged the existence of implied shared competences in its Lugano Opinion in 2006, i.e. at a point in time at which the current provision of Art. 216 (1) TFEU was already contained, in equal wording, in the signed but not yet ratified, Constitutional Treaty of 2004. In other words, it is very unlikely that Art. 216 (1) TFEU rules out the existence of a competence category, which was explicitly recognized by the ECJ after this provision had been drafted. Third, the relevant part of Art. 216 (1) TFEU cannot relate to implied shared competences as it refers to a different competence, namely the extension of the competence sweeping clause of ex-Art. 308 EC to embrace also external competences. Although ex-Art. 308 EC only provided for EU competence if EU action was *necessary* to *attain, in the course of the operation of the common market, one of the objectives of the Community*, Art. 352 (1) TFEU, the provision replacing ex-Art. 308 EC, now provides for EU competence if *action (...) should prove necessary, within the framework of the policies defined in the Treaties, to attain one of the objectives set out in the Treaties*. It therefore follows, on the one hand, that the competence sweeping clause, which was purely an internal competence before the entry into force of the Lisbon Treaty owing to its formulation, is now also an external competence. On the other hand, the extension to now cover also external competence matters in Art. 352 (1) TFEU is replicated in the same terms and meaning in Art. 216 (1) TFEU, namely that the EU has competence if *the conclusion of an agreement is necessary in order to achieve, within the framework of the Union's policies, one of the objectives referred to in the Treaties* (...). This exact replication in Art. 216 (1) TFEU of Art. 352 (1) TFEU is systematically speaking correct as Art. 216 (1) TFEU lists all general

[78]For a continued existence of implied shared competences apparently Herrmann, Die Zukunft der mitgliedstaatlichen Investitionspolitik nach dem Vertrag von Lissabon, EuZW (2010) 6, p. 210. Arg.: *Investitionen, die diese Schwelle nicht erreichen, sind als Portfolioinvestitionen zu bezeichnen und sind von den ausschließlichen Kompetenzen nach Art. 206 und Art. 207 I AEUV nicht abgedeckt. Damit soll die Union nach ganz überwiegender Auffassung im Schrifttum nicht über eine ausschließliche Kompetenz zur Regelung von Portfolioinvestitionen verfügen. Eine solche Kompetenz könne sich allenfalls als geteilte Zuständigkeit aus den Bestimmungen über die Kapitalverkehrsfreiheit ergeben*. Herrmann does not make any reference whatsoever to Art. 216 (1) TFEU.

external EU competences as opposed to those special EU external competences, which are listed in the various chapters on EU policies, such as the chapter on the EU's Common Commercial Policy. In sum, the relevant part of Art. 216 (1) TFEU refers to a competence category very different from implied shared external competence, namely the competence sweeping clause of Art. 352 (1) TFEU, and can therefore, owing to its very nature and function, not rule against the existence of implied shared competences as developed by the ECJ. It is therefore safe to assume that the ECJ's jurisprudence with respect to implied shared competence remains fully valid also after the entry into force of the Lisbon Treaty and as such also the existence and requirements of exercise of implied shared competence remain unaffected by the Lisbon Treaty.

The Significance of Implied Shared Competences for Portfolio Investment

One can look at the EU's external competences in the area of international investment law in several ways, one of which being drawn along the distinction between explicit and implied EU competences. Although there has been considerable debate in recent literature with respect to the EU's explicit external competences, in particular centred around but not limited to Art. 207 TFEU, little attention, if any at all, has been paid to the impact of the EU's implied competences on its international investment law competences.[79] This paper will therefore focus on the interplay of this later competence category with international investment law. Portfolio investment, as opposed to foreign direct investment, represents the major area of interest for this task as the EU's explicit competence is limited to foreign direct investment in Art. 207 TFEU. In other words, the EU, without Members States being contracting parties as well could only conclude international agreements on investment promotion and protection embracing foreign direct investment but not portfolio investment if one were to look only at explicit competences

[79]To the knowledge of the authors, no publication has discussed the foundations and impact of implied shared competences after the entry into force of the Lisbon Treaty on the EU's competences in the field of international investment law in detail. Herrmann, without providing a dogmatic explanation, seems to argue that the EU's external competence also covers portfolio investment, which would eventually even be covered by exclusive EU competence: Herrmann, Die Zukunft der mitgliedstaatlichen Investitionspolitik nach dem Vertrag von Lissabon, EuZW (2010) 6, p. 210. With respect to explicit competences, see Eilmansberger, Bilateral Investment Treaties and EU Law, CMLRev (2009), pp. 394 et seq.; Bungenberg, Außenbeziehungen und Außenhandelspolitik, Beiheft EuR 1/2009, pp. 207 et seq. For a comparative analysis between explicit and implied external EU competences with respect to international investment law, see Hindelang/Maydell, Die Gemeinsame Europäische Investitionspolitik – Alter Wein in neuen Schläuchen?, in: Bungenberg/Griebel/Hindelang (eds.), *Internationaler Investitionsschutz und Europarecht*, 2010, pp. 11 et seq.

following the mainstream view in the literature.[80] Although indeed Art. 207 TFEU covers foreign direct investment, it cannot be argued that, as a consequence, EU competence is limited to foreign direct investment. This would neglect an entire type of competences, namely implied shared competences, a type of competence which has not been terminated or modified by the Lisbon Treaty, as shown above. Implied exclusive competences, on the other hand, have been codified by the Lisbon Treaty and shall not be analysed further here as the very strict requirements for their exercise are explicitly enshrined in the Lisbon Treaty and are most likely not met in the context of international investment agreements. As will be shown in the remainder of this paper, EU competence also embraces portfolio investment based on its implied shared competence and the EU is thus in a position to conclude state-of-the-art investment agreements alone, i.e. without Member States' participation.

The underlying assumptions are as follows: first, the existence of implied shared external competences as established above; second, the facilitation test laid out above for when such competences can be exercised; and third, the Lisbon Treaty has not terminated the existence or altered the requirements of exercise of implied shared competences. Treatment standards regularly established in BITs referring to foreign direct investment as well as portfolio investment, such as non-expropriation, "fair and equitable treatment", "national treatment" and "most favoured nation treatment" provisions, correspond to core "treatment standards" in EU law, such as the provisions regarding the fundamental freedoms and competition law, in particular state aid, including numerous secondary legislation and individual decisions based upon these treaty provisions. In other words, core provisions of BITs are regularly also covered by EU law. Although EU law generally goes into much greater regulatory depth, by means of primary or secondary EU law, EU law and BITs overlap in terms of subject matter area to be regulated, such as not to discriminate against different investors. These EU law and BIT provisions can and regularly do conflict with each other, such as in the case of the *Eastern Sugar* arbitration.[81] In the case of conflict between EU law and BIT provisions, the Member State concerned is faced with the dilemma, at least in case of third-country as opposed to intra-EU investment, of either not applying EU provisions, and thus being in breach of EU law, or applying the EU provision, therefore violating the applicable BIT and thus facing potential financial sanctions by the investor concerned through arbitration proceedings.[82] Both constellations are negatively affecting the effectiveness of EU law. To be more precise, conflict negatively affects the

[80]With a comprehensive overview on relevant literature following this view, see Tietje, *Die Außenwirtschaftsverfassung der EU nach dem Vertrag von Lissabon*, Beiträge zum Transnationalen Wirtschaftsrecht, Heft 83, January 2009, pp. 13 et seq.

[81]Partial award of 27 March 2007, *Eastern Sugar v. Czech Republic*, SCC No. 088/2004, para. 156; for a detailed analysis, see: Eilmansberger, Bilateral Investment Treaties and EU Law, CMLR 46 (2009), pp. 383 et seq. (388 et seq.).

[82]Eilmansberger, Bilateral Investment Treaties and EU Law, CMLR 46 (2009), pp. 383 et seq. (398 et seq.).

effectiveness of the EU's exercise of its internal competence with respect to those areas of law regulated in both the BIT and EU law, such as the EU's state aid law.

EU law regularly extends to both foreign direct investment and portfolio investment in these areas of regulation. Although such analysis is not warranted for foreign direct investment owing to the EU's explicit exclusive competence in Art. 207 TFEU, it is argued that the exercise of the EU's internal competences in those areas of law covered by BITs concluded by its Member States is facilitated in the sense of the above-established facilitation test by the EU concluding such international investment agreements itself. Such facilitation is achieved by the EU being able to conclude only such international agreements on investment which do not contradict EU law. This is of particular importance as Member States' BITs regularly aim to generally regulate the treatment of foreign investors, an area which is also of prominent regulatory significance under EU law as described before. In other words, the conclusion of international investment agreements applying also to portfolio investments fulfils the requirements of the exercise of implied shared external competences by the EU under the facilitation test.

It cannot be argued, however, that the requirements for (formerly implied) exclusive competence under Art. 216 (1) TFEU in connection with Art. 3 (2) TFEU are met, namely that the conclusion of an international agreement is "necessary", i.e. the only way for the internal competence to be exercised. Apart from the central criterion of the facilitation test, the facilitation of exercise of internal competence by the EU's exercise of its external competence, the other criteria of the test are also met: Internal competence norms with a scope comprising all those areas to be included in the international agreement exist, in particular Art. 114 TFEU (ex-Art. 95 EC), and the – fictional – exercise of such internal competence with respect to those subject matters to be covered by the international agreement would not contradict the principle of subsidiarity.

Evaluation

The implied shared competence for portfolio investment distilled on this basis would be rather broad in its horizontal scope of application, but equally narrow in its vertical depth of application. In fact, the implied shared competence for portfolio investment is limited to the treatment standards mentioned before common to Member States' state-of-the-art BITs which are equally contained, in EU law, in particular in its fundamental freedoms and its competition law provisions, including state aid. The EU's implied shared competence thus enables the EU to conclude international agreements on portfolio investment. This competence is, contrary to the explicit external competence for foreign direct investment, shared with the Member States, i.e. Member States could – in theory – continue to conclude BITs containing portfolio investment only. Together with its exclusive competence under Art. 207 (1) TFEU, the EU can, thus, conclude state-of-the-art international investment agreements, containing both foreign direct investment and portfolio investment, without Member States' involvement. In other words, the EU does not have to conclude mixed agreements together with the Member States but can be the only treaty party on the European side.

The actual "function" of these comprehensive competences of the EU to conclude international agreements on investment, however, strongly depends on one's understanding of free movement of capital in a third-country context as outlined above. Only if one follows the restrictive approach apparently favoured by the ECJ, the EU would have the "justification" to develop a comprehensive CIP determining both the conditions of access to and postaccess treatment of foreign investment in the EU through international agreements and autonomous legislation. Further steps towards liberalization with third countries would be discussed on the basis of reciprocity under this approach as opposed to a more "unilateral outcome" if one follows a reading (favoured in this paper) of the free movement of capital provisions as already granting access and treatment standards for third country and EU investors alike.

Conclusion

This paper has attempted to bridge the gap between the EU's competence with regard to third-country investment under the Lisbon Treaty and its predecessor constitutional order. For this purpose, we have linked both fundamental freedom and competences as well as portfolio investment and foreign direct investment to provide a comprehensive picture. That said, the two following main conclusions are to be drawn:

Although the more convincing arguments speak in favour of a liberal reading of free movement of capital in a third-country context, and hence the unilateral liberalization of the Internal Market towards non-EU countries, the ECJ has chosen to lend a narrow reading to the freedom of capital movement in a third-country context: third-country direct investment is largely excluded from the protective scope of Art. 63 (1) EC, the protection of third-country portfolio investments is limited in comparison with such occurring within the EU. Hence, the function of regulation in the context of a CIP shifts from attending to liberalization to allowing for it, both through internal regulation as well as through international agreements.

Concerning the scope of the EU's external competences, although implied exclusive competences have been codified in the Lisbon Treaty, implied shared competences have continued to exist since the entry into force of the Lisbon Treaty and can be exercised under the standard developed by the ECJ and further developed in this paper, the so-called facilitation test. Under this standard, the EU has shared competence to conclude international agreements if, among others, the conclusion would enable the exercise of an internal competence with the same subject matter scope. As has been shown in this paper, the facilitation test is met with regard to portfolio investment as commonly included in Member States' BITs. Implied shared competence together with the EU's exclusive competence of Art.

207 (1) TFEU thus enables the EU to conclude state-of-the-art international agreements on investment – alone, without the necessity of mixed agreements together with Member States.

Combining these two main conclusions, one is left with a picture of an EU which is in the context of the CIP comprehensively empowered to regulate foreign investment independent of the Member States. In exercising these powers the EU relies on the idea that it is charged not just with attending to already liberalized third-country investments by way of regulation, but in essence of allowing for such economic activity, most likely on the basis of reciprocity through international agreements. Such a setting lends much power to the Commission as "negotiator-in-chief " for international agreements in this area and Member States' representatives in the Council in respect of a future design of the CIP. Whether such power will be used wisely remains to be seen, in particular in light of an ever-changing international consensus on the pros and cons of cross-border investment.

The Division of Competences Between the EU and Its Member States in the Area of Investment Politics

Marc Bungenberg

Even though the EC competences for investment treaty-making "before Lisbon" were limited, the Commission had nevertheless already been heading towards a broad and proactive approach on this issue.[1] The EU was making efforts in developing its own foreign investment promotion and protection policy by including rules on investment in Preferential Trade Agreements (PTAs) as well as by setting up its own "EU Minimum Platform on Investment" (MPoI).[2] With the entry into force of the Treaty of Lisbon on 1 December 2009, multiple questions resulting from a new division of competences between the EU and its Member States in the area of international investment policy have to be answered. This paper discusses the reason for the transfer of these specific competences (theses 1 and 2) and then addresses specific issues such as the scope of application of this Article 207 competence (thesis 3), the competences for the renegotiation of existing Member States' Bilateral Investment Treaties (BITs) and the conclusion of new EU international investment agreements (thesis 4) and for the regulation of market access of sovereign wealth funds (thesis 5). It is shown that the current division of competences is still insufficient for a coherent and efficient investment policy (thesis 6). Therefore, cooperation between the EU and its Member States is necessary. Ideas for new modes of investment protection are left for discussion

[1]See, in this volume, S. Hindelang and N. Maydell, The EU's Common Investment Policy – Connecting the Dots, p. 1 et seq. and C. Nowak, Legal Arrangements for the Promotion and Protection of Foreign Investments within the Framework of the EU Association Policy and European Neighbourhood Policy, in this volume, p. 105 et seq.

[2]Minimum Platform on for the EU FTAs, revised version of 6 March 2009; on this in general N. Maydell, The European Community's Minimum Platform on Investment or the Trojan Horse of Investment Competence, in: A. Reinisch/C. Knahr (eds.), *International Investment Law in Context*, 2008, pp. 73–92; M. Burgstaller, European Law and Investment Treaties, JIA 26 (2009), pp. 181 et seq. (204 et seq.); the MPoI serves as a standardized negotiation proposal for ongoing and future PTA negotiations with third states.

M. Bungenberg
Chair for Public Law, European Law, Public International Law and International Economic Law, University of Siegen, Germany
e-mail: Marc.Bungenberg@gmx.de

M. Bungenberg et al. (eds.), *International Investment Law and EU Law*,
DOI 10.1007/978-3-642-14855-2_2, © Springer-Verlag Berlin Heidelberg 2011

by *Tillmann R. Braun*[3] and *Jörn Griebel*,[4] and the need for the inclusion of "non-investment issues" in investment politics is discussed by *Lars Markert*.[5]

First Thesis: The inclusion of the provisions on foreign direct investments into the chapter on the Common Commercial Policy reflects reciprocal synergistic effects between foreign investments and international trade

The increasing importance of investment policy in international economic negotiations is obvious.[6] Rules on investment promotion and protection can stimulate trade relations and have an influence on the quality and quantity of investments.[7] Rules on the freedom of capital movement were, for example, part of the Treaty Establishing the European Economic Community signed in Rome in 1957, even though trade in goods at that time was still the centre of attention. However, one element of "economic globalization" is the globalization of capital; capital is a production factor and its free transfer stimulates trade in goods – at least in the long run.[8] The synergic effect of the expansion of trade and investment is supposed to lead to further economic growth.[9] Limits on the ability of governments to interfere with the operation of foreign investors reduce the political risks associated with an investment, which should result in greater levels of investment in a given economy.[10]

The number of pure BITs continues to rise,[11] but because of their interrelation with trade rules chapters on investment more and more often form an integral part

---

[3]T.R. Braun, For a Complementary European Investment Protection, in this volume, at 95 et seq.

[4]J. Griebel, The Great New Challenge after the Entry Into Force of the Treaty of Lisbon: Bringing About a Multilateral EU-Investment Treaty, in this volume, p. 139 et seq.

[5]L. Markert, The Crucial Question of Future Investment Treaties: Balancing Investors' Rights and Regulatory Interests of Host States, in this volume, at 145 et seq.

[6]On this, see for example A. Newcombe and L. Paradell, Law and Practice of Investment Treaties, 2008, p. 41 et seq.

[7]M. Lesher/S. Miroudot, The Economic Impact of Investment Provisions in Regional Trade Agreements, OECD Trade Policy Working Paper No. 36/2006.

[8]On the relationship between trade and investment, see for example, the Report (1998) of the (WTO) Working Group on the Relationship between Trade and Investment to the General Council, WT/WGTI/2.

[9]P. Gugler/J. Chaisse, Foreign Investment Issues and WTO Law - Dealing with Fragmentation while waiting for a Multilateral Agreement, in: J. Chaisse/T. Balmelli (eds.), *Essays on the Future of the World Trade Organization*, Vol. I, 2008, pp. 135 et seq.

[10]S. McGuire/M. Smith, *The European Union and the United States – Competition and Convergence in the Global Arena*, 2008, p. 142.

[11]See UNCTAD, Recent developments in international investment agreements (2008 - June 2009), IIA Monitor (2009) 3, p. 2 figure 1; in 2008, 59 new BITs were concluded, the total number of BITs rose to 2,676 at the end of 2008.

of new "Free Trade Agreements" (FTAs) and Preferential Trade Agreements (PTAs). Thus, the inclusion of competences on foreign investments reflects today's reality regarding international economic agreements. FTAs very often are not "pure" any more, but broader "international economic agreements" or PTAs do contain rules on investment promotion and protection as well. Reflecting this trend, "investment" has been on the WTO agenda since the WTO Singapore Conference in 1996 and later was included in the Doha Ministerial Declaration of 2001:[12]

> Relationship between trade and investment
>
> 20. Recognizing the case for a multilateral framework to secure transparent, stable and predictable conditions for long-term cross-border investment, particularly foreign direct investment, that will contribute to the expansion of trade, and the need for enhanced technical assistance and capacity-building in this area as referred to in para. 21, we agree that negotiations will take place after the Fifth Session of the Ministerial Conference on the basis of a decision to be taken, by explicit consensus, at that session on modalities of negotiations.

Due to strong synergies of trade and investments, the "European Convention for a Treaty Establishing a Constitution for Europe", which completed its work on 10 July 2003, included in its proposal at a very late stage the competences for foreign direct investments within the chapter on the Common Commercial Policy. The comments of the Secretariat of the European Convention confirm this position, stating that the added reference to foreign direct investments was made *in recognition of the fact that financial flows supplement trade in goods and today represent a significant share of commercial exchanges.*[13] Furthermore the European Convention took into account the necessary competences for a future final agreement to the Doha Round.

Some delegates to the European Convention – the at that time French foreign minister *Dominique de Villepin* as well as the at that time German foreign minister *Joschka Fischer* and others – suggested deleting "foreign direct investments" from the chapter on the Common Commercial Policy, with no success.[14] It was left as it stood in the Constitutional Treaty even during the Lisbon Treaty negotiations. This was surprising, because (a) the consequences were already starting to be discussed[15] and (b) investment policy was no longer on the WTO Doha Agenda: in the aftermath of the WTO Ministerial Conference in Cancún (10–14 September 2003)[16] the trade ministers of the WTO Member States decided to exclude "trade

---

[12]WTO approach see WT/MIN(01)/DEC/1 of 20 November 2001, point 20.

[13]CONV 685/03, Document of 23 April 2003, comments on Article 23.

[14]See CONV 707/03, 13 May 2003; CONV 821/03, 27 June 2003.

[15]See as the first ones examining this new development J. Ceyssens, Towards a Common Foreign Investment Policy? – Foreign Investment in the European Constitution, Legal Issues of Economic Integration (2005), pp. 259 et seq. (278 et seq.); J. Karl, The Competence for Foreign Direct Investment, JWT&I 5 (2006), pp. 413 et seq.

[16]See for example, P. Sauvé, Multilateral Rules on Investment: Is forward Movement possible, J Int Economic Law 9 (2006) 2, pp. 325 et seq.; on the Cancun Ministerial Summit in general see,

and investments" from the Doha Agenda.[17] Therefore the inclusion of (only) "foreign direct investments" into the Common Commercial Policy even after the entry into force of the Lisbon Treaty is more than surprising regarding the far-reaching effects this transfer has, as will be shown in the following subsections of this paper.

Second Thesis: The transfer of investment policy competences to the EU is supposed to give the EU the necessary legal basis to conclude international investment agreements as well as broader PTAs in an international competition of systems

The protection of foreign investments via "special" international investment agreements is of growing importance, since the attempt to find a multilateral solution to the problem of the fragmentation of investment law[18] has failed on various occasions already, and general public international law does not give sufficient protection for investors, as is pointed out in recent books on investment law by, for example, *Dolzer* and *Schreuer*[19] and *Griebel*.[20] Thus, it is up to governments to individually preserve their undertakings and investors with the best legal setting of rules on investment promotion and protection possible.

Competition between the USA, China and the EU as well as other players for their positions in the new economic order of the twenty-first century in trade as well as foreign investments is a situation to which all actors in the global arena must adapt. In general, the globalization of markets leads to regulatory competition in the field of economic law. Investors seek locations for production, distribution, research and development on the basis of efficiency criteria only. The possibility of almost global market access for business affects governments. These have to present investors with legal systems offering stability, freedom and protection of inward and outward investments. Therefore, governments also have the role of system providers to attract investment.[21] Today's globalization of markets for

for example. J. Bhagwati, Don't Cry for Cancún, Foreign Affairs 83 (2004), pp. 52 et seq., R. Sally, The End of the Road for the WTO? World Economics 5 (2004), pp. 1 et seq.

[17]Decision Adopted by the General Council on 1 August 2004, Doc. WT/L/579; on the "July Package" see F. Ismail, A Development Perspective on the WTO July 2004 General Council Decision, JIEL 8 (2004), pp. 377 et seq.

[18]See on this A. van Aaken, Fragmentation of International Law: The Case of International Investment Protection, Finnish Yearbook of International Law (2008), pp. 93 et seq.

[19]R. Dolzer/C. Schreuer, *Principles of International Investment Law*, 2008, pp. 11 et seq.

[20]J. Griebel, *Internationales Investitionsrecht*, 2008, pp. 14 et seq.

[21]For an explanation of the regulatory factors liable to channel economic activities to certain locations, see C. Tiebout, A pure Theory of Local Expenditures, J. Pol. Econ. 64 (1956), pp. 416 et seq.; for an overview on the economic theory on interjurisdictional competition and legal federalism see S. Sinn, *Competition for Capital, On the Role of Governments in an Integrated World*

goods and capital imposes a merciless "competition of systems".[22] In the areas of trade and investment this leads to a "competitive liberalization" with a liberal trade and investment regime.[23]

The possible escape[24] from a competition of economic law systems by harmonizing certain areas of international investment law has failed,[25] as already mentioned and as pointed out in length in other publications. "Trade and investment" was finally removed from the Doha Agenda. Ever since, the main actors in the global arena have given priority to bilateral and regional trade negotiations to promote inward investments and to provide their economy with better business opportunities.[26] The offers that existing global players can make to the states of the emerging economies and developing countries individually will be a relevant factor for the future economic world order.[27] Thus, the struggle for agreements with emerging markets, especially on market access, (exploration of) resources and investments and their protection are of significant importance for the position of nation states and international organizations as economic actors in their global competition. The EU, China and the USA are building separate networks of free trade relations and PTAs as "superhubs".[28] This is not only true for trade relations but at the same time for the liberalization of foreign investments and their protection, all actors being aware of the importance of an internationalized legal investment setting.

The USA is using "pure" BITs parallel to including investment promotion and protection chapters in broader FTAs.[29] After 2003, the US government concluded

Economy, 1993; H. Siebert (ed.), *Locational Competition in the World Economy*, 1995; L. Gerken, *Der Wettbewerb der Staaten*, 1999; V. Vanberg/W. Kerber, *Institutional Competition Among Jurisdictions*, Constitutional Political Economy 10 (1994), pp. 219 et seq. Especially on the role of economic law in the competition of systems, see K.M. Meessen, Economic Law as an Economic Good, in: K.M. Meessen/M. Bungenberg/A. Puttler (eds.), *Economic Law as an Economic Good: The Rule and the Tool Function in the Competition of Systems*, 2009, p. 5.

[22] K.M. Meessen, *Economic Law in Globalizing Markets*, 2004, p. 9.

[23] F. Bergsten, *Competitive Liberalization and Global Free Trade: A Vision for the Early 21st Century*, Institute for International Economics Working Paper 96-15.

[24] W. Kerber, The Theory of Regulatory Competition and Competition Law, in: K. Meessen/M. Bungenberg/A. Puttler (eds.), *Economic Law as an Economic Good: The Rule and the Tool Function in the Competition of Systems*, 2009, p. 28.

[25] On the OECD approach see Chapter III Article 1 MAI Negotiating Text, http://www1.oecd.org/daf/mai/pdf/ng/ng987r1e.pdf; see on this P. Muchlinski, The Rise and Fall of the MAI: Lessons for the Regulation of International Business. in: I. Fletcher/L. Mistelis/M. Cremona (eds.), *Foundations and Perspectives in International Trade Law*, 2001, pp. 114 et seq.

[26] On this, see also S. Woolcock, *European Union policy towards free Trade Agreements*, ECIPE Working Paper No. 03/2007.

[27] On this, see P. Khanna, *The Second World, Empires and Influence of the New Global Order*, 2008.

[28] On the USA and the EU as superhubs, see P.J. Lloyd/D. MacLaren, The EU's New Trade Strategy and Regionalisation in the World Economy, Aussenwirtschaft (2006), pp. 423 et seq.

[29] S. McGuire/M. Smith, *The European Union and the United States – Competition and Convergence in the Global Arena*, 2008, p. 142; See on this A. Capling/K.M. Nossal, Investor-State Dispute Mechanisms in International Trade Agreements, Governance 19 (2006) 2, p. 57.

PTAs containing investment chapters with Australia,[30] various Central American states and the Dominican Republic,[31] Morocco,[32] Oman[33] and Peru.[34] PTAs with Colombia,[35] Korea[36] and Panama[37] have been signed but as of this writing are still awaiting Congressional approval and implementing legislation. The US Trade Representative gave a clear example for this "competition of investment laws" as he stated on the "Korea-EU Free Trade Agreement": *There is no investment chapter or investor-state dispute settlement provisions in the Korea-EU FTA (competency for investment matters rests with the individual EU Member States), whereas KORUS features investor protections.*[38]

The EU Commission communication on "Global Europe" reflects this trend of a stronger competition of systems as well.[39] The EU Commission observed in 2006, *in comparison to NAFTA countries' agreements, EU agreements and achievements in the area of investment lag behind because of their narrow content. As a result, European Investors are discriminated vis-à-vis their foreign competitors and the EU is loosing market shares.*[40] Therefore, the EU Commission had been taking a new approach to the establishment of its own investment policy even before the entry into force of the Lisbon Treaty. This had already started with the EU–Chile Agreement,[41] and continued with EU ambitions to set up an EU investment platform ("EU Minimum Platform on Investment") and the inclusion of investment chapters in EU PTAs currently being negotiated. The Commission has stressed that *Future FTAs should also include new provisions for investment.... A new, ambitious model EU investment agreement should be developed in close coordination with Member States. It could be usefully complemented by a dialogue on investment promotion and facilitation.*[42]

The EU did not possess the necessary competences for an effective EU investment policy in terms of a competition of systems before the entry into force of the Lisbon Treaty nor does it possess such competences since the entry

[30]United States–Australia Free Trade Agreement (AFTA), 18 May 2004.

[31]United States–Dominican Republic–Central America Free Trade Agreement (CAFTA), 5 August 2004. In addition to the Dominican Republic and the U.S., the parties are Costa Rica, El Salvador, Guatemala, Honduras, Nicaragua.

[32]United States–Morocco Free Trade Agreement (MFTA), 14 June 2004.

[33]United States–Oman Free Trade Agreement (OFTA), 19 January 2006.

[34]United States–Peru Trade Promotion Agreement (PTPA), 12 April 2006.

[35]United States–Colombia Trade Promotion Agreement (CTPA), 22 November 2006.

[36]United States–Republic of Korea (KORUS FTA), 30 June 2007.

[37]United States–Panama Trade Promotion Agreement, 11 July 2007.

[38]USTR-release Preliminary Analysis of KOREA-EU Free Trade Agreement, October 2010 (http://www.ustr.gov/about-us/press-office/press-releases/2009/october).

[39]EU Commission, Global Europe: Competing in the World, COM (2006) 567 final.

[40]Commission, Upgrading the EU Investment Policy, Note for the Attention of the 133 Committee, Brussels, 30 May 2006.

[41]OJ 2002 L-352, signed on 18 November 2002.

[42]European Commission, Staff Working Document SEC (2006) 1230, 18.

into force of the Lisbon Treaty, as will be demonstrated in the third thesis. The USA seems to be more flexible and regarding its external competences it is "better equipped" than the EU. The latter is facing the difficulty of being an economic superpower, without being capable of negotiating with a single voice, due to the distribution of competences between itself and the Member States. To conclude: From a competition of systems perspective, a coherent trade and investment policy is necessary and has to lead to a sufficient transfer of competences to the European level to allow the EU to act in its external economic relations as efficiently as its main competitors, the USA and China. This "sufficient transfer" has not taken place so far.

Third Thesis: The notion "Foreign Direct Investments" is not defined in the Treaty on the European Union nor in the Treaty on the Functioning of the European Union. An interpretation of Article 207 TFEU leads to the conclusion that the competence covers the regulation of market access, material standards of protection and dispute settlement

Since the entry into force of the Lisbon Treaty, the EU possesses the exclusive competence in the field of "foreign direct investment" (Article 207 TFEU). Nevertheless, the scope of application of the EU foreign investment policy is not yet clear. Most BITs in force use the much broader term "investment" or the narrower terms "establishment" and "enterprise".[43] Neither the IMF interpretation given to the term "foreign direct investment" (reflecting the objective of obtaining a lasting interest by a resident entity in one economy in an enterprise resident in another economy)[44] nor EU secondary law in the capital directive[45] provides clear guidance with respect to the kind of policy instruments the EU would have at its disposal,[46] except for a wide interpretation of the notion "direct investment". Irrespective of the fact that a final definition of "foreign direct investment" does not seem possible, it is common understanding that foreign direct investments need to serve "to establish or to

[43] J. Karl, The Competence for Foreign Direct Investment – New Powers for the European Union? JWT&I 5 (2006) 3, pp. 413 et seq. (420).

[44] IMF Balance of Payments Manual (1993).

[45] Council Directive 88/361/EEC, 1988 OJ L-187/5: "Direct investments: Investments of all kinds by natural persons or commercial, industrial or financial undertakings, and which serve to establish or to maintain lasting and direct links between the person providing the capital and the entrepreneur to whom or the undertaking to which the capital is made available in order to carry on an economic activity. This concept must therefore be understood in its widest sense. ..."

[46] J. Karl, The Competence for Foreign Direct Investment – New Powers for the European Union? JWT&I 5 (2006), pp. 413 et seq. (421).

maintain lasting and direct links"[47] between the investor and the entrepreneur to whom or the undertaking to which the capital is made available in order to carry on an economic activity. This is underlined by a communication from the EC and its Member States to the WTO Working Group on Trade and Investments[48]:

> Foreign direct investment is the category of international investment that reflects the objective of a resident entity in one economy (direct investor) obtaining a lasting interest in an enterprise resident in another economy (direct investment enterprise). The two criteria incorporated in the notion of "lasting interest" are: the existence of a long-term relationship between the direct investor and the enterprise and, the significant degree of influence that gives the direct investor an effective vice in the management of the enterprise.

Furthermore, the distinction between portfolio investments and foreign direct investments is generally accepted[49] and a decision has to be made on a case-by-case basis.

The wording of Article 207 TFEU does not contain any explicit limitation regarding the extent of competences for "foreign direct investments". For reasons of efficiency and practicability (*effet utile*) the EU should possess the competence for all possible aspects of (foreign direct) investment promotion and protection.[50] The intention of this far-reaching transfer of competences in the field of foreign direct investment is to strengthen the EU as an actor in bilateral and multilateral negotiations on investment policy.[51] As noted, chapters on investment are increasingly often part of PTAs and the EU's bargaining power with third countries is stronger than that of individual Member States, in particular the smaller ones. Therefore there might be a better chance to obtain more favourable conditions for EU investors.[52]

Furthermore, Article 345 TFEU does not exclude the extension of the new competences to the protection from expropriation[53]; it does not preserve exclusive powers for Member States to determine expropriation and has been interpreted narrowly so far.[54] The scope of Article 345 TFEU concerns the right of Member States to nationalize private property or to privatize public property only.[55] This

---

[47]Council Directive 88/361/EEC, 1988 OJ L-187/5

[48]See Communication from the EC and its Member States to the WTO Working Group on Trade and Investments, WT/WGTI/W/115, point 8.

[49]See R. Dolzer/C. Schreuer, *Principles of International Investment Law*, 2008, p. 64.

[50]J. Karl, The Competence for Foreign Direct Investment – New Powers for the European Union?, JWT&I 5 (2006) 3, pp. 413 et seq. (422).

[51]European Commission, Draft Articles Concerning External Action, CONV 685/03, 23 April 2003.

[52]J. Karl, The Competence for Foreign Direct Investment – New Powers for the European Union? JWT&I 5 (2006) 3, pp. 413 et seq. (425).

[53]See also C. Herrmann, Die Zukunft der mitgliedstaatlichen Investitionspolitik nach dem Vertrag von Lissabon, EuZW (2010), pp. 207 et seq. (211).

[54]See on this I. Brinker, Artikel 295, in: J. Schwarze (ed.), *EU-Kommentar*, 2000, Rn. 6.

[55]ECJ, Case 182/83 – *Fearon*, (1984) ECR, p. 3677.

narrow scope of application has been recognized in the field of intellectual property rights and protection, where the European Court of Justice (ECJ) found that the regulation of intellectual property rights concerning not only their existence can be adopted at the EU level.[56] As pointed out, Article 345 TFEU does not deal with the determination of the conditions under which an expropriation might take place; in international investment law it is the condition under which expropriation might take place and that forms a material standard of almost all BITs. Thus, the determination of this condition does not fall within the scope of Article 345 TFEU,[57] but falls within the scope of possible regulation covered by Article 207 TFEU.[58] This extensive interpretation can also be based on the broad EU competences for the regulation of intellectual property rights that are strongly related to property protection themselves.[59]

This leads to the conclusion that the EU, at least in the area of market access and material standards of protection (market access, pre- and postestablishment standards of treatment, possible performance requirements and the question of protection in terms of the conditions under which expropriation takes place) for foreign direct investments, is capable of concluding agreements similar to the standards included in US FTAs and BITs.[60] On the other hand, the extension of the scope of application of the Common Commercial Policy to portfolio investments[61] and other forms of investment (for example intellectual property rights) will not be covered by the scope of application of the term "foreign direct investment". Furthermore, the competences of the ECJ have to be respected when international investment agreements containing rules and mechanisms for investor–state/EU dispute settlement are negotiated.[62]

---

[56] ECJ, Case C-92/92 and C-326/92 – *Phil Collins*, (1993) ECR I, p. 5155, para. 22; Case C-30/90 – *Commission v. UK*, (1992) ECR I, p. 829, para. 18.

[57] A. Dimopoulus, The Common Commercial Policy after Lisbon: Establishing Parallelism between Internal and External Economic Relations?, Croatian Yearbook of European Law and Policy 4 (2008), pp. 101 et seq. (text at footnote 48).

[58] On this, see, for example, C. Herrmann, Die Zukunft der mitgliedstaatlichen Investitionspolitik nach dem Vertrag von Lissabon, EuZW (2010), pp. 207 et seq.

[59] A. Dimopoulus, The Common Commercial Policy after Lisbon: Establishing Parallelism between Internal and External Economic Relations?, Croatian Yearbook of European Law and Policy 4 (2008), pp. 101 et seq. (text at footnote 46); see also J. Karl, The Competence for Foreign Direct Investment – New Powers for the European Union?, JWT&I 5 (2006) 3, pp. 413 et seq. (421); J. Ceyssens, Towards a Common Foreign Investment Policy? – Foreign Investment in the European Constitution, Legal Issues of Economic Integration (2005), pp. 259 et seq. (278 et seq.).

[60] See, for example, J. Karl, The Competence for Foreign Direct Investment – New Powers for the European Union? JWT&I 5 (2006) 3, pp. 413 et seq. (422).

[61] See, for example, H.G. Krenzler/C. Pitschas, Die Gemeinsame Handelsolitik im Verfassungsvertrag, in: C. Herrmann/H.G. Krenzler/R. Streinz (eds.), *Die Außenwirtschaftspolitik der Europäischen Union nach dem Verfassungsvertrag*, 2006, pp. 11 et seq. (27).

[62] On the role of the ECJ in international dispute settlement, see ECJ, Case C-459/03, *Commission v. Ireland* (MOX Plant decision), [2006] ECR I, p. 4635.

Fourth Thesis: The EU Member States have lost their competence to negotiate or conclude international agreements on foreign direct investments. The EU Member States cannot renegotiate existing BITs with third countries (outside the EU) that were concluded before the entry into force of the Lisbon Treaty, except if permission to do so is given by the EU

A first and direct consequence of the transfer of exclusive competences to the EU level in this field is that EU Member States are not allowed to conclude new BITs any more – this has been the common understanding of what the transfer of competences would lead to.[63] Irrespective of the entry into force of the Lisbon Treaty on 1 December 2010, Austria and Germany keep on signing BITs: Germany signed a BIT with Pakistan on 1 December 2009, and Austria followed the German example by signing a new BIT with Kazakhstan in January 2010. Both countries pointed out that the EU Commission gave its "consent" to the signature of those agreements. Nevertheless, on different occasions the EU Commission has stressed that its "consent" covers only the signature of the agreements and not their entry into force. However, before the entry into force of these new German and Austrian BITs, explicit permission from the EU adopted in an ordinary legislative procedure needs to be given to Germany and Austria; in any other case an entry into force of the agreements would violate EU law.

In addition, there is no provision recognizing the right of Member States to keep in place their existing agreements. Nevertheless, Member States' BITs not violating specific rules of EU law need to remain in force until the EU has concluded new international investment agreements with the third countries involved. It is argued that for reasons of legal certainty a "transmission regulation" is needed, as Commissioner for External Trade *Karel de Gucht* pointed out during the parliamentary hearings before being appointed Commissioner[64]: *There are existing investment agreements, by which I mean agreements for protecting investments. There are about a thousand of them. ... First of all we will preserve legal certainty, then we will look closely at what initiatives we should take, and towards which countries. Within our prerogatives with respect to investment, legal certainty for investments in third countries is a main topic that we should certainly address very soon because, for example, it has a lot to do also with energy security. ...*

[63] See, for example, M. Bungenberg, Going Global? The EU Common Commercial Policy After Lisbon, in: C. Herrmann/J. Terhechte (eds.), *European Yearbook of International Economic Law 2010*, pp. 123 et seq. (147); J. Karl, The Competence for Foreign Direct Investment – New Powers for the European Union?, JWT&I 5 (2006) 3, pp. 413 et seq.; A. de Mestral, The Lisbon Treaty and the Expansion of EU Competence over Foreign Direct Investment, in. K. Sauvant (ed.), *Yearbook on International Investment Law and Policy 2009/2010.*

[64] http://www.europarl.europa.eu/hearings/static/commissioners/cre/de_gucht.pdf.

In its decisions of March 2009 the ECJ pointed out that BITs violating EU law have to be modified or terminated.[65] From a legal point of view, the Member States have lost their competence to renegotiate their BITs (for example, if material standards were to be modified; not though if single provisions in contradiction to EU law were simply to be terminated) – even if they violate EU law. Either the EU empowers the EU Member States to renegotiate and modify the BITs in question or these BITs have to be terminated by the Member States.

Fifth Thesis: EU Member States do not have the competence to control foreign direct investments of Sovereign Wealth Funds in the EU market

With the entry into force of the Lisbon Treaty the "control of market access" of non-EU/non-EFTA investments in the EU market is exclusively on the EU level. The regulation of investments made by sovereign wealth funds as well as of private enterprises from abroad is covered by the EU Common Commercial Policy if they are determined as "foreign direct investments" and thus fall within the exclusive sphere of the EU.[66]

For example the German control of market access mechanism contradicts the current distribution of competences. Germany has introduced into its Foreign Trade and Payments Act (Außenwirtschaftsgesetz, AWG) a control mechanism for non-EU/non-EFTA investments in German enterprises that lead to a 25% or greater equity ownership.[67] The amendment of the AWG establishes a review procedure, administered by the Federal Ministry of Economic Affairs and Technology, for investments that threaten public policy or public security. The Ministry may prohibit acquisitions or subject them to mitigation measures. The procedure complements an existing review procedure that addresses investments in certain military goods and cryptographic equipment; the new procedure is not limited to specific industries only any more.

Three solutions in conformity with EU law to the "control of market access problem" seem possible. The first option is that the Member States abolish all kinds of market access control mechanisms and totally liberalize capital transfer and thus foreign direct investments from abroad as well. The second option is the introduction of a market access control system on the EU level, comparable to the Merger Control Regulation in competition law. The third option is a redelegation of powers

---

[65] ECJ, Case C-249/06, *Commission v. Sweden*, (2009) ECR I, p. 1335; Case C-205/06, *Commission v. Austria*, (2009) ECR I, p. 1301.

[66] See also C. Herrmann, Die Zukunft der mitgliedstaatlichen Investitionspolitik nach dem Vertrag von Lissabon, EuZW (2010), pp. 207 et seq. (209).

[67] On this, see T. Müller-Ibold, Foreign Investment in Germany: Restrictions Based on Public Security Concerns and Their Compatibility with EU Law, in: C. Herrmann/J. Terhechte (eds.), *European Yearbook of International Economic Law 2010*, pp. 103 et seq.

for such a mechanism to the Member States. This option is already foreseen in Article 2 TFEU: according to the definition given to "exclusive competence" by Article 2 TFEU *only the Union may legislate and adopt legally binding acts, the Member States being able to do so themselves only if so empowered by the Union or for the implementation of Union acts.* Such a "share of policy" in a field of European exclusivity has been practised in other fields of the Common Commercial Policy. At least until the WTO Opinion of 1994 the ECJ gave a broad interpretation to the matters covered by the (already then) exclusive EU competence for trade in goods in ex-Article 133 TCE.[68] Nevertheless the General Export Regulation[69] gives the possibility to take into consideration a national *ordre public* when granting an export license to the Member States. The same is foreseen in the Regulation on the Export of Cultural Goods[70] and the Dual-Use Regulation.[71] The ECJ has already agreed to such a possibility of a redelegation, which is now as mentioned above laid down in Article 2 TFEU,[72] whereas the literature stayed reserved towards such an approach.[73] Nevertheless, a "Member States market access control mechanism" for foreign direct investments requires empowerment of the Member States by the EU in an ordinary legislative procedure.

Sixth Thesis: EU investment agreements comparable with US investment agreements in their scope of application and quality can only be concluded as "mixed agreements". Thus, a further transfer of competences from the Member States to the EU seems necessary to allow the EU to have a coherent and efficient investment policy in its international economic relations

The intention of the Lisbon Treaty's far-reaching transfer of competences in aspects of foreign direct investment is to strengthen the EU as an actor in bilateral and multilateral negotiations on investment policy.[74] As noted, chapters on investment are

[68]See ECJ, Opinion 1/78, (1979) ECR, p. 2871, para. 44.

[69]Council Regulation (EC) 1061/2009 establishing common rules for exports, OJ 2009 L 291, pp. 1 et seq.

[70]Council Regulation (EC) 116/2009 on the export of cultural goods, OJ 2009 L 39, pp. 1 et seq.

[71]Council Regulation (EC) 428/2009 setting up a Community regime for the control of exports of dual-use items and technology, OJ 2009 L 134, pp. 1 et seq.

[72]ECJ, Case 41/76 - *Donckerwolcke*, (1976) ECR, p. 1921, paras. 31/37; Case 174/84 – *Bulk Oil*, (1986) ECR, p. 559; Case C-70/94 – *Werner*, (1995) ECR I, p. 3189; Case C-83/94 – *Leifer*, (1995) ECR I, p. 3231.

[73]See Schaefer, *Die nationale Kompetenz zur Ausfuhrkontrolle nach Art. 133 EG*, 2009, pp. 113 et seq.

[74]European Commission, Draft Articles Concerning External Action, CONV 685/03, 23 April 2003.

increasingly often part of PTAs[75] and the EU's bargaining power is stronger than that of individual Member States, in particular the smaller ones, which is why it is more likely that the EU will obtain more favourable conditions for EU investors than the smaller Member States could.[76] The question is therefore to what degree the EU will be able to negotiate new agreements and if it will be capable of narrowing down the existing differences between EU and NAFTA countries' BITs.

The US approach is more coherent than the EU one. Both BITs and investment chapters in PTAs follow the US Model BIT (2004).[77] The objective of this Model BIT is to provide a consistent approach between the investment chapters of the PTAs and future US BITs.[78] The US Model BIT, generally "concerning the encouragement and reciprocal protection of investment", uses a broad definition of investment that extends to all "investments". The treatment provisions of the US Model BIT apply to the pre-establishment phase as well – in its Articles 4 and 5, the 2004 US Model BIT[79] explicitly stipulates the national treatment and most favoured nation treatment also for "establishment, acquisition, and expansion" of investments.[80] Furthermore US BITs in general contain rules on investor–state dispute settlement.

Obviously, the EU possesses an explicit exclusive competence only in the area of foreign direct investments. Most of today's approximately 2,700 BITs not only cover foreign direct investments, but also portfolio investments and their protection. Therefore, it is almost unanimously argued that future EU agreements that cover all forms of investments and their protection would not in their entirety fall under exclusive EU competences.[81] In conclusion, future agreements on investments even after the entry into force of the Lisbon Treaty are troublesome to negotiate if the objective of those future EU BITs is investment protection in its entirety. Treaty-making powers as well as competences for an autonomous regulation of portfolio investments are not part of the exclusive Common Commercial

[75] See above thesis 1 and 2.

[76] J. Karl, The Competence for Foreign Direct Investment – New Powers for the European Union? JWT&I 5 (2006) 3, pp. 413 et seq. (425).

[77] 19 U.S.C.S. § 3801.

[78] On this see M. Kantor, The New Draft Model U.S. BIT: Noteworthy Developments, Journal of International Arbitration 21 (2004), pp. 383 et seq.; critical on this approach see S.M. Schwebel, The US 2004 Model Bilateral Investment Treaty, in: Liber amicorum in honour of R. Briner, *Global Reflections on International Law*, 2005, pp. 815 et seq.

[79] http://www.ustr.gov/assets/Trade_Sectors/Investment/Model_BIT/asset_upload_file847_6897.pdf.

[80] P. Gugler/V. Tomsik, The North American and European Approaches in International Investment Agreements, NCCR Working Paper No. 2006/04, p. 5.

[81] See C. Tietje, Die Außenwirtschaftsverfassung der EU nach dem Vertrag von Lissabon, Beiträge zum Transnationalen Wirtschaftsrecht (2009), Heft 83 p. 16, http://www.wirtschaftsrecht.uni-halle.de/Heft83.pdf; M. Burgstaller, The Future of Bilateral Investment Treaties of EU Member States, in this volume, at p. 66.

Policy competences. Implicit treaty-making powers for this area of investment law could probably be based – as *Hindelang* and *Maydell*[82] have pointed out – on the provisions of the free movement of capital. Irrespective the general implicit external competence for the regulation of portfolio investments, it is questionable if the inclusion of a mechanism for state/EU-investor dispute settlement for the protection of portfolio investments would be covered by such a competence; the ECJ will have to give an opinion on this issue. Thus, it is most probable that new agreements comparable to US agreements need to be negotiated by the EU together with its Member States and will have to be concluded as mixed agreements.

Conclusion

It is obvious that EU investment protection is still facing multiple problems. Before 1 December 2009 it was a difficult situation, but at least the EU Member States were quite successful in concluding BITs. However, neither the EU nor its Member States were able to negotiate international investment agreements comparable to those of other actors on their own for a matter of distribution of competences. This has not changed. With the Lisbon Treaty in force, the EU's task for the coming years is how to solve this unsatisfactory post-Lisbon situation. The Lisbon transfer of competences in the area of investments does not enable the EU to position itself as a global actor in today's global investment politics. Further "problems" of a future EU investment policy are the politicization of the entire Common Commercial Policy including investment politics[83] and the new "powers" of the European Parliament.[84]

To conclude, the new EU international investment policy has to be shaped and developed – by the EU and its Member States together for reasons of insufficient EU competences. A solution might be a PLURILATERAL INVESTMENT PROMOTION AND PROTECTION PLATFORM, an agreement signed by both the EU and its Member States which is open for signature to third countries, too.[85] Such an EU-based approach could then develop into a multilateral solution.

[82]S. Hindelang/N. Maydell, The EU's Common Investment Policy – Connecting the Dots, in this volume, at p. 1.

[83]On this, see L. Markert, The Crucial Question of Future Investment Treaties:Balancing Investors' Rights and Regulatory Interests of Host States , in this volume, at p. 145.

[84]On this, see M. Bungenberg, Going Global? The EU Common Commercial Policy After Lisbon, in: C. Herrmann/J. Terhechte (eds.), *European Yearbook of International Economic Law 2010*, pp. 123 et seq. (128); S. Woolcock, EU Trade and Investment Policymaking After the Lisbon Treaty, Intereconomics 2010, pp. 1 et seq. (p. 2).

[85]On this topic, see J. Griebel, Überlegungen zur Wahrnehmung der neuen EU-Kompetenz für ausländische Direktinvestitionen nach Inkrafttreten des Vertrags von Lissabon, RIW 55 (2009), pp. 473 et seq.

The Division of Powers Between the EU and Its Member States "After Lisbon"

August Reinisch

Introduction

The question of the allocation of powers between the centre and the periphery, i.e. between the EU and its Member States, with regard to regulating and protecting investments has attracted the attention of many EU as well as investment law scholars.[1] This rather recent interest may have been the result of the fact that the

[1]See Bungenberg, Centralizing European BIT Making under the Lisbon Treaty, Draft Paper to be presented at the 2008 Biennial Interest Group Conference in Washington, D.C., November 13–15, 2008; Bungenberg, Going Global? The EU Common Commercial Policy After Lisbon, in: Hermann/Terhechte (eds.), *European Yearbook of International Economic Law*, 2010, pp. 123–151; Bungenberg, Außenbeziehungen und Außenhandelspolitik, EuR Beiheft 1 (2009), pp. 195–218; Ceyssens, Towards a Common Foreign Investment Policy? – Foreign Investment in the European Constitution, Legal Issues of Economic Integration 32 (2005), pp. 259–291; Dimopoulus, The Common Commercial Policy after Lisbon: Establishing Parallelism between Internal and External Economic Relations? Croatian Yearbook of European Law and Policy 4 (2008), pp. 101–131; Ehlers/Wolffgang/Schröder, *Bilaterale und regionale Handelsabkommen als Kernstück der "neuen" EG-Handelspolitik*, 2009; Griebel, Überlegungen zur Wahrnehmung der neuen EU-Kompetenz für ausländische Direktinvestitionen nach Inkrafttreten des Vertrags von Lissabon, Recht der Internationalen Wirtschaft (2009), pp. 469–474; Karl, The Competence for Foreign Direct Investment: New Powers for the European Union?, Journal of World Investment and Trade 5 (2004), pp. 413–448; Klamert/Maydell, Lost in Exclusivity: Implied Non-Exclusive External Competences in Community Law, European Foreign Affairs Review 13 (2008), pp. 493–513; Krajewski, External Trade Law and the Constitution Treaty: Towards a Federal and More Democratic Common Commercial Policy?, Common Market Law Review 42 (2005), pp. 91–127; Maydell, The European Community's Minimum Platform on Investment or the Trojan Horse of Investment Competence, in: Reinisch/Knahr (eds.), *International Investment Law in Context*, 2008, pp. 73–92; Mola, Which role for the EU in the development of international investment law? SIEL Inaugural Conference 2008, Online Proceedings Working Paper No. 26/08, available at http://papers.ssrn.com/sol3/papers.cfm?abstract_id=1154583; Shan, Towards a Common European Community Policy on Investment Issues, Journal of World Investment and Trade 2 (2001), pp. 603–625; Tietje, Die Außenwirtschaftsverfassung der EU nach dem Vertrag von Lissabon, in: Tietje/Kraft (eds.), *Beiträge zum Transnationalen Wirtschaftsrecht, Heft 83*,

A. Reinisch
University of Vienna, Dr.-Karl-Lueger-Ring 1, 1010, Vienna, Austria
e-mail: August.Reinisch@univie.ac.at

M. Bungenberg et al. (eds.), *International Investment Law and EU Law*,
DOI 10.1007/978-3-642-14855-2_3, © Springer-Verlag Berlin Heidelberg 2011

"new" investment power was inserted into the framework of the existing Common Commercial Policy (CCP) in a fairly low key style during the convention deliberations on a Constitution for Europe,[2] probably going unnoticed by many, though opposed by some.[3]

The result is a new version of the Treaty's CCP provision, Article 133 TEC, now to be renumbered as Article 207 Treaty on the Functioning of the European Union (TFEU),[4] which contains a new EU power with regard to "foreign direct investment" (FDI).

The two main articles of the new CCP after the entry into force of the Lisbon Treaty are as follows. Article 206 TFEU provides:

By establishing a customs union in accordance with Articles 28–32, the Union shall contribute, in the common interest, to the harmonious development of world trade, the progressive abolition of restrictions on international trade and on foreign direct investment, and the lowering of customs and other barriers.

Article 206 TFEU provides:

1. The common commercial policy shall be based on uniform principles, particularly with regard to changes in tariff rates, the conclusion of tariff and trade agreements relating to trade in goods and services, and the commercial aspects of intellectual property, foreign direct investment, the achievement of uniformity in measures of liberalisation, export policy and measures to protect trade such as those to be taken in the event of dumping or subsidies. The common commercial policy shall be conducted in the context of the principles and objectives of the Union's external action.
2. The European Parliament and the Council, acting by means of regulations in accordance with the ordinary legislative procedure, shall adopt the measures defining the framework for implementing the common commercial policy.
3. Where agreements with one or more third countries or international organisations need to be negotiated and concluded, Article 218 shall apply, subject to the special provisions of this article.

2009; Woolcock, The potential impact of the Lisbon Treaty on EU External Trade policy, SIEPS – European Policy Analysis 8/2008.

[2]Treaty Establishing a Constitution for Europe, OJ 2004 C 310/1.

[3]See French, German, and other objections: Proposition d'amendement à l'article III-212 Déposée par Monsieur de Villepin, available at http://european-convention.eu.int/docs/treaty/pdf/866/Art%20III%20212%20de%20Villepin%20FR.pdf; Suggestion for amendment of Article 24 by Mr. Joschka Fischer, CONV 685/03, available at http://european-convention.eu.int/Docs/Treaty/pdf/866/Art24Fischer.pdf; Suggestion for amendment of Article 24 by Mr David Heathcoat-Amory, available at http://european-convention.eu.int/Docs/Treaty/pdf/866/Art24Heathcoat-Amory%20EN.pdf; see also Krajewski, External Trade Law and the Constitution Treaty: Towards a Federal and more Democratic Common Commercial Policy?, Common Market Law Review 42 (2005), p. 91 (103–104); Ceyssens, Towards a Common Foreign Investment Policy? – Foreign Investment in the European Constitution, Legal Issues of Economic Integration 32 (2005), p. 259 (273).

[4]Consolidated versions of the Treaty on European Union and the Treaty on the Functioning of the European Union, OJ 2008 C 115/1.

The Commission shall make recommendations to the Council, which shall authorise it to open the necessary negotiations. The Council and the Commission shall be responsible for ensuring that the agreements negotiated are compatible with internal Union policies and rules.

The Commission shall conduct these negotiations in consultation with a special committee appointed by the Council to assist the Commission in this task and within the framework of such directives as the Council may issue to it. The Commission shall report regularly to the special committee and to the European Parliament on the progress of negotiations.

4. For the negotiation and conclusion of the agreements referred to in para. 3, the Council shall act by a qualified majority.

   For the negotiation and conclusion of agreements in the fields of trade in services and the commercial aspects of intellectual property, as well as foreign direct investment, the Council shall act unanimously where such agreements include provisions for which unanimity is required for the adoption of internal rules.

   The Council shall also act unanimously for the negotiation and conclusion of agreements:

   (a) In the field of trade in cultural and audiovisual services, where these agreements risk prejudicing the Union's cultural and linguistic diversity
   (b) In the field of trade in social, education and health services, where these agreements risk seriously disturbing the national organisation of such services and prejudicing the responsibility of Member States to deliver them
5. The negotiation and conclusion of international agreements in the field of transport shall be subject to Title VI of Part Three and to Article 218.
6. The exercise of the competences conferred by this article in the field of the common commercial policy shall not affect the delimitation of competences between the Union and the Member States, and shall not lead to harmonisation of legislative or regulatory provisions of the Member States in so far as the Treaties exclude such harmonisation.

Three core issues

Marc Bungenberg has addressed many of the legal issues arising from this legislative change in his contribution to this special issue[5] as well as in other publications.[6] As a commentator on his remarks at the 2009 Tübingen Workshop, I suggest restricting my remarks concerning this vast new field at the crossroads of EU and investment law to three main aspects:

1. What is the scope of the new investment power? Is it really limited to FDI and, if so, what kind of implications may flow from this subject-matter limitation?

[5] See Bungenberg, in this special issue, pp. 29 et seq.

[6] See supra footnote 1.

2. Is the "new" EU investment power limited to questions of market access or does it extend to the so-called post-investment phase as well?
3. Will future EU investment treaties contain investor–state dispute settlement mechanisms? If not, what are the expected implications for the future of investment protection for European investors abroad?

As is evident from the type of questions posed here, the following short comments will not be restricted to legal aspects. Rather, they clearly address policy implications, testing whether the intended strengthening of the EU's CCP powers was worth the price of its Member States' loss of powers.

The scope of the new investment competence – FDI versus a modern broad concept of investment

Literally, the new investment competence is limited to FDI. Article 206 as well as Article 207(1) and (4) TFEU use the term "foreign direct investment" (FDI). FDI is a well-known, traditional concept in investment law and economics which is generally considered to encompass investment with a certain degree of control to the exclusion of portfolio and other broader notions of investment covered by most bilateral investment treaties (BITs) and international investment agreements (IIAs).[7]

FDI is, however, a new term in the context of the CCP and uncertainty about its precise meaning could stem from the fact that it is nowhere defined in the TFEU. The only place where the related term "direct investment" appears already is in Article 57 of the currently valid TEC, which contains derogations from the free movement of capital under Article 56 TEC.[8] Also in this context, the term "direct investment" is not defined. An EU law meaning of this notion may rather be found indirectly in secondary law. For instance, Annex I of the Capital Liberalization Directive 88/361/EEC refers to "direct investments" and defines this term – at least

[7]See, e.g. Pollan, *Legal Framework for the Admission of FDI*, 2006; Shihata, Recent Trends relating to Entry of Foreign Investment, ICSID Review-FILJ 9 (1994), p. 48; Alfaro/Chanda/Kalemli-Ozcan/Sayek, How does Foreign Direct Investment Promote Economic Growth? – Exploring the Effects of Financial Markets on Linkages, Working Paper Series 12522, National Bureau of Economic Research, Cambridge, Mass., 2006; Blomström, The Economics of Foreign Direct Investment Incentives, Centre for Economic Policy Research, London, 2003; Graham, Foreign Direct Investment in the World Economy, IMF Working Paper, 1995; UNCTAD, The Determinants of Foreign Direct Investment – A Survey of Evidence, 1992.

[8]Article 57(1) TEC, Treaty Establishing the European Community (consolidated version), OJ 2002 C 325/1, provides: "The provisions of Article 56 shall be without prejudice to the application to third countries of any restrictions which exist on 31 December 1993 under national or Community law adopted in respect of the movement of capital to or from third countries involving direct investment – including in real estate – establishment, the provision of financial services or the admission of securities to capital markets".

for the purposes of the directive – as "investments of all kinds [. . .] which serve to establish or to maintain lasting and direct links between the person providing the capital and the entrepreneur to whom or the undertaking to which the capital is made available in order to carry on an economic activity".[9]

This notion is in fact very close to the OECD Benchmark Definition, speaking of "a strategic long-term relationship" as a crucial element of direct investment.[10] The IMF manual expresses this lasting interest element, which is crucial for the definition of direct investment in terms of a 10% minimum ownership requirement.[11]

---

[9]Council Directive 88/361/EEC of 24 June 1988 for the implementation of Article 67 of the Treaty, OJ 1988 L 178/5, provides in full: "Investments of all kinds by natural persons or commercial, industrial or financial undertakings, and which serve to establish or to maintain lasting and direct links between the person providing the capital and the entrepreneur to whom or the undertaking to which the capital is made available in order to carry on an economic activity. This concept must therefore be understood in its widest sense.

The undertakings mentioned under I-1 of the Nomenclature include legally independent undertakings (wholly-owned subsidiaries) and branches.

As regards those undertakings mentioned under I-2 of the Nomenclature which have the status of companies limited by shares, there is participation in the nature of direct investment where the block of shares held by a natural person of another undertaking or any other holder enables the shareholder, either pursuant to the provisions of national laws relating to companies limited by shares or otherwise, to participate effectively in the management of the company or in its control.

Long-term loans of a participating nature, mentioned under I-3 of the Nomenclature, means loans for a period of more than five years which are made for the purpose of establishing or maintaining lasting economic links. The main examples which may be cited are loans granted by a company to its subsidiaries or to companies in which it has a share and loans linked with a profit-sharing arrangement. Loans granted by financial institutions with a view to establishing or maintaining lasting economic links are also included under this heading".

[10]OECD Benchmark Definition of Foreign Direct Investment, 4th edition, April 2008, para. 11, available at http://www.oecd.org/dataoecd/26/50/40193734.pdf. ("11. Direct investment is a category of cross-border investment made by a resident in one economy (the direct investor) with the objective of establishing a lasting interest in an enterprise (the direct investment enterprise) that is resident in an economy other than that of the direct investor. The motivation of the direct investor is a strategic long-term relationship with the direct investment enterprise to ensure a significant degree of influence by the direct investor in the management of the direct investment enterprise. The 'lasting interest' is evidenced when the direct investor owns at least 10% of the voting power of the direct investment enterprise. Direct investment may also allow the direct investor to gain access to the economy of the direct investment enterprise which it might otherwise be unable to do. The objectives of direct investment are different from those of portfolio investment whereby investors do not generally expect to influence the management of the enterprise".) (Emphasis added).

[11]International Monetary Fund, Balance of Payments Manual, 5th edition, 1993, para. 362, available at http://www.imf.org/external/np/sta/bop/BOPman.pdf. ("362. Reflecting the difference noted previously, a direct investment enterprise is defined in this Manual as an incorporated or unincorporated enterprise in which a direct investor, who is resident in another economy, owns 10 percent or more of the ordinary shares or voting power (for an incorporated enterprise) or the equivalent (for an unincorporated enterprise). Direct investment enterprises comprise those entities that are subsidiaries (a nonresident investor owns more than 50 percent), associates (an investor own 50 percent or less) and branches (wholly or jointly owned unincorporated enterprises) either directly or indirectly owned by the direct investor. [. . .]".).

Although the distinction between portfolio and direct investment is thus a traditional one, the limitation to FDI appears curious, or at least surprising, to the scholars and practitioners of international investment law. Over the last few years, if not decades, investment law – both via IIAs and investor–state arbitration – has contributed to broadening the scope of investment protection. Many BITs and IIAs contain broad, so-called asset-based definitions of investments which are clearly not limited to FDI, but include portfolio investment as well.[12] In a parallel development, investment tribunals, in particular those under the ICSID Rules, have found ways to free the jurisdictional requirement of an "investment" under Article 25 of the ICSID Convention[13] from limited notions of direct investment and have held that also loans,[14] promissory notes,[15] etc. may be covered by the ICSID notion of "investment", which is equally undefined in the ICSID Convention.[16]

---

[12]See, e.g. Article 1 US Model BIT 2004: "For the purpose of this Treaty (...) 'investment' means every asset that an investor owns or controls, directly or indirectly, that has the characteristics of an investment, including such characteristics as the commitment of capital or other resources, the expectation of gain or profit, or the assumption of risk. Forms that an investment may take include:
(a) an enterprise;
(b) shares, stock, and other forms of equity participation in an enterprise;
(c) bonds, debentures, other debt instruments, and loans;
(d) futures, options, and other derivatives;
(e) turnkey, construction, management, production, concession, revenue-sharing, and other similar contracts;
(f) intellectual property rights;
(g) licenses, authorizations, permits, and similar rights conferred pursuant to domestic law; and
(h) other tangible or intangible, movable or immovable property, and related property rights, such as leases, mortgages, liens, and pledges".

[13]Article 25(1) Convention on the Settlement of Investment Disputes Between States and Nationals of Other States (ICSID Convention), 18 March 1965, UNTS 575 (1966), p. 159; ILM 4 (1965), p. 532, provides: "The jurisdiction of the Centre shall extend to any legal dispute arising directly out of an investment, between a Contracting State (or any constituent subdivision or agency of a Contracting State designated to the Centre by that State) and a national of another Contracting State which the parties to the dispute consent in writing to submit to the Centre. When the parties have given their consent, no party may withdraw its consent unilaterally".

[14]See, e.g. *Ceskoslovenska obchodni banka v. Slovak Republic*, ICSID Case No. ARB/97/4, Decision on Objections to Jurisdiction, 24 May 1999, ICSID Review – FILJ 14 (1999), p. 251.

[15]See, e.g. *Fedax N.V. v. Republic of Venezuela*, ICSID Case No. ARB/96/3, Decision on Objections to Jurisdiction, 11 July 1997, ICSID Reports 5 (2002), p. 186.

[16]Certain restrictive elements remain relevant as far as the interpretation of the term "investment" under the ICSID Convention is concerned. ICSID tribunals have developed a test, often referred to as *Salini* test, according to which the following elements indicate the existence of an investment: a certain duration, a regularity of profit and return, an element of risk for both sides as well as a substantial commitment and significance for the host state's development. See *Salini Costruttori S.p.A. and Italstrade S.p.A. v. Kingdom of Morocco*, ICSID Case No. ARB/00/4, Decision on Jurisdiction, 23 July 2001, Journal du droit international 129 (2002), p. 196, English translations of the French original in ILM 42 (2003), p. 609, ICSID Reports 6 (2004), p. 400. See also *Saipem S.p.A. v. The People's Republic of Bangladesh*, ICSID Case No. ARB/05/07, Decision on Jurisdiction and Recommendation on Provisional Measures, 21 March 2007, para. 99 ("[T]he notion of investment implies the presence of the following elements: (a) a contribution of money

Against this background it is surprising to see that the EU reform of the CCP appears to stick to an increasingly obsolete distinction and one may wonder where this comes from. A possible reason for this limitation may be seen in the CCP-related negotiations within the WTO framework. Since the Doha Round, the Community has participated in preliminary discussions on trade and investment which included market access negotiations for investments modelled after the GATS positive list approach.[17] In this forum, the Community suggested a limitation to FDI.[18] It thus appears likely that the trade-oriented Community simply relied on the WTO paradigm of foreign investment, in the form of FDI, without taking into account the more recent developments in investment law.

However, whatever the historical reasons for the limitation to FDI, the more important policy question is whether the regulation of FDI only makes practical sense. This seems at least questionable. If the EU wants to conclude BITs in the future which also provide protection for a broad scope of EU investments abroad, it

---

or other assets of economic value, (b) a certain duration, (c) an element of risk, and (d) a contribution to the host State's development".).

This test largely corresponds to the criteria developed by Schreuer in the first edition of his ICSID commentary. Schreuer, *The ICSID Convention: A Commentary*, 2001, p. 140. On the notion of "investment" in general see also Rubins, The Notion of "Investment" in International Investment Arbitration, in: Horn/Kröll (eds.), *Arbitrating Foreign Investment Disputes*, 2004, p. 283–324; Yala, The Notion of "Investment" in ICSID Case Law: A Drifting Jurisdictional Requirement? Some "Un-Conventional" Thoughts on Salini, SGS and Mihaly, Journal of International Arbitration 22 (2005) 2, p. 105; Dolzer, The Notion of Investment in Recent Practice, in: S. Charnovitz/Steger/van den Bossche (eds.), *Law in the Service of Human Dignity: Essays in Honour of Florentino Feliciano*, 2005, p. 261; Krishnan, A Notion of ICSID Investment, in: T. Weiler (ed.), *Investment Treaty Arbitration and International Law*, 2008, p. 61–84. Recently, some tribunals have displayed a more restrictive attitude, disqualifying economic activities as investments if they did not "contribute" to the development of the host state. Cf. *Patrick Mitchell v. Democratic Republic of the Congo*, ICSID Case No. ARB/99/7, Decision on the Application for Annulment of the Award, 1 November 2006; *Malaysian Historical Salvors, SDN, BHD v. Malaysia*, ICSID Case No. ARB/05/10, Award on Jurisdiction, 17 May 2007. See also Reinisch, Back to Basics: From the Notion of "Investment" to the Purpose of Annulment – ICSID Arbitration in 2007, The Global Community Yearbook of International Law & Jurisprudence (2008), p. 1591.

[17]According to the Doha Ministerial Conference the "Working Group on the Relationship Between Trade and Investment will focus on the clarification of: scope and definition; transparency; non-discrimination; modalities for pre-establishment commitments based on a GATS-type, positive list approach; development provisions; exceptions and balance-of-payments safeguards; consultation and the settlement of disputes between members. [...]". Doha Ministerial Declaration, para. 22, adopted on 14 November 2001, WT/MIN(01)/DEC/1, 20 November 2001, available at http://www.wto.org/english/thewto_e/minist_e/min01_e/mindecl_e.htm.

[18]See Communication from the European Community and its Member States to the Working Group on the Relationship between Trade and Investment: "Concept paper on the definition of investment", WT/WGTI/W/115, 16 April 2002, 4. ("Should a direct investor control the company with less than 10 per cent of the ordinary shares the following criteria could be taken into account to determine whether a direct investment relationship exists: (a) representation in the Board of Directors; (b) participation in policy-making processes; (c) inter-company transactions; (d) interchange of managerial personnel; (e) provision of technical information; (f) provision of long-term loans at lower than existing market rates".).

will have to conclude mixed agreements since the power to enter into agreements concerning portfolio investment is evidently not conferred to the EU.[19] Whether this will support the wish to strengthen the decision-making process with regard to investment agreements by transferring treaty-making powers to the EU may be doubted.

The scope of the new investment competence – market access versus investment protection

The actual formulation of the EU's post-Lisbon investment powers has given rise to considerable interpretation difficulties which are exacerbated by the fact that there are practically no *travaux preparatoires* available which would assist in the interpretation of the relevant treaty provisions. Given the fact that the Community has already been engaged in market-access negotiations concerning services with an impact on investment, it appears possible to consider the new investment powers as a continuation of such narrow trade-related powers regulating access of investments. At the other end of the spectrum, one may regard the new investment competence as a power which extends over all aspects of regulating investments.

On this background it is not surprising that diverging views have been adopted. Some authors are advocating a narrow reading of the substantive scope of the investment powers under the CCP.[20] They would stress the trade context in which this power has been conferred; it forms part of the chapter on the CCP, i.e. the Community's – now the EU's – external trade powers. This systematic argument is supported by the first programmatic CCP article in the new TFEU, Article 206, which mentions the long-term goal of the "progressive abolition of restrictions on international trade and on foreign direct investment".[21] This may be regarded as a reference to powers to regulate FDI access in parallel to market access in trade negotiations. In international investment law, such powers would be referred to as powers relating to the pre-establishment or access phase of investments which are

[19]Bungenberg, Centralizing European BIT Making under the Lisbon Treaty, Draft Paper to be presented at the 2008 Biennial Interest Group Conference in Washington, D.C., November 13–15, 2008, p. 20; Griebel, Überlegungen zur Wahrnehmung der neuen EU-Kompetenz für ausländische Direktinvestitionen nach Inkrafttreten des Vertrags von Lissabon, RIW (2009), p. 470; Tietje, Die Außenwirtschaftsverfassung der EU nach dem Vertrag von Lissabon, in: Tietje/Kraft (eds.), *Beiträge zum Transnationalen Wirtschaftsrecht, Heft 83*, 2009, p. 16.

[20]See, e.g. Krajewski, External Trade Law and the Constitution Treaty: Towards a Federal and more Democratic Common Commercial Policy? Common Market Law Review 42 (2005), p. 91 (112 et seq.).

[21]Article 206 TFEU: "By establishing a customs union in accordance with Articles 23 to 27, the Union shall contribute, in the common interest, to the harmonious development of world trade, the progressive abolition of restrictions on international trade and on foreign direct investment, and the lowering of customs and other barriers". (Emphasis added).

often not regulated in traditional BITs.[22] If the reference to "restrictions on foreign direct investment" is seen as referring to market access or to the pre-establishment phase, it is plausible to argue that *e contrario* the post-establishment phase, i.e. the substantive treatment standards, is not covered by such an investment power.

For the purpose of ascertaining the scope of the EU's new investment power, it is primarily the text of Article 207 para. 1 as well as para. 4 TFEU which has given rise to interpretative problems. Article 207(1) provides in full:

The common commercial policy shall be based on uniform principles, particularly with regard to changes in tariff rates, the conclusion of tariff and trade agreements relating to trade in goods and services, and the commercial aspects of intellectual property, foreign direct investment, the achievement of uniformity in measures of liberalisation, export policy and measures to protect trade such as those to be taken in the event of dumping or subsidies. The common commercial policy shall be conducted in the context of the principles and objectives of the Union's external action.

Article 207(4) TFEU provides in its relevant parts:

For the negotiation and conclusion of agreements in the fields of trade in services and the commercial aspects of intellectual property, as well as foreign direct investment, the Council shall act unanimously where such agreements include provisions for which unanimity is required for the adoption of internal rules.

Those advocating a narrow reading of the new investment powers along the access or pre-establishment line of argument tend to stress that Article 207(1) TFEU refers to "the conclusion of tariff and trade agreements" and that in spite of a rather awkward wording the reference to FDI may be seen as one of the fields in which such trade agreements are to be concluded just like those "relating to trade in goods and services" or those relating to "commercial aspects of intellectual property".

Similarly, they would emphasize that Article 207(4) TFEU confers a treaty-making power building on the existing trade powers of the Community. Thus, the Treaty now confers powers with regard to the "commercial aspects" of foreign direct investment just like the "commercial aspects" of intellectual property.

In support of such a limiting interpretation, one might add that such a division of powers between the EU and its Member States would be meaningful because it would create an EU market access investment power which is complementary to the Member States' power to regulate treatment in the post-establishment phase.

[22]See, e.g. Article 3 (1) Bolivia-Netherlands BIT: "Each Contracting Party shall ensure fair and equitable treatment to the investments of nationals of the other Contracting Party and shall not impair, by unreasonable or discriminatory measures, the *operation, management, maintenance, use, enjoyment, or disposal thereof* by those nationals". Article 3 (3) Austria-Georgia BIT: "Each Contracting Party shall accord to investors of the other Contracting Party and to their investments treatment no less favourable than that it accords to its own investors and their investments or to investors of any third country and their investments with respect to the *management, operation, maintenance, use, enjoyment, sale and liquidation of an investment*, whichever is more favourable to the investor". (Emphasis added).

This would also confirm the policy obviously adopted by the Community in its negotiations within the WTO[23] and it could be seen as a continuation of the policy apparently pursued by the EU Council in adopting the 2006 Minimum Platform on Investment[24] as a negotiating basis for future investment rules "affecting establishment".[25]

However, the wording of the two provisions cited above may equally lend itself to a different interpretation. The comma before the words "foreign direct investment" instead of a phrase such as "as well as of" indicates that FDI is not another item like "intellectual property", the commercial aspects of which may be regulated in trade agreements. Rather, it suggests that FDI is one of the elements of the CCP which shall be based on uniform principles. Similarly, Article 207(4) TFEU may be seen as a provision conferring powers for the "negotiation and conclusion of agreements" in the fields of FDI just like in the fields of trade in services and the commercial aspects of intellectual property. In fact, this reading appears to be closer to what a literal interpretation of Articles 206 and 207 requires.

In fact, such broader treaty-making powers of the EU would certainly enhance the bargaining power of the EU in future investment negotiations.

Dispute settlement in future EU investment treaties

In modern investment law it is clear that investor–state arbitration is one of the most import tools for an effective investment protection regime. It turns bilateral or sometimes multilateral treaty obligations of an interstate character into enforceable rights of private investors. By transferring the enforcement and compliance mechanism from the diplomatic protection paradigm to the directly pursued mixed arbitration, it also contributes to the depoliticization of investment disputes.[26] In fact, the latter concept is considered to be one of the major achievements of the ICSID Convention.[27]

It is thus no surprise that the majority of modern BITs as well as multilateral IIAs contain both interstate dispute settlement – rarely used in practice – as well as investor–state arbitration provisions. If the new post-Lisbon investment powers are

[23]See supra footnote 17.

[24]Council of the EU, Minimum Platform on Investment, 15375/06, 27 November 2006.

[25]See Maydell, The European Community's Minimum Platform on Investment or the Trojan Horse of Investment Competence, in: Reinisch/Knahr (eds.), *International Investment Law in Context*, 2008, p. 73 (75 et seq.).

[26]See already Shihata, Towards a Greater Depoliticization of Investment Disputes: The Roles of ICSID and MIGA, ICSID Review-FILJ 1 (1986), p. 1.

[27]See, e.g. Schreuer/Malintoppi/Reinisch/Sinclair, *The ICSID Convention – A Commentary*, 2009, (2nd ed.) p. 416; Schreuer, Investment Protection and International Relations, in: Reinisch/Kriebaum (eds.), *The Law of International Relations – Liber Amicorum Hanspeter Neuhold*, 2007, p. 345 (346 et seq.).

regarded as broad powers not limited to the establishment or access phase, but rather extending to the post-establishment treatment, there is no reason why this should not encompass the power to agree on dispute settlement, be it interstate or investor–state. In fact, the jurisprudence of investment tribunals with regard to most-favoured-nation clauses indicates that access to dispute settlement may be regarded as a crucial element of investment protection.[28]

However, there are external limits to the power of the EU to agree on mixed arbitration. For instance, investor–state arbitration under the ICSID Convention is only open to states that are parties to the ICSID Convention.[29] Opening ICSID dispute settlement to the EU would require a treaty revision which would be theoretically possible but, practically, very unlikely.[30]

Quite apart from the legal basis for future investor–state arbitration, there seems to be a question with regard to the political will of the EU to provide for such a form of dispute settlement. Although it appears that the EU is currently planning to provide for interstate dispute settlement, there are no perceptible signs of EU plans to include investor–state arbitration in future investment treaties or investment chapters of trade agreements.

If that is the case, one may wonder whether future EU investment agreements can be regarded as instruments providing for protection equivalent to that enjoyed under the current BITs of Member States. However, it is certainly not too late to ensure that this crucial element of investment protection be included in future EU investment agreements.

---

[28]*Maffezini v. Kingdom of Spain*, ICSID Case No. ARB/97/7, Decision on Objections to Jurisdiction, 25 January 2000, ICSID Review-FILJ 16 (2001), p. 212; ICSID Reports 5 (2002), p. 396; ILR 124 (2003), p. 9; ILM 40 (2001), p. 1129; *Siemens A.G. v. Argentine Republic*, ICSID Case No. ARB/02/8, Decision on Jurisdiction, 3 August 2004, ILM 44 (2005), p. 138. According to the *Siemens* tribunal BITs included "as a distinctive feature special dispute settlement mechanisms not normally open to investors. Access to these mechanisms is part of the protection offered under the Treaty. It is part of the treatment of foreign investors and investments and of the advantages accessible through a MFN clause". (*Siemens v. Argentina*, para. 120).

[29]See Article 25 ICSID Convention, supra note 13; Article 67 ICSID Convention: "This Convention shall be open for signature on behalf of States members of the Bank. [. . .]" (Emphasis added).

[30]The practical difficulties of revising the ICSID Convention were discussed earlier this decade when the introduction of an appellate body was debated. See, e.g. Legum, Options to Establish an Appellate Mechanism for Investment Disputes, in: Sauvant (ed.), *Appeals Mechanism in International Investment Disputes*, 2008, pp. 231–239; Bishop, The Case for an Appellate Panel and its Scope of Review, TDM 2 (2005) 2; Tams, An Appealing Option? The Debate about an ICSID Appellate Structure, in: Tietje/Kraft/Sethe (eds.), *Beiträge zum Transnationalen Wirtschaftsrecht, Heft 57*, Juni 2006; Gantz, An Appellate Mechanism for Review of Arbitral Decisions in Investor-State Disputes: Prospects and Challenges, Vanderbilt Journal of Transnational Law 39 (2006) 1, p. 39.

Conclusion

The new FDI powers of the EU after the entry into force of the Lisbon Treaty are a "leftover" from the deliberations in the convention debates on the Treaty Establishing a Constitution for Europe, where they originally entered the draft treaty text rather unnoticed. The text finally adopted in the TFEU of the Lisbon Treaty is everything but clear and unambiguous. Nevertheless, a consensus opinion seems to form according to which the EU will have exclusive competence to enter into treaties concerning FDI, not portfolio investments as part of its new CCP powers. This new investment power is likely to encompass not only market access, but also post-establishment rules. It should thus be possible for the EU to enter into fully fledged investment protection treaties which include in addition to the usual substantive treatment standards not only interstate dispute settlement, but also investor–state arbitration.

The Future of Bilateral Investment Treaties of EU Member States

Markus Burgstaller

Introduction

The era of modern investment treaties began when Germany and Pakistan concluded a bilateral agreement that entered into force in 1962. Germany's interest in investment treaties was grounded in the loss of its earlier foreign investment in negotiated settlements after 1949 owing to the damage it had caused in World War II. In an investment treaty the host state renounces part of its sovereignty to attract foreign investment. In turn, for an investor an investment treaty provides legal protection against state interference, which can come in a range of different forms, including expropriation, conversion and transfer of assets or any forms of unfair, inequitable, discriminatory or arbitrary treatment. Today, these investment guarantees are contained in large part in the approximately 2,000 bilateral investment treaties (BITs) that are currently in force worldwide. Germany has the most comprehensive network, with around 130 BITs in force, whereas other EU Member States also concluded a great number of BITs and continue to conclude such treaties.[1]

Prior to the entry into force of the Treaty of Lisbon, the then European Community had never concluded an investment treaty or an international agreement that predominantly regulated investment with third states. Indeed, from Opinion 1/94 it followed that the Community competence for the common commercial policy (CCP) did not extend to foreign direct investment (FDI) involving

This contribution draws on Burgstaller, European Law and Investment Treaties, Journal of International Arbitration 26 (2009) 2, pp. 181–216 and Burgstaller, European Law Challenges to Investment Arbitration, in: Waibel/Kaushal/Chung/Balchin (eds.), *The Backlash Against Investment Arbitration* (2010).

[1] Other European states with a comprehensive BIT programme are the UK, Italy and France, all of which have around 100 BITs in force. In 2007 the Netherlands (five), Finland, Germany and Spain (three each) together accounted for the majority of the new BITs concluded by EU Member States. See UNCTAD, Recent developments in international investment agreements (2007 to June 2008), available at http://www.unctad.org/en/docs/webdiaeia20081_en.pdf.

M. Burgstaller
Hogan Lovells, London, UK
e-mail: markus.burgstaller@hoganlovells.com

M. Bungenberg et al. (eds.), *International Investment Law and EU Law*,
DOI 10.1007/978-3-642-14855-2_4, © Springer-Verlag Berlin Heidelberg 2011

third states.[2] The Community and the Member States together, however, concluded several international agreements with third states that contain provisions in the field of FDI.[3] Regardless of these agreements, the Member States have been the dominant factor in shaping the EU's investment relations with third states. Nevertheless, even prior to the entry into force of the Treaty of Lisbon certain developments casted doubt on Member States' competence to conclude, amend and uphold their BITs.

First, on 3 March 2009, the European Court of Justice (ECJ) rendered its judgments in infringement cases brought by the Commission against Austria and Sweden. The cases concern some BITs entered into by the two Member States, on the one hand, and various third states, on the other hand, under which investors are guaranteed the free transfer of capital connected with their investments. All of the BITs concerned predate the accession of the Member States to the EU and were therefore governed by Article 307 EC (equivalent to Article 351 Treaty on the Functioning of the European Union; TFEU). Under this provision, Member States are obliged to take all appropriate steps to eliminate any incompatibility with the EC Treaty contained in such agreements. The Commission contended that Austria and Sweden infringed that obligation inasmuch as their agreements do not provide for the restrictions on the free movement of capital to and from third states envisaged in Articles 57(2), 59 and 60(1) EC and they had not acted to rectify that situation. In its judgments the ECJ declared that the Member States had failed to fulfil their obligations under Article 307(2) EC.[4] On 19 November 2009, the ECJ confirmed its view in its judgment in parallel infringement proceedings against Finland.[5] With a view to the ECJ's jurisprudence on Article 307 EC, in effect, Austria, Finland and Sweden may have to terminate the BITs in question. In its judgments, the ECJ clarified that the incompatibilities with the EC Treaty to which the BITs with third states give rise are not limited to the defendants in these cases.[6] Therefore, the ECJ's judgments may have consequences for BITs of all EU Member States.

---

[2]ECJ, Opinion 1/94, *WTO*, [1994] ECR I, 5267.

[3]The EU-Chile Association Agreement, OJ 2002 L 352/3, is the most advanced bilateral free trade agreement currently in force including investment issues. On the multilateral level, the most important agreement is the Energy Charter Treaty (ECT), a multilateral treaty with 47 contracting parties, including the European Communities and all Member States. Both the European Communities and all Member States are contracting parties to the ECT as it was concluded as a mixed agreement, falling within the scope of both Community and Member State competence. See Council and Commission Decision 98/181/EC, ECSC, EURATOM of 23 September 1997 on the conclusion by the European Communities, of the Energy Charter Treaty and the Energy Charter Protocol on energy efficiency and related environmental aspects, OJ 1998 L 69/1.

[4]ECJ, C-205/06, *Commission v. Austria*, not yet in the official reports; ECJ, C-249/06, *Commission v. Sweden*, not yet in the official reports. The author represented Austria in these proceedings up until but not inclusive of the oral hearing before the ECJ.

[5]ECJ, C-118/07, *Commission v. Finland*, not yet in the official reports.

[6]ECJ, C-205/06, *Commission v. Austria*, not yet in the official reports, para. 43; ECJ, C-249/06, *Commission v. Sweden*, not yet in the official reports, para. 43; ECJ, C-118/07, *Commission v. Finland*, not yet in the official reports, para. 34.

Secondly, on 1 December 2009, the Treaty of Lisbon entered into force.[7] The Treaty of Lisbon shifts the allocation of competences between the EU and its Member States in the field of FDI towards the EU. Article 207(1) TFEU states: "The common commercial policy shall be based on uniform principles, particularly with regard to changes in tariff rates, the conclusion of tariff and trade agreements relating to trade in goods and services, and the commercial aspects of intellectual property, *foreign direct investment*, [. . .]" (emphasis added). The extension of the CCP to FDI under the Treaty of Lisbon means that the EU has exclusive competence to negotiate and conclude investment treaties with respect to FDI.[8] Member States will lose the competence to negotiate and conclude treaties covered by the EU competence. But although the extent of the EU's competence is not yet clear, it would seem that the continued applicability of BITs of Member States in force with third states is not endangered,[9] subject to possible infringement proceedings commenced by the Commission against Member States.

Predominantly as a result of the EU's more recent enlargement process, there are currently around 190 BITs in force between Member States.[10] Prior to the entry into force of the Treaty of Lisbon, it was assumed that these so-called intra-EU BITs would continue to be applicable.[11] But the Treaty of Lisbon does not only extend the CCP to FDI, it also amends Article 60(1) EC insofar as it deletes the reference to third states. Article 75(1) TFEU states: "Where necessary to achieve the objectives set out in Article 67 [. . .] the European Parliament and the Council [. . .] shall define a framework for administrative measures with regard to capital movements and payments, such as the freezing of funds, financial assets or economic gains belonging to, or owned or held by, natural or legal persons, groups or non-State entities." It may be that, as a result, intra-EU BITs come under increased scrutiny of the Commission following the ECJ's judgments.

This article will analyse the future of BITs of EU Member States. First, it will deal with the external dimension, i.e. with the future of BITs of Member States as a result of the ECJ's judgments in the infringement proceedings against Member States and as result of the entry into force of the Treaty of Lisbon. Second, it will look at the internal dimension, i.e. at the future of intra-EU BITs, not least in the

---

[7]Treaty of Lisbon amending the Treaty on European Union (TEU) and the Treaty Establishing the European Community, signed in Lisbon on 13 December 2007, entered into force on 1 December 2009.

[8]Article 2(1) TFEU states: "When the Treaties confer on the Union exclusive competence in a specific area, only the Union may legislate and adopt legally binding acts, the Member States being able to do so themselves only if so empowered by the Union or for the implementation of Union acts." The TFEU put an end to the three-pillar-structure of the EU. Reference in the context of the TFEU is therefore made to "Union," "EU" and "EU law" rather than "Community" and "EC law".

[9]BVerfG, 2 BvE 2/08, *Organstreit*, NJW (2009), pp. 2267 et seq., para. 380.

[10]Wehland, Intra-EU Investment Agreements and Arbitration: Is European Community Law an Obstacle? ICLQ 58 (2009) 2, pp. 297–320.

[11]*Eastern Sugar B.V. (Netherlands) v. The Czech Republic*, Partial Award of 27 March 2007, available at http://ita.law.uvic.ca/documents/EasternSugar.pdf.

light of the Treaty of Lisbon. It will argue that for the time being in both dimensions BITs of Member States will continue to play a role.

The External Dimension: The Future of BITs with Third States

The Infringement Proceedings against Certain Member States

Prior to the entry into force of the Treaty of Lisbon, the scope of the CCP did not *explicitly* extend to FDI. Both the Treaty of Amsterdam and the Treaty of Nice extended the scope of the CCP. These two extensions, however, only had limited relevance for foreign investment policy.[12] To the contrary, the Commission's proposals regarding the expansion of the CCP to FDI at the intergovernmental conferences in Amsterdam and Nice were rejected.[13] In Opinion 1/94 the ECJ ended the expansion of Community competence under the CCP.[14] The ECJ thereafter indicated that trade measures would not necessarily be perceived as trade or commercial policy measures if they pursue other objectives. According to the ECJ's jurisprudence, a Community measure fell within the competence in the field of the CCP provided for in Article 133 EC "only if it relates specifically to international trade in that it is essentially intended to promote, facilitate or govern trade and has direct and immediate effects on trade in the products concerned."[15]

Besides explicit external competence, the Community also could have *implied* external competence. Implied *exclusive* competence arose either as a result of internal legal acts of the Community[16] or because external action was deemed necessary for achieving Community objectives.[17] Several competences of the Community provided for the adoption of measures that affected inward investment

---

[12]Ceyssens, Towards a Common Foreign Investment Policy? – Foreign Investment in the European Constitution, Legal Issues of Economic Integration 32 (2005) 3, p. 259 (261).

[13]Cremona, EC External Commercial Policy after Amsterdam: Authority and Interpretation within Interconnected Legal Orders, in: Weiler (ed.), *The EU, the WTO, and the NAFTA: Towards a Common Law of International Trade*, 2000, p. 5 (15); Herrmann, Common Commercial Policy after Nice: Sisyphus Would have Done a Better Job, CMLR 39 (2002) 1, p. 7 (14).

[14]In the early cases concerned with the interpretation of the scope of the CCP, the ECJ took a rather liberal stance when it held that the CCP had the same content as the commercial policy of a state. ECJ, Opinion 1/75, *Local Costs*, [1975] ECR, 1355; ECJ, Opinion 1/78, *International Agreement on Natural Rubber*, [1979] ECR, 2871.

[15]ECJ, Opinion 1/94, *WTO*, [1994] ECR I, 5267, para. 57; ECJ, Opinion 2/00, *Cartagena Protocol*, [2001] ECR I, 9713, para. 40; ECJ, C-281/01, *Commission v Council*, [2002] ECR I, 12049, paras. 40 and 41; ECJ, C-347/03, *Regione autonoma Friuli-Venezia Giulia and ERSA*, [2005] ECR I, 3785, para. 75; ECJ, Joined Cases C-402/05 P and C-415/05 P, *Kadi and Al Barakaat*, not yet in the official reports, para. 301.

[16]ECJ, 22/70, *AETR*, [1971] ECR 263.

[17]ECJ, Opinion 1/76, *Laying-up Fund*, [1977] ECR, 741.

to the EU.[18] These competences conferred certain external competences to the Community, but were far from covering all fields that are typically covered by a BIT.[19] However, the consequences of the implied exclusive competence of the Community were illustrated in the BIT infringement proceedings.

The Commission had originally commenced infringement proceedings not only against Austria, Finland and Sweden, but also against Denmark. The reasons why the cases against Austria and Sweden were combined whereas the case against Finland proceeded on a separate, somewhat delayed track remain unclear. Unlike Austria, Finland and Sweden, Denmark appears to have taken a more conciliatory approach. The Commission had argued that the 1968 Denmark–Indonesia BIT violated Denmark's obligation under Article 307 EC. In response, Denmark terminated the BIT and negotiated a new BIT with Indonesia, which was signed on 22 January 2007.[20]

In the cases against Austria and Sweden the BITs at issue contain provisions that guarantee the free transfer, without undue delay and in freely convertible currency, of payments connected with an investment. In its judgments the ECJ noted that the BITs were consistent with the wording of Articles 56(1) and 56(2) EC. Under these provisions all restrictions on the movement of capital and payments between Member States and between Member States and third states were prohibited.[21] Articles 57(2), 59 and 60(1) EC, however, conferred on the Council the power to restrict, in certain circumstances, movements of capital and payments between Member States and third states. As the BITs at issue do not contain any provision reserving such possibilities to restrict such movements, the ECJ found that it was necessary to examine whether Austria and Sweden were under an obligation to take the appropriate steps in accordance with Article 307(2) EC.

The ECJ observed that to ensure the effectiveness of Articles 57(2), 59 and 60(1) EC measures restricting the free movement of capital, where adopted by the Council, had to be capable of being applied immediately with regard to the state to which they relate.[22] The ECJ found that there was an incompatibility in a situation in which the BIT did not contain a provision allowing the Member State to exercise its rights and to fulfil its obligations and in which there was no international law mechanism which made that possible.[23] The ECJ noted that the Member States' measures did not fulfil their Community obligations. First, the time involved in any

[18]See, for example, Articles 47(2), 48 and 56–60 EC.

[19]See ECJ, Opinion 2/92, *OECD*, [1995] ECR I, 521.

[20]To the author's knowledge, the new Denmark–Indonesia BIT has not yet entered into force. Whereas the BIT does not require ratification by the Danish Parliament, it still appears to be awaiting ratification by Indonesia.

[21]ECJ, C-205/06, *Commission v. Austria*, not yet in the official reports, para. 26; ECJ, C-249/06, *Commission v. Sweden*, not yet in the official reports, para. 27.

[22]ECJ, C-205/06, *Commission v. Austria*, not yet in the official reports, para. 36; ECJ, C-249/06, *Commission v. Sweden*, not yet in the official reports, para. 37.

[23]ECJ, C-205/06, *Commission v. Austria*, not yet in the official reports, para. 37; ECJ, C-249/06, *Commission v. Sweden*, not yet in the official reports, para. 38.

international negotiations which would be required to reopen discussion of the BITs was incompatible with the practical effectiveness of measures to restrict the free movement of capital.[24] Second, international law mechanisms such as suspension or termination of the BITs or of some of their provisions were "too uncertain [...] to guarantee that the measures adopted by the Council could be applied effectively".[25]

The ECJ concluded that Austria and Sweden by not having taken appropriate steps to eliminate incompatibilities concerning the provisions on transfer of capital contained in the BITs at issue failed to fulfil their obligations under Article 307(2) EC. The ECJ did not indicate what consequences such failure would have. According to the ECJ's jurisprudence, once there is an incompatibility, there is an obligation under Article 307 EC to terminate incompatible prior international agreements. This obligation was reinforced by the ECJ in *Kadi and Al Barakaat*. In these joined cases, the court acknowledged that it had previously recognised that Article 307 EC "could, if the conditions for application have been satisfied, allow derogations from even primary law, for example from [Article 133 of the EC Treaty] on the common commercial policy."[26] It then, however, went on to observe that "Article 307 EC may in no circumstances permit any challenge to the principles that form part of the very foundations of the Community legal order [...]."[27]

Importantly, in the BIT infringement cases the court noted that the incompatibilities with the EC Treaty to which the BITs with third states give rise are not limited to the Member States which were defendants in these cases. Put differently, although the ECJ explicitly stated that the BITs violate Article 307 EC, all BITs of Member States with third states that contain similar free movement of capital clauses violate EU law. In the case against Finland the ECJ clarified the required scope of such a provision. Finland had argued that a clause with the following wording would ensure compliance with Community law: "Every contracting party guarantees under all circumstances, within the limits authorised by its own laws and decrees and in conformity with international law, a reasonable and appropriate treatment of investments made by citizens or companies of the other Contracting Party."[28] The ECJ acknowledged Finland's argument that restrictive measures adopted on the basis of Articles 57(2), 59 and 60 EC form part of the Finnish legal order.[29] However, the court ultimately found that since the interpretation of

[24]ECJ, C-205/06, *Commission v. Austria*, not yet in the official reports, para. 39; ECJ, C-249/06, *Commission v. Sweden*, not yet in the official reports, para. 40.

[25]ECJ, C-205/06, *Commission v. Austria*, not yet in the official reports, para. 40; ECJ, C-249/06, *Commission v. Sweden*, not yet in the official reports, para. 41.

[26]ECJ, Joined Cases C-402/05 P and C-415/05 P, *Kadi and Al Barakaat*, not yet in the official reports, para. 301.

[27]ECJ, Joined Cases C-402/05 P and C-415/05 P, *Kadi and Al Barakaat*, not yet in the official reports, para. 304.

[28]ECJ, C-118/07, *Commission v. Finland*, not yet in the official reports, para. 5.

[29]ECJ, C-118/07, *Commission v. Finland*, not yet in the official reports, para. 38.

those provisions was too uncertain, they are not sufficient to ensure compatibility of the BITs with Community law.[30]

Austria, Finland and Sweden ultimately may have to terminate the challenged BITs, even if termination should be considered an *ultima ratio*. Therefore, the immediate consequence will be felt by these Member States.[31] Because their efforts to amend these BITs had not been successful up until the commencement of the infringement proceedings, it seems unlikely that they will be able to do so in the foreseeable future. Thus, they may be forced to terminate these BITs.[32] In the light of the ECJ's reasoning, however, the intermediate-term consequences may well be felt not only by some, but by all Member States. BITs of Member States that do not contain a provision allowing them to exercise their rights and to fulfil their obligations under EU law (a so-called REIO clause) violate EU law. Although more recent BITs tend to contain such a clause, there are numerous BITs of Member States with third states in force that do not contain such a clause or a clause that does not adequately take into account Member States' obligations under EU law.[33] Potentially, therefore, numerous BITs of all Member States may be challenged by the Commission in infringement proceedings before the ECJ.

---

[30]ECJ, C-118/07, *Commission v. Finland*, not yet in the official reports, paras. 42 and 43.

[31]Typically, the BITs at issue remain in force for a further period of 10 years (see, for example, Article 12(3) of the Austria-Turkey BIT, signed on 16 September 1988, entered into force on 1 January 1992, available at http://www.unctad.org/sections/dite/iia/docs/bits/austria_turkey_ger.pdf) to 20 years (see, for example, Article 11(3) of the Sweden-Vietnam BIT, signed on 8 September 1993, entered into force on 2 August 1994, available at http://www.unctad.org/sections/dite/iia/docs/bits/sweden_vietnam.pdf) from the date when the termination of the BIT becomes effective in respect of investments made prior to the effective termination date. However, investments of, say, Austrian investors in Turkey after the termination of the Austria–Turkey BIT would not be protected under the BIT until the entry into force of a new BIT.

[32]There is no exact timeframe until when such termination has to take place. However, if Member States do not comply with ECJ judgments, the Commission may institute proceedings under Article 260 TFEU (equivalent to Article 228 EC) for non-compliance. According to the ECJ's jurisprudence, it has no jurisdiction under this article to require Member States to comply with its judgment within a specified period of time. ECJ, C-473/93, *Commission v. Luxembourg*, [1996] ECR I, 3207, paras. 46 and 47. However, although Article 260 TFEU does not specify the period within which a judgment must be complied with, the ECJ ruled that the interest in the immediate and uniform application of Community law required compliance as soon as possible. ECJ, C-291/93, *Commission v. Italy*, [1996] ECR I, 859, para. 6. Judgments in proceedings pursuant to the said article may well result in hefty fines for Member States; see ECJ, C-304/02, *Commission v. France*, [2005] ECR I, 6263. However, under Article 260 TFEU the court does not have the power either to seek an injunction or to order a Member State to take specific action. ECJ, C-105/02, *Commission v. Germany*, [1996] ECR I, 9659, paras. 44 and 45.

[33]It would seem that a clause such as the one contained in Article 7(c) of the most recent UK Model BIT of 2005 ("The provisions of this Agreement relative to the grant of treatment not less favourable than that accorded to the nationals or companies of either Contracting Party or of any third State shall not be construed so as to oblige one Contracting Party to extend to the nationals or companies of the other the benefit of any treatment, preference or privilege from any requirements of European Community law resulting from the United Kingdom's membership of the European Union prohibiting, restricting or limiting the movement of capital to or from any third country.") might be interpreted so as to comply with the UK's obligations under EU law even

The EU's FDI Competence under the Treaty of Lisbon

Limitation to FDI

The extension of the CCP under the Treaty of Lisbon has one significant limitation: the EU competence is limited to foreign *direct* investment (FDI).[34] Thus, agreements which cover forms of investment other than FDI are not covered by the exclusive EU competence. The TFEU, however, does not define the term "direct investment." Neither was the term defined in the EC Treaty. The term is referred to in Article 64 TFEU (equivalent to Article 57 EC). The explanatory notes of Council Directive 88/361/EEC, the secondary legislation passed with respect to Article 57 EC, define the term in the following way: "Investments of all kinds by natural persons or commercial, industrial or financial undertakings, and which serve to establish or to maintain lasting and direct links between the person providing the capital and the entrepreneur to whom or the undertaking to which the capital is made available in order to carry on an economic activity. This concept must therefore be understood in its widest sense."[35] Annex I to Directive 88/361/EEC gives some examples for direct investments such as "[e]stablishment and extension of branches or new undertakings belonging solely to the person providing the capital, and the acquisition in full of existing undertakings," "[p]articipation in new or existing undertakings with a view to establishing or maintaining lasting economic links,"[36] "[l]ong-term loans with a view to establishing or maintaining

---

though it remains unclear why this provision limits its scope of application to treatment not less favourable.

[34]In the draft articles of the Convention's Praesidium it was explained that FDI was included in the scope of the CCP "in recognition of the fact that financial flows supplement trade in goods and today represent a significant share of commercial exchanges." European Convention, draft articles on external action in the Constitutional Treaty, CONV 685/03. The Treaty of Lisbon did not change the Constitutional Treaty's provisions in respect of the EU's competence for FDI, which is why the Convention's deliberations are a useful point of reference for the interpretation of the EU's competence for FDI.

[35]Council Directive 88/361/EEC of 24 June 1988 for the implementation of Article 67 of the Treaty, OJ 1988 L 178/5. The ECJ has endorsed this definition of direct investment. See ECJ, C-446/04, *Test Claimants in the FII Group Litigation*, [2006] ECR I, 11753, paras. 179–182; ECJ, C-157/05, *Holböck*, [2007] ECR I, 4051, paras. 33 and 34; ECJ, C-112/05, *Commission v. Germany*, [2007] ECR I, 8995, para. 18; ECJ, C-101/05, *Skatteverket v. A*, [2007] ECR I, 11531, para. 46.

[36]According to the explanatory notes "there is participation in the nature of direct investment where the block of shares held by a natural person of another undertaking or any other holder enables the shareholder, either pursuant to the provisions of national laws relating to companies limited by shares or otherwise, to participate effectively in the management of the company or in its control." Council Directive 88/361/EEC of 24 June 1988 for the implementation of Article 67 of the Treaty, OJ 1988 L 178/5.

lasting economic links"[37] and "[r]einvestment of profits with a view to maintaining lasting economic links."[38]

The ECJ summarised the scope of direct investment in the following terms: "[T]he concept of direct investments concerns investments of any kind undertaken by natural or legal persons and which serve to establish or maintain lasting and direct links between the persons providing the capital and the undertakings to which that capital is made available in order to carry out an economic activity. As regards shareholdings in new or existing undertakings [...] the objective of establishing or maintaining lasting economic links presupposes that the shares held by the shareholder enable him, either pursuant to the provisions of the national laws relating to companies limited by shares or otherwise, to participate effectively in the management of that company or in its control."[39] The ECJ also ruled that a participation of 25% constitutes direct investment. At the same time, the ECJ was willing to adopt a flexible approach.[40] Overall, however, it is not entirely clear what "effective management" or "control" of a company means under EU law.

It seems therefore sensible to look at other definitions of the term "direct investment" in international legal instruments. Notably, the IMF defines FDI as "an incorporated or unincorporated enterprise in which a direct investor, who is resident in another economy, owns 10 percent or more of the ordinary shares or voting power (for an incorporated enterprise) or the equivalent (for an unincorporated enterprise)."[41] Similarly, pursuant to the OECD's definition, FDI is characterised by a long-term participation of at least 10% in a foreign enterprise.[42] Consequently, there appear to be good reasons why FDI means participation in a company through an investment of at least 10% in that company.[43]

[37]The explanatory notes explain that the term "long-term loans" means "loans for a period of more than 5 years which are made for the purpose of establishing or maintaining lasting economic links. The main examples which may be cited are loans granted by a company to its subsidiaries or to companies in which it has a share and loans linked with a profit-sharing arrangement. Loans granted by financial institutions with a view to establishing or maintaining lasting economic links are also included under this heading." Council Directive 88/361/EEC of 24 June 1988 for the implementation of Article 67 of the Treaty, OJ 1988 L 178/5.

[38]See also ECJ, C-463/00, *Commission v. Kingdom of Spain*, [2003] ECR I, 4581.

[39]ECJ, C-446/04, *Test Claimants in the FII Group Litigation*, [2006] ECR I, 11753, paras. 181 and 182.

[40]ECJ, C-492/04, *Lasertec*, [2007] ECR I, 3775, paras. 22–24.

[41]IMF, *Balance of Payments Manual*, (5th ed.) 1993, p. 86.

[42]OECD, *Benchmark Definition of Foreign Direct Investment*, 1999 (3rd edition), p. 7.

[43]Tietje, Die Außenwirtschaftsverfassung der EU nach dem Vertrag von Lissabon, in: Tietje/Kraft (eds); *Beiträge zum Transnationalen Wirtschaftsrecht, Heft 83*, 2009, p. 16 (discussing systematic problems with this interpretation).

Further Limitations to the EU's FDI Competence?

The wording of Article 207 TFEU does not contain any further limitation to the EU competence. Some commentators, however, argue that further restrictions to the EU's competence would apply. For example, it has been argued that the EU's competence would be limited in a sense that FDI has to be connected to international trade law. This limitation would be justified because the CCP traditionally concerned trade agreements and because the Convention deliberations would support such a reading.[44] But it is unclear why the traditional scope of the CCP should limit the EU competence for FDI. Rather, it would seem that precisely because the drafters intended to broaden the EU competence, such a limitation can hardly be justified.[45] Indeed, the Convention deliberations show that several representatives proposed the exclusion of FDI from the draft chapter on the CCP.[46] One representative emphasised the need for a clarification in the treaty to the extent it was not the intention to remove the competence of Member States to conduct bilateral investment activity.[47] No clarification, however, was made. Neither was any limitation included. This reinforces the view that the EU's competence is not limited to the extent that FDI has to be connected to international trade law.

Another possible limitation may flow from the parallelism clause contained in Article 207(6) TFEU which reads as follows: "The exercise of the competences conferred by this Article in the field of the common commercial policy shall not affect the delimitation of internal competences between the Union and the Member States, and shall not lead to harmonisation of legislative or regulatory provisions of Member States insofar as the Treaties exclude such harmonisation." The most important question with regard to international investment law is to what extent this clause may limit the scope of investment treaties which the EU is competent to conclude. It has been argued that by virtue of Article 207(6) TFEU substantive treatment standard provisions against expropriation would be excluded from the

---

[44]Krajewski, External Trade Law and the Constitution Treaty: Towards a Federal and more Democratic Common Commercial Policy? CMLR 42 (2005) 1, p. 91 (113–114).

[45]The fact that Article 207 TFEU, unlike Article 133 EC, does not distinguish between trade in goods and other areas of the CCP supports the view that the Treaty of Lisbon put an end to the traditional approach of the CCP which henceforth expands towards other areas of economic activity.

[46]Fischer, Amendment Form: Suggestion for amendment of Article: 24, available at http://european-convention.eu.int/Docs/Treaty/pdf/866/Art24Fischer.pdf; De Villepin, Fiche Amendement: Proposition d'amendement à l'article III-211, available at http://european-convention.eu.int/Docs/Treaty/pdf/866/Art%20III%20211%20de%20Villepin%20FR.pdf; Palacio, Fiche Amendement: Proposition d'amendement à l'Article: 23: Chapitre 2, Titre B, Partie, available at http://european-convention.eu.int/Docs/Treaty/pdf/866/Art23Palacio%20FR.pdf.

[47]Hain, Amendment Form: Suggestion for amendment of Article: Part II, Title B, Article 23, available at http://european-convention.eu.int/Docs/Treaty/pdf/866/Art23Hain.pdf.

EU's competence.[48] Indeed, Article 345 TFEU (equivalent to Article 295 EC) states that "[t]he Treaties shall in no way prejudice the rules in Member States governing the system of property ownership." But the better interpretation of this article is that it does not preserve exclusive powers for Member States to determine expropriation. According to the ECJ's settled case law, the right to property is one of the general principles of Community law. However, it is not absolute, but must be viewed in relation to its social function. The exercise of the right to property may be restricted, provided that those restrictions in fact correspond to objectives of general interest pursued by the Community and do not constitute in relation to the aim pursued a disproportionate and intolerable interference, impairing the very substance of the rights guaranteed.[49] More specifically, the ECJ has interpreted Article 295 EC narrowly so that its scope does not reserve for Member States the power to decide the conditions under which an expropriation takes place.[50] In *Kadi and Al Barakaat*, the court emphasised that even temporary measures which entail a restriction of the exercise of the right to property need to be justified under Community law. There must exist a reasonable relationship of proportionality between the means employed and the aim sought to be realised.[51] There is one more reason why expropriation is covered by the EU's competence for FDI. Before the Treaty of Lisbon was opened for signature, a footnote to Article 207 TFEU excluded expropriation from the scope of the reference to FDI.[52] The footnote, however, does not appear in the final text of the Treaty of Lisbon. For these reasons, the better view is that the EU competence extends to expropriation.

Neither does the parallelism clause in Article 207(6) TFEU mean that the lack of exercise of EU internal competence limits the existence or the exercise of EU external competence. As said, the drafters of the treaty deliberately extended the scope of the CCP to all sectors of the service economy. To interpret the clause as a limitation to the external and internal competences of the EU would limit the EU's external competences. Such an interpretation would contradict the express intention of the drafters of the treaty. Therefore, the better interpretation is that Article 207(6) TFEU may limit the internal, but not the external competence of the EU. As a consequence, the EU's external competence extends beyond the scope of the

[48]Ceyssens, Towards a Common Foreign Investment Policy? – Foreign Investment in the European Constitution, Legal Issues of Economic Integration 32 (2005) 3, p. 259 (279–281); Tietje, Die Außenwirtschaftsverfassung der EU nach dem Vertrag von Lissabon, in: Tietje/Kraft (eds.), *Beiträge zum Transnationalen Wirtschaftsrecht, Heft 83*, 2009, p. 14–15.

[49]ECJ, C-306/93, *SMW Winzersekt*, [1994] ECR I, 5555, para. 22; ECJ, Joined Cases C-37/02 and C-38/02, *Di Lenardo and Dilexport*, [2004] ECR I, 6911, para. 82; ECJ, C-347/03, *Regione autonoma Friuli-Venezia Giulia and ERSA*, [2005] ECR I, 3785, para. 119; ECJ, Joined Cases C-402/05 P and C-415/05 P, *Kadi and Al Barakaat*, not yet in the official reports, para. 355.

[50]See ECJ, 4/73, *Nold*, [1974] ECR 491; ECJ, C-84/95, *Bosphorus*, [1996] ECR I, 3953.

[51]ECJ, Joined Cases C-402/05 P and C-415/05 P, *Kadi and Al Barakaat*, not yet in the official reports, paras. 358 and 360.

[52]In addition, this footnote also excluded investor–state arbitration from the EU's FDI competence.

internal competence.[53] This interpretation is in line with the jurisprudence of the ECJ[54] and Article 3(2) TFEU.[55] An external competence may exist without a parallel internal competence.

In conclusion, under the Treaty of Lisbon the EU is competent to conclude comprehensive investment treaties. The competence covers market access, pre- and postestablishment standards of treatment, performance requirements, investor–state dispute settlement provisions and the terms of the conditions under which expropriation may take place.[56] The major apparent limitation of the EU's competence results from the term "foreign direct investment" (FDI). Because of this limitation, the EU's competence does not cover portfolio investments. The limitation is mitigated owing to the broad interpretation which should be given to this term. Nevertheless, owing to this limitation, investment treaties that cover all forms of investments will have to be concluded as mixed agreements. Mixed agreements have to be ratified by the EU and all 27 Member States. Therefore, the EU and its Member States will have to sign and ratify agreements with coverage beyond the exclusive EU competence for FDI.[57] In the process of negotiation, conclusion and application of mixed agreements, Member States are bound by the duty of cooperation. They are under a duty, if not to abstain from action, at the very least to

[53]Krajewski, External Trade Law and the Constitution Treaty: Towards a Federal and more Democratic Common Commercial Policy? CMLR 42 (2005) 1, p. 91 (116–117).

[54]ECJ, Case 22/70, *AETR*, [1971] ECR 263; ECJ, Opinion 1/75, *Local Costs*, [1975] ECR 1355.

[55]Article 3(2) TFEU states: "The Union shall also have exclusive competence for the conclusion of an international agreement when its conclusion is provided for in a legislative act of the Union or is necessary to enable the Union to exercise its internal competence, or in so far as its conclusion may affect common rules or alter their scope".

[56]It should not be overlooked that the EU's action on the international scene has to respect some non-economic principles enshrined in Article 21 TEU. Article 21(1) TEU states: "The Union's action on the international scene shall be guided by the principles which have inspired its own creation, development and enlargement, and which it seeks to advance in the wider world: democracy, the rule of law, the universality and indivisibility of human rights and fundamental freedoms, respect for human dignity, the principles of equality and solidarity, and respect for the principles of the United Nations Charter and international law." Further, Article 21(2) TEU states: "The Union shall define and pursue common policies and actions, and shall work for a high degree of cooperation in all fields of international relations, in order to [inter alia] foster the sustainable economic, social and environmental development of developing countries, with the primary aim of eradicating poverty; [...] help develop international measures to preserve and improve the quality of the environment and the sustainable management of global natural resources, in order to ensure sustainable development; [...]." It is unclear, however, to what extent these principles may in effect limit the EU's competence to conclude investment treaties with third states.

[57]As far as negotiation is concerned, the division of competence under a mixed agreement does not, generally, influence participation in negotiations. Although the practice is decided on a case-by-case-basis, it is accepted that the Commission may act as a sole negotiator for the whole agreement according to the mandate given to it by the Council. See Craig/de Burca, *EU Law*, 2008, pp. 198–199. See also Article 218 TFEU. On the problems with regard to mixed agreements generally see, for example, Weiler, The External Legal Relations of Non-Unitary Actors: Mixity and the Federal Principle, in: Weiler (ed.), *The Constitution of Europe: Do the New Clothes Have an Emperor?*, 1999, pp. 168–183.

cooperate closely with the EU's institutions to "facilitate the achievement of the [Union] tasks and to ensure the coherence and consistency of the action and its international representation."[58] Consequently, the result of the vertical allocation of competences under the Treaty of Lisbon may be an increased cooperation on foreign investment policy between the EU and the Member States.

Consequences of the EU's FDI Competence for the BITs of Member States and European Foreign Investment Policy

Upon the entry into force of the Treaty of Lisbon, existing BITs of Member States with third states remain valid under international law.[59] Further, without further qualification, these BITs are compatible with EU law since they were concluded before the new EU competence for FDI entered into force and thus do not violate the vertical allocation of competences between the EU and its Member States. The issue of compatibility with EU law cannot arise because the supervening external EU competence in matters previously regulated by BITs of Member States does not suffice in itself to render those agreements incompatible with the rules and principles governing the division of powers.[60] However, under Article 351(2) TFEU (equivalent to Article 307(2) EC) Member States will be under an obligation to terminate these BITs. Following the ECJ's judgments in the infringement cases and the entry into force of the Treaty of Lisbon, it remains to be seen whether the Commission will move on to challenge comprehensively the compatibility of BITs between Member States and third states with EU law. Until the Commission does, from its point of view, successfully challenge these BITs, they will remain in force, at least until the EU exercises its new competence in this field under the Treaty of Lisbon. Thus, investors may rely upon and commence arbitration under such BITs.

It is important to note that the Treaty of Lisbon does not contain a provision that would recognise the right of Member States to keep in place their existing agreements.[61] Neither does the Treaty of Lisbon contain a transition period. To that extent, the situation is different from the situation upon the full entry into force of the CCP. Then, two Council decisions were issued. The Council Decision of

---

[58]ECJ, C-266/03, *Commission v. Luxembourg*, [2005] ECR I, 4805, para. 60; ECJ, C-433/03, *Commission v. Germany*, [2005] ECR I, 6985, para. 66; ECJ, C-459/03, *Commission v. Ireland*, [2006] ECR I, 4635, para. 174. The principle of cooperation can be seen as a constitutional principle within EU external relations law. See Koutrakos, The Elusive Quest for Uniformity in EC External Relations, Yearbook of European Law 4 (2001), p. 243 (258).

[59]Compare Eeckhout, *External Relations of the European Union*, 2004, p. 335; but see Manzini, The priority of pre-existing treaties of EC Member States within the framework of international law, EJIL 12 (2001) 4, p. 781 (785).

[60]ECJ, C-466/08, *Commission v. United Kingdom*, Opinion of AG Tizzano [2002], ECR I, 9427, para. 113.

[61]Again, it should be emphasised that most BITs contain post-termination protection clauses.

9 October 1961 set out the guidelines on the duration of trade agreements with third states in light of the transitional period of 12 years under Article 111 EEC combined with Article 8 Treaty EEC. Article 1 of the Council Decision prohibited Member States from concluding trade agreements with third states beyond the transitional period. Article 2 provided for a default rule of a 1-year termination period for agreements which neither foresaw the entry into force of the CCP nor allowed for an "annual notice of termination." Article 3 determined the joint examination by Member States and the Commission of the Member States' international agreements to ensure "that they [did] not constitute an obstacle to introduction of the common commercial policy provided for in the Treaty." Finally, Article 4 stated that the Member States, in consultation with the Commission, shall arrange that the terminal dates of their agreements with third states coincide.[62] A second decision, the Council Decision of 29 December 1969, shows that some flexibility in the regime set out in the previous Council Decision was adopted. In particular, Article 3 of this Council Decision stated that if the Member State instrument did not constitute an obstacle to the implementation of the CCP, the Commission may propose to the Council that the Member State concerned be authorised, by way of derogation from Article 1 of the Council Decision of 9 October 1961, to extend, expressly or tacitly, for a period to be specified, the provisions in question of agreements of Member States.[63]

It may well be that these Council decisions of 1961 and 1969 will be used as a template to set time limits and guidelines for the termination and/or renegotiation of BITs of Member States with third states, even if the Treaty of Lisbon does not contain a transition period to that effect. Another possibility in the transitory stage of transfer of competence would be to conclude an EU investment framework agreement with third states while leaving details to the individual Member States. Such a framework agreement would lay down the basic conditions of investment protection with a third state, whereas the necessary details concerning the actual investment guarantees may be better agreed by the Member State and the third state in question. There are also precedents for the application of this latter model, which has sometimes been called the Community's multilevel governance reflected in a multilevel conclusion of international agreements.[64]

[62]Council Decision of 9 October 1961 on standardisation of the duration of trade agreements with third countries, OJ 1961 71/1274.

[63]Council Decision of 16 December 1969 on the progressive standardisation of agreements concerning commercial relations between Member States and third countries and on the negotiation of Community agreements (69/494/EEC), OJ 1969 L 326/42.

[64]See, for example, the example of readmission agreements described by Kuijper, Fifty Years of EC/EU External Relations: Continuity and the Dialogue Between Judges and Member States as Constitutional Legislators, Fordham International Law Journal 31 (2008) 6, p. 1571 (1597). In the context of international trade see, for example, Petersmann, Multilevel Judicial Governance of International Trade Requires a Common Conception of Rule of Law and Justice, Journal of International Economic Law 10 (2007) 3, p. 529 (551).

Yet another possibility would be to look at treaty partners individually and conclude an EU investment treaty only in selected cases. For example, in the case of aviation policy, one outcome of the ECJ's AETR jurisprudence was that the new "Open Skies" agreement with the USA was concluded as a mixed agreement.[65] Contrarily, aviation agreements with smaller treaty partners, in which only a few Member State carriers would be interested, could be left to these Member States, constrained by some principle rules of Community law laid down in a regulation.[66] To be sure, an approach used in one policy area may not be equally suitable for another policy area because the economics, the history and any other factors are different. But such an approach may nevertheless be useful and be it for the consistency and coherence of the EU's external relations policy alone. Further, it may well be that the EU will face severe practical constraints in the exercise of its new competence for FDI under the Treaty of Lisbon. In this context, it would seem unlikely that the EU has the resources to enter into BIT negotiations with third states on a broad scale. Rather, it would seem more likely that the EU focuses on selected third states, thereby adopting a piecemeal approach.

In the end, from an EU policy perspective, an enhanced EU competence is to be welcomed because the negotiating power of the Commission is likely to be stronger than that of individual Member States, in particular smaller ones. A strengthened EU competence will also contribute to the development of an integrated policy approach concerning trade and investment. As was recognised by the drafters of the Constitutional Treaty (and thus, by implication the drafters of the Treaty of Lisbon), there are strong linkages between these two areas and an increased EU competence for investment might make it easier for the EU to conclude combined international agreements on trade and investment. Indeed, the main rationale for including investment into the CCP was to strengthen the EU as an actor in multilateral negotiations on foreign investment.[67] Thereby, the drafters followed a proposal which the Commission has made for many years.[68]

An extension of the CCP to investment will also lead to efficiency gains, since an investment treaty between the EU and a third state will cover 27 Member States at once. The multiplying effect will be particularly beneficial for those Member States with few BITs.[69] An EU competence for investment will also reduce distortions

---

[65] See Council Decision No. 2007/339/EC, OJ 2007 L 134/1.

[66] See Council Regulation No. 847/2004, OJ 2004 L 157/7.

[67] European Convention, Draft Articles on external action in the Constitutional Treaty, CONV 685/03.

[68] The Commission made proposals to that effect for example during the intergovernmental conferences leading to the Treaty of Amsterdam and the Treaty of Nice. See European Commission, Report on the operation of the Treaty on European Union, SEC (95) 731, 57–60 and European Commission, Commission Opinion in accordance with Article 48 EU, COM (2000) 34, 27.

[69] On the other hand, Member States might have different priorities in the respective third state, depending how extensively their investors are engaged in that state and how strongly they are

between EU investors in third states through replacing the existing BITs of Member States with EU BITs. This will remedy a comparative advantage which a few Member States enjoy compared with other Member States. Such competence will also improve the transparency at the global level, as the total number of BITs will be reduced significantly. A common EU investment policy will further increase the attractiveness of the EU as a location for FDI from third states because a harmonised investment scheme on an EU level will create an equal level playing field for foreign investors in the EU. Economies with more transparent trade and FDI regimes attract more FDI compared with those economies with less transparent trade and FDI regimes.[70]

But even upon the entry into force of the Treaty of Lisbon, the continued fragmentation of competences between the EU and its Member States, in particular due to the limitation of the EU competence to FDI under the Treaty of Lisbon, is likely to cause confusion both within the EU and with the EU's treaty partners. Because the EU's exclusive competence to conclude investment treaties with third states only covers FDI, and does not cover portfolio investments, BITs comparable to the US Model BIT covering all kinds of investments will have to be concluded as mixed agreements. On the other hand, if the EU were to conclude BITs with third states alone, without the involvement of Member States, the most significant problem would be Article 67 of the International Centre for Settlement of Investment Disputes (ICSID) Convention. The ICSID is the most important arbitral institution in the field of investment disputes. The availability of the ICSID presents numerous advantages for the settlement of investment disputes.[71] According to its Article 67, the ICSID Convention is open "for signature on behalf of States members of the Bank." Notably, the ICSID Convention is not open for signature for a supranational organisation such as the EU. It is doubtful, at least, whether Article 67 of the ICSID Convention would allow for the EU to sign "on behalf of States." Rather, it would seem that the EU cannot become a member of the ICSID Convention. Until and unless it may do so, however, the EU may not offer its treaty

---

interested in attracting investors from there. Individual Member States may also have different preferences for political and historical reasons. See the discussion by Karl, The Competence for Foreign Direct Investment – New Powers for the European Union, JWIT 5 (2004) 3, p. 413 (425–426).

[70]Drabek/Payne, The Impact of Transparency on Foreign Direct Investment, World Trade Organization Economic Research and Analysis Division Staff Working Paper ERAD-99-02, available at http://www.wto.org/english/res_e/reser_e/erad-99-02.doc.

[71]For example, the rules of procedure for arbitral proceedings are specifically tailored for arbitration with the participation of a government party; oversight by the ICSID Secretariat and the availability of the institution's resources and experienced personnel represent a major asset in investment arbitration; and the self-contained enforcement regime of the ICSID Convention means that enforcement of ICSID awards will generally be smoother than enforcement of non-ICSID awards. See McLachlan/Shore/Weiniger, *International Investment Arbitration*, 2007, pp. 4–5; Muchlinski, Policy Issues in: Muchlinski/Ortino/Schreuer (eds.), *The Oxford Handbook of International Investment Law*, 2008, pp. 4–48; Dolzer/Schreuer, *Principles of International Investment Law*, 2008, pp. 20–21; Schreuer/Malintoppi/Reinisch/Sinclair, *The ICSID Convention – A Commentary*, (2nd ed.) 2009, pp. 1117–1150.

partners to arbitrate under the ICSID arbitration rules. Moreover, according to Article 66(1) ICSID Convention, each amendment to the ICSID Convention requires that all Contracting States have ratified, accepted or approved the amendment. Therefore, in practice such an amendment is unlikely. Potentially, the non-availability of the ICSID dispute settlement mechanism may be a drawback for investors protected only under an EU investment treaty.

The Internal Dimension: The Future of Intra-EU BITs

On 27 March 2007, an arbitral tribunal constituted under the authority of the Arbitration Institute of the Stockholm Chamber of Commerce issued a partial award in the matter of an ad hoc arbitration in the case *Eastern Sugar B.V. (Netherlands) v. The Czech Republic.*[72] The tribunal quoted extensively from a letter by the Commission Directorate-General Internal Market and Services of 13 January 2006 (2006 Letter) and a note by Commission Directorate-General Internal Market and Services of November 2006 (2006 Note). In the end, the tribunal rejected the Czech Republic's objections to the tribunal's jurisdiction. At heart, the tribunal rejected the Czech Republic's argument that the applicable BIT in force between the Netherlands and the Czech Republic ("Netherlands–Czech Republic BIT")[73] would not be applicable after the accession of the Czech Republic to the EU. The tribunal held that therefore, "the BIT, including its arbitration clause, is still in force".[74]

In *Eastern Sugar* the Czech Republic did not argue that the Netherlands–Czech Republic BIT had been expressly terminated. Rather, it invoked Article 59(1) of the Vienna Convention on the Law of Treaties (VCLT)[75] and argued that the BIT was

[72]*Eastern Sugar B.V. (Netherlands) v. The Czech Republic*, Partial Award of 27 March 2007, available at http://ita.law.uvic.ca/documents/EasternSugar.pdf. The Final Award dated 12 April 2007 dealt merely with the arbitration costs, available at http://ita.law.uvic.ca/documents/FinalAward_EasternSugar.pdf.

[73]Agreement on encouragement and reciprocal protection of investments between the Kingdom of the Netherlands and the Czech and Slovak Federal Republic, signed on 29 April 1991, entered into force on 1 October 1992. As of 1 January 1993 the Czech Republic succeeded into the Czech and Slovak Federal Republic's international obligations, including those arising from the BIT.

[74]*Eastern Sugar B.V. (Netherlands) v. The Czech Republic*, Partial Award of 27 March 2007, para. 172.

[75]Article 59 VCLT ("Termination or suspension of the operation of a treaty implied by conclusion of a later treaty") states: "1. A Treaty shall be considered as terminated if all the parties to it conclude a later treaty relating to the same subject matter and: (a) it appears from the later treaty or is otherwise established that the parties intended that the matter should be governed by that treaty; or (b) the provisions of the later treaty are so far incompatible with those of the earlier one that the two treaties are not capable of being applied at the same time. 2. The earlier treaty shall be considered as only suspended in operation if it appears from the later treaty or is otherwise established that such was the intention of the parties".

not applicable beyond the Czech Republic's accession to the EU, i.e. beyond 1 May 2004. The Czech Republic was of the view that the BIT should be considered as terminated following its accession to the EU and that Dutch investments in the Czech Republic should be governed by Community law. As of the date of its accession to the EU, the intra-EU investment regime would supersede the obligations in the BIT.[76] Moreover, if earlier treaties survived after its accession to the EU, this might distort the principle of equality of treatment.[77] The application of the BIT would also breach the principle of mutual trust. This principle would imply that Eastern Sugar would have to bring its claim before a Czech national court. There would be no room for international arbitration in this area. The Czech Republic concluded that the BIT was not applicable and that the arbitral tribunal did not have jurisdiction.[78]

The tribunal quoted extensively from the 2006 Letter. The 2006 Letter noted that the date of the Czech Republic's accession to the EU was the decisive date. For facts occurring after accession, the BIT was not applicable to matters falling under Community competence. The Commission stated: "Only certain residual matters, such as diplomatic representation, expropriation and eventually investment promotion, would appear to remain in question. Therefore, where the EC Treaty or secondary legislation are in conflict with some of these BITs' provisions - or should the EU adopt such rules in the future - Community law will automatically prevail over the non-conforming BIT provisions. [. . .] intra-EU BITs should be terminated in so far as the matters fall under Community competence. However, the effective prevalence of the EU *acquis* does not entail, at the same time, the automatic termination of the concerned BITs or, necessarily, the non-application of all their provisions. Without prejudice to the primacy of Community law, to terminate these agreements, Member States would have to strictly follow the relevant procedure for this in regard in the agreements themselves."[79]

With regard to dispute settlement procedures between Member States, the 2006 Letter observed that Member States, in the light of Article 292 EC,[80] cannot apply the dispute settlement procedures in the BIT insofar as the dispute concerns a matter falling under Community competence. With regard to investor–state

---

[76]*Eastern Sugar B.V. (Netherlands) v. The Czech Republic*, Partial Award of 27 March 2007, paras. 101–104.

[77]In *Matteucci v. Belgium* the ECJ concluded that "[a] bilateral agreement which reserves the scholarships in question for nationals of the two Member States which are the parties to the agreement cannot prevent the application of the principle of equality of treatment between national and Community workers established in the territory of one of those two Member States." ECJ, 235/87, *Matteucci v. Begium*, [1988] ECR, 5589, para. 23.

[78]*Eastern Sugar B.V. (Netherlands) v. The Czech Republic*, Partial Award of 27 March 2007, paras. 106–108.

[79]*Eastern Sugar B.V. (Netherlands) v. The Czech Republic*, Partial Award of 27 March 2007, para. 119.

[80]Article 292 EC (= Article 344 TFEU) states: "Member States undertake not to submit a dispute concerning the interpretation or application of this Treaty to any method of settlement other than those provided for therein".

dispute settlement, the Commission stated: "Since Community law prevails from the time of accession, the dispute should be decided on basis of Community law (which indirectly also follows from Article 8(6) first bullet point in the agreement between the Czech Republic and the Netherlands).[81] However, it may be argued that the private investor could continue to rely on the settlement procedures provided for in the agreement until formal termination of the BIT if the dispute concerns facts which occurred before accession."[82]

The *Eastern Sugar* tribunal found the 2006 Letter "for the most part diplomatic and ambiguous."[83] Although the tribunal was right to emphasise that it was not bound by the 2006 Letter, some of its reasoning lacks support. The tribunal's notion that the Commission "did not start infringement proceedings against the Netherlands and the Czech Republic and other Member States for failure to terminate their BITs"[84] does not support its position. It is well established that the Commission has a *right*, but *no obligation* to commence infringement proceedings against Member States. In fact, the Commission has substantial leeway to commence proceedings against Member States and the discretion of the Commission is not even subject to judicial review.[85] Similarly, the tribunal's observation that "neither the Czech Republic nor the Netherlands, nor anybody else, did file a complaint to the European Commission, against the Netherlands and the Czech Republic"[86] does not support its position, as there is no obligation of Member States or "anybody else" to that effect.

In the 2006 Note, the Commission reiterated its view, expressed in the 2006 Letter, that most of the content of intra-EU BITs was superseded by Community law upon accession of the respective Member State and that there "appears to be no need for agreements of this kind in the single market and their legal character after accession is not entirely clear".[87] The Commission feared that investor–state

[81] Article 8(6) of the Netherlands-Czech Republic BIT states: "The arbitral tribunal shall decide on the basis of the law, taking into account in particular though not exclusively:

- the law in force of the Contracting Party concerned;
- the provisions of this Agreement, and other relevant Agreements between the Contracting Parties;
- the provisions of special agreements relating to the investment;
- the general principles of international law."

It bears emphasising that the Commission referred only to the first bullet point of this provision.

[82] *Eastern Sugar B.V. (Netherlands) v. The Czech Republic*, Partial Award of 27 March 2007, para. 119 (footnote added).

[83] *Eastern Sugar B.V. (Netherlands) v. The Czech Republic*, Partial Award of 27 March 2007, para. 120.

[84] *Eastern Sugar B.V. (Netherlands) v. The Czech Republic*, Partial Award of 27 March 2007, para. 121.

[85] See, for example, CFI, T-126/95, *Dumez v. Commission*, [1995] ECR II, 2863.

[86] *Eastern Sugar B.V. (Netherlands) v. The Czech Republic*, Partial Award of 27 March 2007, para. 122.

[87] *Eastern Sugar B.V. (Netherlands) v. The Czech Republic*, Partial Award of 27 March 2007, para. 126.

dispute settlement procedures could lead to arbitration taking place without relevant questions of Community law being submitted to the ECJ, with unequal treatment of investors among Member States as a possible outcome. "In order to avoid such legal uncertainties and unnecessary risks for Member States, it is strongly recommended that Member States exchange notes to the effect that such BITs are no longer applicable, and also formally rescind such agreements. The [Economic and Financial] Committee is invited to endorse this approach and Member States are asked to communicate to the Commission by 30 June 2007 which actions have been taken in that regard and which of their intra-EU investment agreements still remain to be terminated."[88]

The *Eastern Sugar* tribunal, without giving any reasons, rightly concluded that the 2006 Note did not support the view that intra-EU BITs are all automatically superseded.[89] The tribunal went on to reject the Czech Republic's submission to refer the matter to the ECJ.[90] Indeed, under the ECJ's case law, an arbitral tribunal is not a "court or tribunal of a Member State" within the meaning of Article 267 TFEU (equivalent to Article 234 EC). The reason put forward by the ECJ is that the parties are under no obligation, in law or in fact, to refer their dispute to arbitration and the public authorities of the Member States concerned are not involved in the decision to opt for arbitration nor are they required to intervene of their own accord in the proceedings before an arbitral tribunal.[91]

After the tribunal had found that neither the BIT nor the Czech Republic's preaccession agreement with the Commission (the "Europe Agreement") nor the Accession Treaty had dealt expressly with the question of whether the BIT was still valid, it noted that the effect of the Czech Republic's accession to the EU would have to be judged by international law, and in particular Article 59 VCLT.[92] The tribunal rejected the Czech Republic's argument that EU law would relate to the

[88] *Eastern Sugar B.V. (Netherlands) v. The Czech Republic*, Partial Award of 27 March 2007, para. 126. Subsequently, the Czech Ministry of Finance proposed to the Czech Government that it terminate Czech intra-EU BITs. As a consequence, Italy and the Czech Republic terminated their BIT and Denmark is in the process of terminating its BIT with the Czech Republic. Slovenia and Malta announced their agreement with the Czech position, and their intent to unwind their own BITs. Italy also has indicated that it intends to terminate a number of other intra-EU BITs. However, not all EU member states concur with the Czech Republic's approach, including, according to public reports, Belgium, Germany, the Netherlands and the UK.

[89] *Eastern Sugar B.V. (Netherlands) v. The Czech Republic*, Partial Award of 27 March 2007, para. 128.

[90] *Eastern Sugar B.V. (Netherlands) v. The Czech Republic*, Partial Award of 27 March 2007, para. 138.

[91] ECJ, Case 102/81, *Nordsee*, [1982] ECR 1095, paras. 10–12; ECJ, Case C-126/97, *Eco Swiss China Time Ltd v. Benetton International NV*, [1999] ECR I, 3055, para. 34; ECJ, Case C-125/04, *Denuit and Cordenier v. Transorient*, [2005] ECR I, 923, para. 13.

[92] *Eastern Sugar B.V. (Netherlands) v. The Czech Republic*, Partial Award of 27 March 2007, paras. 144–158.

same subject matter as the BIT.[93] It also noted that it was neither the common intention of the Czech Republic and the Netherlands that the EU Treaty should supersede the BIT nor were the BIT and the EU Treaty incompatible.[94] It did not only reject the Czech Republic's argument based on Article 59 VCLT, but it also rejected its argument based on Article 30 VCLT.[95] Indeed, if the restrictive conditions of Article 59 VCLT are not met, Article 30 VCLT governs treaty relationships. The latter article is concerned with the application of successive treaties relating to the same subject matter, and deals only with the priority of inconsistent obligations in treaties when there is no doubt that both are in force. It therefore comes into play once it has been determined by way of application of Article 59 VCLT that the parties did not intend to abrogate or suspend the earlier treaty.[96] The tribunal, however, neither engaged in an analysis of Article 30 VCLT[97] nor did it refer to Article 307 EC.[98]

Eastern Sugar is not the only arbitral award that deals with the validity and applicability of intra-EU BITs. It is highlighted because to date it appears to be the

---

[93] *Eastern Sugar B.V. (Netherlands) v. The Czech Republic*, Partial Award of 27 March 2007, para. 165.

[94] *Eastern Sugar B.V. (Netherlands) v. The Czech Republic*, Partial Award of 27 March 2007, paras. 167–168.

[95] Article 30 VCLT ("Application of successive treaties relating to the same subject-matter") states in relevant parts: "2. When a treaty specifies that it is subject to, or that it is not to be considered as incompatible with, an earlier or later treaty, the provisions of that other treaty prevail. 3. When all the parties to the earlier treaty are parties also to the later treaty but the earlier treaty is not terminated or suspended in operation under Article 59, the earlier treaty applies only to the extent that its provisions are compatible with those of the later treaty".

[96] Anthony Aust, *Modern Treaty Law and Practice*, 2007, p. 293. On the problems regarding the application of Article 30 VCLT see Vierdag, The time of the "conclusion" of a multilateral treaty: Article 30 of the Vienna Convention on the Law of Treaties and related provisions, BYIL 59 (1988), p. 75 (110–111). It has been suggested that owing to the highly integrated nature of Community secondary law the implications of Member States' duties under Community law should be considered in the light of Article 27 VCLT ("A party may not invoke the provisions of its internal law as justification for its failure to perform a treaty.") rather than Article 30 VCLT. Licková, European Exceptionalism in International Law, EJIL 19 (2008) 3, p. 463 (470). However, the better view seems to be that EU law constitutes a highly developed order of international law.

[97] The tribunal shrugged off Article 30 VCLT and confined itself to stating that: "The Arbitral Tribunal moreover does not believe that it can accept the Czech Republic's argument that the treaty can end partially and remain in force otherwise. This situation would be governed by Article 30 of the Vienna Convention." *Eastern Sugar B.V. (Netherlands) v. The Czech Republic*, Partial Award of 27 March 2007, para. 178.

[98] Although Article 307 EC applies to agreements of Member States with third states only, it is nevertheless remarkable that the tribunal did not refer to it, while at the same time rejecting the Czech Republic's arguments by glancing at Article 13(3) of the Netherlands–Czech Republic BIT. *Eastern Sugar B.V. (Netherlands) v. The Czech Republic*, Partial Award of 27 March 2007, paras. 174–175. Article 13(3) of the Netherlands–Czech Republic BIT states: "In respect of investments made before the date of the termination of the present Agreement the foregoing Articles [regulation entry into force, tacit extension and procedure for termination; MB] thereof shall continue to be effective for a further period of fifteen years from that date".

only publicly available award in this regard. There appears to be at least one more award in which the respondent, again the Czech Republic, raised a jurisdictional challenge against the application of an intra-EU BIT. In a dispute between a German national, Mr Binder, and the Czech Republic under the Germany–Czech Republic BIT, an arbitral tribunal appears to have rejected the Czech Republic's argument that its BITs concluded with other EU Member States are no longer applicable following the Czech Republic's accession to the EU. Apparently, the Czech Republic challenged the tribunal's decision on jurisdiction in the Prague courts with a view that the courts ask the ECJ for a preliminary ruling. There is no public information available with regard to the status of the court proceedings in Prague.[99]

In conclusion, under the EC Treaty, intra-EU BITs remain applicable until they are terminated. From a Community perspective, this was not a welcome conclusion. However, Article 75(1) TFEU is unlikely to change this conclusion. Although it deletes the reference to third states, there is no reason to conclude that as a result intra-EU BITs would not be applicable upon the entry into force of the Treaty of Lisbon. Rather, these BITs continue to remain applicable for the reasons stated. Since arbitral tribunals are called upon to apply EU law in intra-EU BIT disputes, central questions of EU law will continue to be decided by arbitral tribunals rather than the ECJ. This result is facilitated by the ECJ's jurisprudence that arbitral tribunals do not qualify as courts or tribunals in the meaning of Article 267 TFEU. On the other hand, EU law does not provide for investor–state dispute settlement. However, if compared with redress before domestic courts or through a complaint to the Commission, investor–state arbitration is not necessarily the better dispute settlement mechanism for investors. Nevertheless, one reason why EU investors prefer their claims to be solved by international arbitral tribunals rather than in domestic courts of another Member State may be their lack of trust in these courts. This may well reflect the current state of the EU.

Conclusion

In both the internal and the external dimensions, BITs of Member States will continue to play a role. With regard to the external dimension, it remains to be seen whether the Commission comprehensively challenges the BITs of Member States with third states following the ECJ's judgments in the infringement cases and the entry into force of the Treaty of Lisbon. Until the Commission does successfully challenge these BITs, they will continue to be applicable. Further, given the limitation of the EU's exclusive external competence to FDI under the Treaty of Lisbon, Member States will continue to play a role in shaping the EU's external

[99]See IA Reporter 1 (July 1, 2008) 4, available at http://www.iareporter.com. It seems likely that in other cases based on intra-EU BITs the respondent argued along these lines. The most recent award based on an intra-EU BIT, though unpublished, appears to be *Austrian Airlines v. Slovak Republic*, Award of 20 October 2009.

investment policy. Although the extended competence under the Treaty of Lisbon is a step towards a comprehensive EU investment policy, further steps will be needed if the EU endeavours to become an efficient player in international investment law. Unless and until such steps are taken, the continued fragmentation of competences between the EU and its Member States is likely to cause confusion both within the EU and with the EU's treaty partners. With regard to the internal dimension, save for few exceptions, Member States have not yet followed the Commission's suggestion to terminate intra-EU BITs. However, even after the entry into force of the Treaty of Lisbon, these BITs continue to be applicable.

Art. 351 TFEU, the Principle of Loyalty and the Future Role of the Member States' Bilateral Investment Treaties

Jörg Philipp Terhechte

Introduction

The transfer of national competences to the European Union or at least the discussion surrounding this contentious issue has been central to almost every revision of the European treaties in recent years. This is in part because none of the Union's traits highlights its special, downright peerless role among other regional integration projects as succinctly as the wide scope of its competences and responsibilities. The transfer of competences often also serves to resolve policy issues that can no longer be adequately dealt with on a purely national level. The establishment of the Union Policy on the Environment by the Single European Act (now Art. 191–193 TFEU),[1] the introduction of the Common Foreign and Security Policy by the Maastricht Treaty (now Art. 21–46 TEU)[2] and the formation of Union Policy on Energy by the Treaty of Lisbon (Art. 194 TFEU)[3] can all be traced to this central dilemma. In the transfer of the said competences to the Union also lies the Member States' acknowledgement of their limited possibilities in a time of increasing fragmentation and globalization. They, thus, yield to an overarching "supranational causality", as *Werner von Simson* has put it.[4]

Several changes to the Common Commercial Policy (CCP) effectuated by the Treaty of Lisbon extend the competences of the Union and are thus in line with this

---

[1]See Scheuing, Umweltschutz auf der Grundlage der Einheitlichen Europäischen Akte, EuR (1989), pp. 152 et seq.; see also Jans/Vedder, *European Environmental Law*, Groningen (3rd ed.) 2008, pp. 3 et seq.

[2]For an overview on the creation of CFSP cf. Koutrakos, *EU International Relations Law*, Oxford 2006, pp. 381 et seq.; Terhechte, in: Schwarze (ed.), *EU-Kommentar*, Baden-Baden (2nd ed.) 2009, Art. 11 EUV para. 3.

[3]Kahl, Die Kompetenzen der EU in der Energiepolitik nach Lissabon, EuR (2009), pp. 601 et seq.

[4]"Überstaatliche Bedingtheit" in the German original, see von Simson, *Die Souveränität im rechtlichen Verständnis der Gegenwart*, Berlin 1965, p. 186 et seq.

J.P. Terhechte
Institute for European Law, University of Hamburg, Rothenbaumchaussee 33, 20148 Hamburg, Germany
e-mail: joerg.terhechte@uni-hamburg.de

M. Bungenberg et al. (eds.), *International Investment Law and EU Law*,
DOI 10.1007/978-3-642-14855-2_5, © Springer-Verlag Berlin Heidelberg 2011

development.[5] According to Art. 207(1) TFEU, the CCP is to be "based on uniform principles", including, but not limited to, the sector of "*foreign direct investment*". The regulation of this sector is novel to the TFEU, as the corresponding stipulation of the TEC (Art. 133 [1]) made no mention of it at all. The Treaty of Lisbon has thus extended the scope of application of the CCP by including foreign direct investment.

Admittedly, the transfer of competences between the Union and Member States is not new to the process of European integration – if anything, the issue of correctly allocating responsibilities to Union or Member State level has always dominated this process.[6] Nonetheless, the development of foreign direct investment is of utmost importance at the moment, for the following reasons:

1. On the one hand, following the Treaty of Lisbon's implementation, several hundred bilateral investment treaties (BITs) remain in force between Member States and third-party states.[7] This can be seen as a direct consequence of the Union's former lack of competences in this policy area, which only allowed for the regulation of a limited field, including, for example, questions of market access. Given the new competency of the Union, one is faced with the fate of these treaties. This paper seeks to focus on this issue. As a first step towards a viable solution, one has to identify the extent of the Union's new competence. This is an endeavour which is complicated by the ambiguous wording of Art. 207(1) S. 1 TFEU with regard to "foreign direct investment". A heated debate has developed over the wording in question. Does Art. 207(1) S. 1 TFEU apply to all kinds of foreign direct investment or only to such investment that leads to an acquisition of control over undertakings? This question must be taken seriously, for it determines whether the Union can act independently in the area

[5]See for example Eilmansberger, Bilateral Investment Treaties and EU Law, CML Rev. 46 (2009), pp. 383 et seq.; Bungenberg, Going Global? The EU Common Commercial Policy after Lisbon, EYIEL 1 (2010), pp. 123 et seq. (135 et seq.); Tietje, Außenwirtschaftliche Dimensionen der europäischen Wirtschaftsverfassung, in: Fastenrath/Nowak (eds.), *Der Lissabonner Reformvertrag – Änderungsimpulse in einzelnen Rechts- und Politikbereichen*, Berlin 2009, pp. 237 et seq.; Griebel, Überlegungen zur Wahrnehmung der neuen EU-Kompetenz für ausländische Direktinvestitionen nach Inkrafttreten des Vertrags von Lissabon, RIW (2009), pp. 469 et seq.; Bungenberg, Außenbeziehungen und Außenhandelspolitik, in: Schwarze/Hatje (eds.), *Der Reformvertrag von Lissabon*, Europarecht-Beiheft 1 (2009), pp. 195 et seq. (202 et seq.); Streinz/Ohler/Herrmann, *Der Vertrag von Lissabon zur Reform der EU*, München (2nd ed.) 2008, pp. 126 et seq. (127 et seq.); Müller-Ibold, Handelsaspekte geistigen Eigentums sowie Investitionen, in: Herrmann/Krenzler/Streinz (eds.), *Die Außenwirtschaftspolitik der Europäischen Union nach dem Verfassungsvertrag*, Baden-Baden 2006, pp. 117 et seq. (126 et seq.).

[6]Every treaty revision has extended the Union's competences, and the Treaty of Lisbon is no exception, cf. Terhechte, Der Vertrag von Lissabon: Grundlegende Verfassungsurkunde der europäischen Rechtsgemeinschaft oder technischer Änderungsvertrag? EuR (2008), pp. 143 et seq. (173 et seq.); in detail on the responsibility and competence structure of the Union, see Nettesheim, in: von Bogdandy/Bast (eds.), *Europäisches Verfassungsrecht*, Berlin/Heidelberg (2nd ed.) 2009, pp. 389 et seq.

[7]Overview by Herdegen, *Internationales Wirtschaftsrecht*, Munich (8th ed.) 2009, § 20 para. 5 et seq.

of foreign direct investment or is forced to act in conjunction with the Member States, by means of so-called *mixed* agreements. The future fate of national BITs also hinges on the interpretation of Art. 207 TFEU as modifications based on Art. 351(2) TFEU (ex-Art. 307(2) TEC) will only be possible if the Union's competences regarding the CCP cover this area.

2. A much more general issue, but of equal importance, is the overall relationship between Union law and those obligations of Member States that are derived from public international law. Namely, are the Member States required to amend or even withdraw from treaties that interfere with the newly extended competences of the Union? How far does the proverbial "new legal order of international law"[8] have to commit to the principle of "commitment to international law" (*Völkerrechtsfreundlichkeit*) without neglecting its own statutes?
3. This leads to the question of which principles of Union law could be used to resolve the arising issues. Here, Art. 351(2) TFEU and its previous incarnations have constituted the main focus of discussion in recent years. It must not be overlooked, though, that this stipulation and its application to specific cases are heavily influenced by the fundamental aims and principles of the Union Treaty, especially comprising the principle of *effet utile*,[9] the principle of union loyalty,[10] the principle of uniform application[11] as well as the general aims and values of the Union (Art. 2 TEU).
4. An interpretation of Art. 351 TFEU cannot be undertaken without at least a look at three (nearly identical) recent judgments of the Court of the European Union (CEU) on the topic of BITs, which focused on Art. 307 TEC (the pre-Lisbon Art. 351 TFEU) and solved many persistent issues regarding the stipulation.[12]
5. Last but not least, the German Federal Constitutional Court's (FCC) famous Lisbon judgment of June 2009 must not go unmentioned, for it intensively discussed – among many other things – the extension of the CCP.[13] If the judgments of the CEU represent the Union's side of the coin, the judgment of the FCC represents the Member States' side. The exact influence of both sides on

[8]ECJ, Case 26/62, *Van Gend & Loos*, [1963] ECR, 1 para. 10.

[9]See Streinz, Der effet utile in der Rechtsprechung des Gerichtshofs der EG, in: Due/Lutter/Schwarze (eds.), *Festschrift für Ulrich Everling*, Baden-Baden 1995, pp. 1491 et seq.; Terhechte, *Die ungeschriebenen Tatbestandsmerkmale des europäischen Wettbewerbsrechts*, Baden-Baden 2004, pp. 64 et seq. with further references.

[10]Unruh, Die Unionstreue – Anmerkungen zu einem Rechtsgrundsatz der Europäischen Union, EuR (2002) 1, p. 41; Hatje, *Loyalität als Rechtsprinzip in der Europäischen Union*, Baden-Baden 2002, pp. 17 et seq.

[11]In detail, see Hatje, *Die gemeinschaftsrechtliche Steuerung der Wirtschaftsverwaltung*, Baden-Baden 1998, pp. 35 et seq.

[12]ECJ, C-249/06, *Commission/Sweden*, [2009] ECR I, 1335; ECJ, C-205/06, *Commission/Austria*, [2009] ECR I, 1301.

[13]Bundesverfassungsgericht 123, 267; extensively on the judgment Hatje/Terhechte (eds.), *Grundgesetz und europäische Integration – Die EU nach dem Lissabon-Urteil des Bundesverfassungsgerichts*, Europarecht-Beiheft (2010) 1; also cf. fn. 50.

the future application of the newly extended Union competences and the fate of the Member States' BITs are closely related to the issues covered here.

Extent of Transferred Competences

Union Competences over Bilateral Investment

European Community law previously did not contain any stipulations that explicitly spelled out the competency to conclude BITs.[14] This resulted in many a claim to the effect that only the Member States themselves were allowed to act in this field or that at the very least the conclusion of BITs was not part of the CCP.[15] The totality of this assertion may seem unattractive, yet it must not be denied that the Community's scope of competence was rather limited in this regard. Not least did the Court of Justice's WTO Opinion reinforce that notion, for it restricted Community activity on CCP to such concerning goods and thus reduced activity on foreign direct investment to a bare minimum.[16]

Extent of the New Competence over "Foreign Direct Investment"

This rather unsatisfactory situation was to be resolved by assigning the competence over "foreign direct investment" directly to the Union, as now manifested in Art. 207(1) TFEU. Still in dispute is the extent of this competence and how it is to be delineated, a question that is nothing less than the hub of *all* discussion regarding foreign direct investment.

For a start, the assignment of the said competence by the Treaty of Lisbon closes a gaping hole in the Union competence system regarding foreign trade, which originally should have been closed by the Treaty of Nice.[17] The assignment, therefore, does not come as a surprise. Rather, it can be considered to close important gaps which had previously been identified as a particular legal drawback.

What exactly is "foreign direct investment"? By choosing this terminology, the Treaty of Lisbon revives a mode of differentiation that was seen as obsolete in the field of international investment protection, namely that between "direct

---

[14]See, for example, Bourgeois, in: von der Groeben/Schwarze (eds.), *EU-/EG-Kommentar*, Baden-Baden (6th ed.) 2003, Art. 133 EG para. 26.

[15]Vedder, in: Grabitz/Hilf/Nettesheim (eds.), *Recht der EU*, Loosleaf, Munich, Art. 133 EGV para. 35.

[16]ECJ, Opinion 1/94, *WTO*, [1994] ECR I, 5267.

[17]See Herrmann, Common Commercial Policy after Nice – Sisyphus Would have done a Better Job, CML Rev. 39 (2002), pp. 7 et seq. (13 et seq.).

investment" and "portfolio investment". This arrangement actually originated in the Constitutional Treaty (cf. Art. III-314 and III-315 TCE).[18] Analysing the Constitutional Treaty in its different language versions reveals that in all cases the reference points straight to explicitly foreign direct investment, eliminating the acceptance of a grander competence encompassing all facets of investment protection.

On the one hand, the structure of the provision, in particular the enumeration of competence fields, does not allow for a limitation to only trade-related aspects of foreign direct investment, but dictates an application to all its aspects.[19] Regarding a more specific definition of the term, a number of reasons suggest that only the acquisition of control in the form of at least 10% of an undertaking be covered by it.[20] In this field the Union does have exclusive competence. If, on the other hand, portfolio investment is to be part of one of the Union's investment protection treaties, a "mixed" agreement will be unavoidable.[21]

All in all, the limitation arising from Art. 207 TFEU seems out of place. It seems to convolute the entire system of competences in the Treaty of Lisbon (and the Constitutional Treaty as its predecessor). The CCP is stated to be an exclusive competence. However, this exclusive competence is not universal but parted on behalf of a traditional understanding of different modes of investment. This goes to show that the structure of the distribution of competences within the Treaty

[18]See Hummer, in: Vedder/Heintschel von Heinegg (eds.), *Europäischer Verfassungsvertrag*, Baden-Baden 2007, Art. III-315, para. 8 et seq.; Herrmann, Die Außenhandelsdimension des Binnenmarktes im Verfassungsentwurf – von der Zoll- zur Weltordnungspolitik, in: Hatje/Terhechte (eds.), *Das Binnenmarktziel in der Europäischen Verfassung*, Europarecht-Beiheft (2004) 3, pp. 175 et seq. (195).

[19]See also Tietje, Außenwirtschaftliche Dimensionen der europäischen Wirtschaftsverfassung, in: Fastenrath/Nowak (eds.), *Der Lissabonner Reformvertrag – Änderungsimpulse in einzelnen Rechts- und Politikbereichen*, Berlin 2009, pp. 237 et seq. (248); Martenczuk, Außenbeziehungen und Außenvertretung, in: Hummer/Obwexer (eds.), *Der Vertrag über eine Verfassung für Europa*, Baden-Baden 2007, p. 188 fn. 31; contra Krajewski, External Trade and the Constitution Treaty: Towards a Federal and More Democratic Common Commercial Policy? CML Rev. 42 (2005), pp. 91 et seq. (114 et seq.).

[20]In detail, see Tietje, Außenwirtschaftliche Dimensionen der europäischen Wirtschaftsverfassung, in: Fastenrath/Nowak (eds.), *Der Lissabonner Reformvertrag – Änderungsimpulse in einzelnen Rechts- und Politikbereichen*, Berlin 2009, pp. 237 et seq. (249 et seq.).

[21]For example, Tietje, Außenwirtschaftliche Dimensionen der europäischen Wirtschaftsverfassung, in: Fastenrath/Nowak (eds.), *Der Lissabonner Reformvertrag – Änderungsimpulse in einzelnen Rechts- und Politikbereichen*, Berlin 2009, pp. 237 et seq. (250); Griebel, Überlegungen zur Wahrnehmung der neuen EU-Kompetenz für ausländische Direktinvestitionen nach Inkrafttreten des Vertrags von Lissabon, RIW (2009), pp. 469 et seq. (470).

of Lisbon does not exhibit the conclusiveness that it sought to establish – a phenomenon that can be observed in other policy areas as well.[22]

The Future Role of National BITs and the Principle of Commitment to International Law (Völkerrechtsfreundlichkeit)

How can the legal relationship between the extended Union competence and national BITs be best described? From the very beginning of the process of European integration, the treaty contained a provision, namely Art. 307(1) TEC (ex-Art. 234 TEEC), stating the invulnerability of Member States' international treaties concluded before the treaty's entry into force on 1 January 1958.[23] This provision was extended during the treaty revision process of Amsterdam, in that the international treaties of Member States that were not founding members should equally not be affected by their accession to the Union.[24] In the course of the drafting of the Treaty of Lisbon, Art. 307 TEC was inducted into Art. 351 TFEU, but the provision itself has stayed unchanged. It is commonly seen as an expression of the fundamental *principle of commitment to international law* (*Grundsatz der Völkerrechtsfreundlichkeit)* that the Union has to adhere to.[25] This principle does not only appear in Art. 351 TFEU, but also resurfaces in ex-Art. 132(1) TEC and Art. 42(2) TEU.[26]

Through these provisions, Union law explicitly accepts that the Member States are bound by a multitude of complex international obligations which – at least at the time of the treaty's entry into force – were not to be negated. Thus, Union law is in accordance with the public international law principle *pacta sunt servanda*.

The Court of Justice emphasized the fundamental role of Art. 351 TFEU (then Art. 234 TEEC) in the *Burgoa* Judgment of 1980 as a provision of "general scope", which can be applied to all such international agreements which are capable of affecting the application of the treaty.[27]

---

[22]See Terhechte, Die Rolle des Wettbewerbsrechts in der Europäischen Verfassung, in: Hatje/ Terhechte (eds.), *Das Binnenmarktziel in der Europäischen Verfassung*, Europarecht-Beiheft (2004) 3, pp. 107 et seq. (110 et seq.).

[23]ECJ, Case 812/79, *Burgoa*, [1980] ECR, 2787, para. 5; ECJ, Case 286/86, *Deserbais*, [1988] ECR, 4907, para. 17.

[24]Petersmann/Spennemann, in: von der Groeben/Schwarze (eds.), *EU/EG-Kommentar*, Baden-Baden (6th ed.) 2003, Art. 307 EGV, para. 6 fn. 18.

[25]Terhechte, in: Schwarze (ed.), *EU-Kommentar*, Baden-Baden (2nd ed.) 2009, Art. 307 EGV, para. 2.

[26]Terhechte, in: Schwarze (ed.), *EU-Kommentar*, Baden-Baden (2nd ed.) 2009, Art. 307 EGV, para. 2.

[27]ECJ, Case 812/79, *Burgoa*, [1980] ECR, 2787, para. 5.

Admittedly, the provision's wording makes a direct application of Art. 351 TFEU impossible, when Member States later transfer powers to the Union, nevertheless leaving room for an analogy with Art. 351 TFEU owing to comparable situations in both cases. Therefore, it has been generally agreed upon among scholars – the Court of Justice apparently has never found the opportunity to concern itself with that particular question – that the provision remains applicable even if older national treaties come into conflict with newer primary Union law.[28] A prime example for this kind of collision is precisely the field of foreign direct investment, as newly introduced by the Treaty of Lisbon.

The content of Art. 307(1) TEC remains nearly entirely unchanged by the Treaty of Lisbon,[29] the sole exception being a change of the provision's field of application in that older international treaties are now to be unaffected by *the treaties*, read TEU and TFEU. This naturally follows from the merger of the Union and the Community into a single entity and the post-Lisbon-Treaty's largely supranational character, entailing newly created instances of material law which could possibly go against the objectives of Art. 351(1) TFEU.

National BITs from the Viewpoint of Art. 351(2) 2 TFEU

Although Art. 351(1) TFEU reiterates the commitment to international law in principle – which includes the possibility of BITs that remain in force next to Union law – the inherent limitations constituted by it are still surprisingly vague. The provision can, for example, not be applied by Member States if an older international treaty grants them different courses of action. In that case, the Member State is obliged to take the course that derogates Union law the least.[30] In addition, the measures taken must not exceed that which is necessary to ensure that the Member State performs its obligations towards third-party states.[31] Equally certain is the necessity of newer international treaties, that are international treaties agreed upon after 1 January 1958 (or in case of non-founding Member States, after their accession to the Union), staying in conformity with Union law – here the limits of the principle of commitment to international law are reached.

[28] Meessen, The Application of Rules of Public International Law within Community Law, CML Rev. 13 (1976), pp. 485 et seq. (491); Bernhardt, Die Europäische Gemeinschaft als neuer Rechtsträger im Geflecht der traditionellen zwischenstaatlichen Beziehungen, EuR (1983), pp. 199 et seq. (205); Terhechte, in: Schwarze (ed.), *EU-Kommentar*, Baden-Baden (2nd ed.) 2009, Art. 307 EGV, para. 15; contra Manzini, The Priority of Pre-Existing Treaties of EC Member States within the Framework of International Law, EJIL 12 (2001), pp. 781 et seq. (786).

[29] Terhechte, in: Schwarze (ed.), *EU-Kommentar*, Baden-Baden (2nd ed.) 2009, Art. 307 EGV, para. 18.

[30] ECJ, C-324/93, *Evans*, [1995] ECR I, 563, para. 32 f.

[31] ECJ, C-124/95, *Centro-Com*, [1997] ECR I, 81, para. 61.

The vital issue of how to solve a "real" collision between a Member State's public international obligation and one of Union law quality is laid down in Art. 351(2) TFEU. This provision stipulates that Member States whose agreements are not compatible with the treaties shall take *any appropriate steps* to eliminate the incompatibilities established. Art. 351(2) S. 2 TFEU adds that the Member States shall assist each other to this end and adopt a common approach where appropriate.

In practical terms, this entails an obligation of Member States to reach amendments of their agreements – in cases of extreme incompatibility with Union law this can mean terminating the agreement in accordance with the Vienna Convention on the Law of Treaties (VCLT). At least some of the problems that are prone to result from this have been anticipated in Art. 351(2) TFEU, for it states the need for a "common attitude" and mutual assistance among the Member States.

The European Court of Justice's Recent Jurisdiction on the Topic

The Court of Justice has shown Art. 351(2) TFEU to be a rather sharp tool in the course of two judgments from March 2009[32]: The subject of these infringement proceedings according to Art. 258 TFEU (then Art. 226 TEC) was Sweden's and Austria's failure to take appropriate measures in the sense of Art. 307(2) TEC to amend BITs they had concluded before acceding to the Union. The proceedings were centered around a clause that was to be found in each of the agreements and under which "each party guarantees to the investors of the other party, without undue delay, the free transfer, in freely convertible currency, of payments connected with an investment". The Commission argued that these clauses were capable of impeding the application of restrictions on movement of capital and on payments according to Art. 64(2), 66, 75 TFEU (then Art. 57(2), 59, 60(1) TEC), which the Council *might* adopt. Ultimately, the criticized treaty infringement was thus of a potential nature.

Nevertheless, the Court of Justice declared that the Member States had in both cases failed to fulfil their obligations under Art. 307(2) TEC. It particularly emphasized the importance of the principles of effectiveness and of uniform application. Not only would the practical effectiveness of the provisions regarding free movement of capital and payments be impaired if Sweden and Austria were obliged to refrain from measures according to Art. 307(2) TEC being taken and to first negotiate new provisions, essentially showing that practical effectiveness requires immediate implementation. Negotiations would also take a long time, giving rise to the Court of Justice's fear that the then-current state of affairs would become

[32]ECJ, C-249/06, *Commission/Sweden*, [2009] ECR I, 1335; ECJ, C-205/06, *Commission/Austria*, [2009], ECR I, 1301; see also Burgstaller, European Law and Investment Treaties, Journal of International Arbitration 26 (2009), pp. 181 et seq. (196 et seq.).

permanent. Any ad hoc measures that could be taken in accordance with public international law were also prone to fail.

Hereby the Court of Justice has clearly shown, given the precedence of these cases (at this time a third proceeding against Finland has been decided[33]), that it is not reluctant to prompt Member States to terminate international treaties even if their infraction of Union law is only of a potential nature. Similarly, the Commission can be expected to initiate a wide-scale screening process and subsequently call for amendments of remaining national agreements that are in conflict with Union law.

For the future, this means that the Member States will have to adhere not only to Art. 207 TFEU, but also to the entirety of Union law when concluding bilateral agreements.[34]

Art. 351 TFEU and the Impact of European Constitutional Principles

The Court of Justice's judgments placed special emphasis on a number of constitutional principles native to Union law which are likely to be of great relevance to the future fate of Member States BITs. Central among these are the principle of uniform application, the principle of loyalty and the principle of practical effectiveness. Each of these played a central role in the aforementioned proceedings and incorporated standards the Member States are highly advised to abide by.

Principle of Uniform Application

The multitude of national BITs[35] poses a constant threat for the principle of uniform application of Union law as required by Art. 4(3) TEU.[36] This principle – rightfully called the "centrepiece" of Union law by *Thomas Oppermann*[37] – branches into three main facets. Firstly, Union law must not tolerate a divergence of national application if its autonomy is not to be endangered. Secondly, the principle of uniform application runs parallel to the principle of the equality of citizens of the Union before the law and is therefore part of the tenet of the rule of

---

[33]ECJ, C-118/07, *Commission/Finland*, [2009] ECR I, not yet published.

[34]For an overview on the consequences in practice see below.

[35]For an overview of the rather complex system of international investment protection laws, see Dolzer/Schreuer, *Principles of International Investment Law*, Oxford 2008; Reinisch, *Standards of Investment Protection*, Oxford 2008; Griebel, *Internationales Investitionsrecht*, Munich 2008.

[36]Hatje, in: Schwarze (ed.), *EU-Kommentar*, Baden-Baden (2nd ed.) 2009, Art. 10 EGV, para. 10.

[37]Oppermann, Die Dritte Gewalt in der Europäischen Union, DVBl. (1994), para. 901 (906); cit. Hatje, *Die gemeinschaftsrechtliche Steuerung der Wirtschaftsverwaltung*, Baden-Baden 1998, p. 35.

law (Art. 2 TEU). Thirdly, tolerating a divergent application in practice would call into question the delicate balance between the Member States with regard to the distribution of burden under European law.[38]

The vastness of the number of BITs currently in force alone demonstrates that the Member States have so far executed a vivid and mostly autonomous policy regarding investment protection. Yet, any kind of uniform behaviour towards non-member states is effectively obstructed by this. Hence, it is most likely that the Court of Justice will try to unitarize the Union's policy regarding investment protection as much as possible, be it to secure uniform standards of protection for the citizens of the Union or to build up a more coherent Union behaviour towards non-member states.

Principle of Loyalty

Further restrictions on the Member States' activities could result from the principle of loyalty and cooperation between Member States and the Union. As is generally known, this concept[39] seeks to facilitate and improve the Union's and Member States' collaboration as well as to contribute to a fair division of tasks between them (see Art. 4(3) TEU). This is possible only if the Member States refrain from any measures liable to compromise Union aims.[40] However, the principle's relevance to national BITs was only marginally touched upon in the Court of Justice's recent judgments. Sweden and Austria explicitly resisted it being brought up by the Advocate General, which would in their opinion have warranted a reopening of the oral procedure, Art. 61 RPCJ, but this was on reasonable grounds rejected by the Court of Justice.[41] One can only speculate why the contesting parties stressed this aspect in particular, but almost certainly the potency of Art. 4(3) TEU is at least partly responsible for it.

Advocate-General *Maduro*'s Opinion on the case of Sweden draws a parallel between the principle of loyalty and the Court of Justice's present jurisdiction as to the preliminary effect of directives, meaning that although a Member State is not obliged to adopt the directive's measures before the end of the period prescribed for

[38] Hatje, *Die gemeinschaftsrechtliche Steuerung der Wirtschaftsverwaltung*, Baden-Baden 1998, pp. 35 et seq.; Hatje, in: Schwarze (ed.), *EU-Kommentar*, Art. 10 EGV, para. 10, with further references from the Court of Justice's jurisdiction.

[39] For an explanation of the terminology, see von Bogdandy, in: Grabitz/Hilf/Nettesheim (eds.), *Das Recht der EU,* Loosleaf, Munich, Art. 10 EGV, para. 6.

[40] Hatje, *Loyalität als Rechtsprinzip in der Europäischen Union*, Baden-Baden 2001, p. 11 with further references.

[41] ECJ, C-249/06, *Commission/Sweden*, [2009] ECR I, 1335, para. 9 et seq.; ECJ, C-205/06, *Commission/Austria*, [2009], ECR I, 1301, para. 9 et seq.

transposition, it must still refrain from any measures liable to compromise seriously the result prescribed.[42] In particular the Advocate-General stated:

> that Member States are obliged to refrain from any measures liable seriously to compromise the exercise of Community competence. In particular, Member States are obliged to take all appropriate steps to prevent their pre-existing international obligations from jeopardising the exercise of community competence.[43]

Thus, following an approach which ultimately classifies Art. 351(2) TFEU as a subcategory of Art. 4(3) TEU, the Advocate-General's Opinion puts the Member States under considerable pressure to comply, for it implies that their duty to amend their BITs does not only follow from the comparatively specific Art. 351(2) TFEU, demanding what is possible under international law, but also that this duty is derived from EU Law itself. When coupled with the principle of uniform application as another subcategory of Art. 4 TFEU, this places systemic pressure on the Member States' obligations from older international treaties.

Most importantly, this results in the Member States' exercise of their competences being tied to the Union system of competences instead of being unrestricted, at least if the field of investment protection is regarded as a shared competence which in turn depends on the subject matter affected. Thus, the Member State's ability to preserve any remaining obligations from older treaties as well as its leeway to play a lone hand in the field of portfolio investment – which in practice should be close to impossible anyway – is significantly reduced. Admittedly, the Court of Justice has not explicitly approved of the Advocate-General's point of view. In conclusion, the principle of loyalty and its influence on the future alignment of Member States' investment policies is seen to be quite far-reaching.

Principle of Effectiveness

Lastly, the supremely important role of the principle of effectiveness (*effet utile)* must not escape mention, for it served as a point of reasoning to establish the Court of Justice's aforementioned judgments several times. It forbids the Member States to frustrate or severely impede the legal effects of Union law and is founded in the principle of uniform application and thereby also in Art. 4(3) TEU.[44]

---

[42]ECJ, C-129/96, *Inter-Environnement Wallonie*, [1997] ECR I, 7411, para. 45.

[43]Advocate-General *Maduro*'s Opinion in C-249/06, [2009], ECR I, 1335, para. 42.

[44]Schwarze, in: Schwarze (ed.), *EU-Kommentar*, Baden-Baden (2nd ed.) 2009, Art. 220 EGV, para. 29; Everling, Richterliche Rechtsfortbildung in der Europäischen Gemeinschaft, JZ (2000), pp. 217 et seq. (223); Hatje, *Die gemeinschaftsrechtliche Steuerung der Wirtschaftsverwaltung*, Baden-Baden 1998, pp. 58 et seq.; Terhechte, *Die ungeschriebenen Tatbestandsmerkmale des europäischen Wettbewerbsrechts*, Baden-Baden 2004, pp. 64 et seq.

Its scope is ever different depending on the respective legal effects, which makes an abstract definition virtually impossible.[45]

Concerning the transfer of an exclusive competence for the field of foreign direct investment to the Union, the principle of effectiveness is likely to affect even the competences that remain with the Member States, for it prohibits the use of the said competences if their use would frustrate or severely impede the Union's foreign direct investment competence. Even in the rather implausible case of newly concluded BITs that specifically regulate portfolio investment, this should cause the Member States to be closely bound to Union standards for foreign direct investment – notwithstanding the profoundly difficult differentiation between the modes of investment. Overall, the superposition of Art. 351 TFEU results in an increase of legal (and factual) Union competences that are much vaster than it may initially seem. This development is less obvious when seen in the light of the usual division between portfolio investment and foreign direct investment.

Consequences of the Transfer of Competences

Finally, the practical consequences of the transfer of competences to the Union must be pointed out, including especially the following questions: Firstly, are the Member States obligated to amend or even terminate existing, older international treaties? Secondly, how far does the binding effect of the existing treaties go and is by any chance the Union itself bound to them? Thirdly, how are the problems illustrated to be prevented from emerging again in the future?

Termination or Amendment of Previously Concluded International Treaties

As previously hinted at, the basis for Member States' activities in the field of foreign direct investment has at least theoretically ceased to exist, following the transfer of the corresponding exclusive competence to the Union. The principle of commitment to international law as in Art. 351(1) TFEU applies here only insofar as the termination or amendment (in accordance with the rules of VCLT) of the existing bilateral treaties is impossible. After that, the treaties' continuing existence, even if compatible with public international law in general, becomes an infringement of the treaties, which is to be answered with the corresponding facilities of Union law. The Court of Justice has pointed out this distinct scenario in the past.[46]

---

[45]See also Hatje, *Die gemeinschaftsrechtliche Steuerung der Wirtschaftsverwaltung*, Baden-Baden 1998, p. 58.

[46]ECJ, C-203/03, *Commission/Austria*, [2005] ECR I, 935, para. 57 et seq.

However, even an exclusive competence does not remove all room for national activity.[47] Given an "authorization" by the Union, Member States can still keep acting in a field that has been exclusively given to the Union. In this context it has been suggested that the Council grants authorizations (in particular the FCC has taken up suggestions of this kind in its Lisbon Judgment; see below). Although it may sound practically plausible, this suggestion puts the Union in a difficult position. Neither can a duty of the Council to grant authorizations be legally established from existing Union law, nor does the Council have any obligation to yield to the FCC's input. It is rather a question of what can be implemented in practice and what is proper in the current political situation. Ultimately, much depends on the creative willpower of the Union, even if it is troubled by concerns about "lowered" standards.

Should the multitude of national BITs actually endure for considerably longer, they will have to be accompanied by an intensive screening process. Insofar as potentially infringing aspects are uncovered, the treaties in question must be amended. To best avoid such clashes in the future it is advisable to include in the treaties so-called REIO clauses, which formulate reservations in favour of obligations spawned from regional integration projects.

Binding Effect of Older International Treaties Beyond the Scope of Art. 351(1) TFEU?

Beyond Art. 351(1) TFEU on the other hand, establishing an obligation of the Union to refrain from taking measures towards the Member States proves much more difficult – in particular, the transfer of competences to the Union does not automatically bind it to the national BITs.[48] Only Art. 4(3) TFEU may lead to a different result if the Union does grant the aforementioned authorizations, the effect of which would thus be important not only for the relationship between the Member State and the Union but also for the level of the international law obligation itself.

Mutual Consideration During the Transition Period

In practice, the Union (more specifically, the Commission) will have to gather first-hand experience in the field of investment protection to reliably execute its competences – in cooperation with the Member States. The lack of any deadlines in

[47]Nettesheim, Kompetenzen, in: von Bogdandy/Bast (eds.), *Europäisches Verfassungsrecht*, Heidelberg/Berlin (2nd ed.) 2009, pp. 389 et seq. (424).

[48]See, generally, Koutrakos, *EU International Relations Law*, Oxford 2006, pp. 301 et seq.; Pache/Bielitz, Das Verhältnis der EG zu den völkerrechtlichen Verträgen ihrer Mitgliedstaaten, EuR (2006), pp. 316 et seq.

the Treaty of Lisbon makes it clear that the implementation in detail is entrusted to the authorities responsible. Here the aforementioned moderating principles can help avoid potential conflicts. This also implies that the Union's institutions need to give the Member States enough time to end their obligations from older treaties, which can only be realized through renegotiations anyway.

The Lisbon Judgment's Influence on the New Competence over Foreign Direct Investment

The subject at hand unexpectedly gained a lot of importance when the FCC passed its Lisbon Judgment in June 2009.[49] Therein the FCC declared the act of assent with the Treaty of Lisbon to be compatible with the German Basic Law, but denied such compatibility for the so-called corollary laws because they supposedly reduced the importance of the parliament's position beyond the threshold necessitated by the Basic Law.[50] It quite surprisingly also discussed the new exclusive Union competence for foreign direct investment, resulting in the following notions. The FCC drew up a limit to this competence, acting from the Member States' perspective. This limit is the invulnerability of existing bilateral treaties, which must be respected by the Union – for example by granting the aforementioned authorizations and concluding new treaties only in cooperation with the Member States – if ultra vires actions are to be avoided. The FCC also tended to a rather restrained interpretation of new Art. 207 TFEU, by insinuating only the investment that leads to acquiring control over undertakings to be part of "foreign direct investment", which leaves the Member States (and, thus, the FCC itself) with some influence on the subject matter.[51] The corresponding parts of the judgment may be presented in subjunctive speech but the FCC's intentions shine through nonetheless.

The judgment has noticeably narrowed the previously existing room for a common European investment policy – lone-hand plays by the Union will be meticulously observed by the constitutional courts, as will be the possible application of Art. 351(2) TFEU (if only by way of analogy). If the Union disregards the formulated constraints, the FCC may, as it has established in the judgment, possibly declare the inapplicability of the Union's measures. The passages in question

[49] Bundesverfassungsgericht 123, 267 (420 et seq.).

[50] See, for example, Thym, In the Name of Sovereign Statehood: A Critical Introduction to the Lisbon Judgement of the German Constitutional Court, CML Rev. 46 (2009), pp. 1795 et seq.; Everling, Europas Zukunft unter der Kontrolle nationaler Verfassungsgerichte? Anmerkung zum Urteil des BVerfG vom 30. Juni 2009 über den Vertrag von Lissabon, EuR (2010), pp. 91 et seq.; Nettesheim, Ein Individualrecht auf Staatlichkeit? Die Lissabon-Entscheidung des BVerfG, NJW (2009), p. 2867 et seq.; Terhechte, Souveränität, Dynamik und Integration – making up the rules as we go along? – Anmerkungen zum Lissabon-Urteil des Bundesverfassungsgerichts, EuZW (2009), pp. 724 et seq.

[51] Bundesverfassungsgericht 123, 267 (421).

actually go so far as to state an *obligation* of the Council to authorize the continued existence of the Member States BITs.[52] Not even the activity of the Council in specific cases could escape the jealous watch of the FCC in Karlsruhe! Whether the new competence of Art. 207 TFEU can take any effective form under these circumstances cannot be determined at this time.

Conclusion: The Treaty of Lisbon and National BITs

The extension of the Union's competences in the field of CCP will conjure up many a heated discussion in the upcoming years. By transferring the competence for foreign direct investment to the Union, the Member States have expressed that they wish it to be a one-stop policy field. The wisdom of this decision becomes clearer when looking back at the hundreds of different BITs and the Member States' completely fragmented approach to non-EU states. Only by this means can a unified outward appearance, one of the main aims of the CCP and the whole Union legal system, be achieved. Although the situation of many BITs will in practice stay the same, at least for now, the changes that ultimately occur will be even more numerous. The diffusion of a technically exclusive Union competence with remaining and hidden Member State influence leads to a difficult field and one that is, from a long-term perspective, prone to fail. Hence, a solid foundation for a common European investment policy is now of the utmost importance. The necessary in-detail cooperation of the Union and the Member States will depend on them loyally standing side by side.

[52]Bundesverfassungsgericht 123, 267 (422); see also Terhechte, Souveränität, Dynamik und Integration – making up the rules as we go along? – Anmerkungen zum Lissabon-Urteil des Bundesverfassungsgerichts, EuZW (2009), pp. 724 et seq. (731).

For a Complementary European Investment Protection

Tillmann Rudolf Braun*

The following seven theses are possible policy recommendations for the future formulation of European investment protection "after Lisbon."

First Thesis: It is worthwhile re-examining the actual purpose of the protection of international investment through treaties in international law and investor–state arbitral tribunals, as the protection given to property by bilateral investment treaties is not provided merely as an end in itself. It is also expressly provided to create an international "rule of law,"[1] which is one of the most important preconditions for the beneficial private direct investment which is essential for the economic development of many countries.[2]

Furthermore, the second generation of bilateral investment treaties since the 1980s/1990s has made an important contribution to the creation of a unique investor–state arbitration system.[3] The task of these international arbitral tribunals

[1]Generally, see Tamanaha, *On the Rule of Law–History, Politics, Theory*, 2004; Dyzenhaus, The Rule of (Administrative) Law in International Law, Law & Contemp. Prob. 68 (2005), p. 127; Raz, The Rule of Law and its Virtue, L. Quart. Rev. 93 (1977), p. 195; Fallon, "The Rule of Law" as a Concept in Constitutional Discourse, Columb. L. Rev. 97 (1997), p. 1.

[2]"The protection of foreign investments is not the sole aim of the Lisbon Treaty, but rather a necessary element alongside the overall aim of encouraging foreign investment and extending and intensifying the parties' economic relations."; *Saluka Investments BV (The Netherlands) v. The Czech Republic*, UNCITRAL (Dutch/Czech BIT), Partial Award, 17 March 2006, Para. 300, http://ita.law.uvic.ca/documents/Saluka-PartialawardFinal.pdf; Koroma, The Effects of Globalization on the Development of International Law, in: Hobe (ed.), *Globalisation–the State and International Law*, 2009, p. 27: "The objective of international investment law is, however, not investor protection for its own sake, but rather protection of the infrastructure of and thereby promotion of economic growth and development. Investment treaties are thus both a product and a motor of globalization."

[3]Regarding the development of international investment law, see Braun, Investitionsschutz durch internationale Schiedsgerichte, TranState Working Papers 89 (2009), Universität Bremen, Sonderforschungsbereich 597, Staatlichkeit im Wandel, passim, http://hdl.handle.net/10419/27911;

T.R. Braun Ass. iur., M.P.A. (Harvard)
*The author's view is exclusively his own and does not necessarily represent the position of his employer
Auswärtiges Amt, Werderscher Markt 1, 10117 Berlin, Germany
e-mail: tillmann.braun@diplo.de

M. Bungenberg et al. (eds.), *International Investment Law and EU Law*,
DOI 10.1007/978-3-642-14855-2_6,

was, and still is, to decide between the interests of the investor in protecting his foreign investment from state intervention, on the one hand, and the interests of the host state in implementing its public aims on the other hand. This led to a dispute arbitration system which denationalizes and depoliticizes conflicts between investors and states. It appears that investors currently view international investor–state arbitral proceedings as *the* most suitable instrument of last resort for the law-based[4] resolution of such problems.[5] The investor can independently assert the standards guaranteed in bilateral investment treaties against the host state directly at the level of international law. The subsequent elevation and recognition of the investor as a partial subject of international law – resulting from globalization – has helped to give international investment law its vigour and current importance and is rightly seen as a paradigm shift[6] in international law.

Moreover, it is noteworthy that today almost a third of all bilateral investment treaties are concluded between developing and emerging nations and also include investor–state arbitration.[7] This reflects the fact that large developing and emerging

---

Braun, Globalization: The Driving Force in International Investment Law, in: Waibel/Kaushal/Chung/Balchin (eds.), *The Backlash against Investment Arbitration*, 2009, Chap. 21.

[4]Regarding other forms and possibilities of dispute resolution, see Braun, Home-State Assisted Negotiations—an Alternative to Mediation?, in: Rovine (ed.), *Contemporary Issues in International Arbitration and Mediation: The Fordham Papers 2009*, 2010; Coe, Towards a Complementary Use of Conciliation in Investor-State Disputes–A Preliminary Sketch, in: (ed.), *Investor-State Arbitration: Perspectives on Legitimacy and Practice*, Suffolk University 2009, pp. 73–112; Salacuse, Is there a better way? Alternative Methods of Treaty-Based Investor-State Dispute Resolution, 31 Fordham Int'l L.J. 31 (2007–2008), pp. 138–185; Schwebel, Is Mediation of Foreign Investment Disputes Plausible? ICSID Journal Fall 2007, pp. 237–241.

[5]UNCTAD, Latest Developments in investor-State dispute settlement, IIA MONITOR (2009) 1, UNCTAD/WEB/DIAE/IIA/2009/6, p. 2: "a trend (…) indicating that international investment arbitration is no longer an exceptional phenomenon, but part of the "normal" investment landscape"; p. 8: "Developments in 2008 confirm the trend towards increased use of international arbitration to resolve investment disputes."

[6]*BG v Argentina*, Award: "The proliferation of bilateral investment treaties has effected a profound transformation of international investment law. Most significantly, under these instruments investors are entitled to seek enforcement of their treaty rights by directly bringing action against the State in whose territory they have invested. Investors may seek redress in arbitration without securing espousal of their claim or diplomatic protection. The Argentina-U.K. BIT is a paradigm of this evolution." Award, 24 December 2007, UNCITRAL, http://ita.law.uvic.ca/documents/BG-award_000.pdf, M.N. 145; Schreuer, Paradigmenwechsel im internationalen Investitionsrecht, in: Hummer (ed.), *Paradigmenwechsel im Völkerrecht zur Jahrtausendwende*, 2002, p. 237; Salacuse/Sullivan, Do BITs Really Work? An Evaluation of Bilateral Investment Treaties and Their Grand Bargain, Harv. Int'l L. J. 46 (2005), p. 67 (88: "revolutionary innovation [whose]…uniqueness and power should not be overlooked"); Wälde, Improving Mechanism for Treaty Negotiation and Investment Disputes, in: Sauvant (ed.), *Yearbook on International Investment Law & Policy 2008/2009*, 2009, p. 505 (509: "[…] it is difficult to deny that we are facing a spectacular success in terms of international institutional and legal reform").

[7]Sachs/Sauvant, BITs, DTTs and FDI flows: an overview, in: Sauvant/Sachs (eds.), *The Impact of Bilateral Investment Treaties and Double Taxation Treaties on Foreign Direct Investment Flows*, 2009, p. xxvii et seq.; UNCTAD, *World Investment Report 2007*, 2007, p. 17; UNCTAD, *South-South Cooperation in International Investment Agreements*, 2005, p. 42.

nations have themselves become capital-exporting nations and they now also find themselves in the situation of having to adapt their investment policy and guarantee the protection of their own foreign investments. China is the classic example, being the number two worldwide behind Germany in terms of the number of bilateral investment treaties concluded. China first included an investor–state arbitration clause in its investment treaties with a developing country in its bilateral investment treaty with Barbados in 1998.[8] Its first treaty of this kind with an industrial state was the bilateral investment treaty with Germany in 2003.[9] The developing nations with the highest number of bilateral investment treaties in place generally tend to be some of the largest investors in other developing nations and have, therefore, become both host countries and countries of origin of investments.[10]

This elevation of the investor and the possibility of an investor–state arbitral proceeding resulting from bilateral investment treaties can also have the interesting consequence that diplomatic protection can be increased *in advance* of potential (arbitral) proceedings: The possibility of an investor initiating independent legal action in a case of arbitration under international law strengthens his negotiating position in relation to the host state – even before potential arbitral proceedings – since in any arbitral proceedings he has rights equal to those of the state and, therefore, usually enjoys international attention in advance.

Furthermore, both states know that, should political efforts to settle the dispute be unsuccessful, the investor can instigate proceedings on the basis of the bilateral investment treaty. Therefore, the present dense network of modern investment treaties which fundamentally allows and enables investor–state arbitral proceedings also performs a *dispute-avoidance* function.[11] An important aim of investment

---

[8]Regarding Chinese investment protection policy, see Schill, Tearing Down the Great Wall—the New Generation Investment Treaties of the People's Republic of China, Cardozo J. Int'l & Comp. L. 15 (2007), pp. 73–118; Berger, China and the Global Governance of Foreign Direct Investment: The Emerging Liberal Bilateral Investment Treaty Approach, Discussion Paper, Deutsches Institut für Entwicklungspolitik, 2008; Congyan, Change of the Structure of International Investment and the Development of Developing Countries' BIT Practice, JWIT 8 (2007), p. 829 (844); Rooney, ICSID and BIT Arbitrations and China, Journal of International Arbitration 24 (2007), p. 689.

[9]Braun/Schonard, Der neue deutsch-chinesische Investitionsförderungs- und -schutzvertrag im Lichte der Entwicklung des völkerrechtlichen Investitionsschutzes, RIW (2007), pp. 561–569; Braun / Schonard, The new Germany-China Bilateral Investment Treaty – A Commentary and Evaluation in Light of the Development of Investment Protection under Public International Law, ICSID Review 22 (Fall 2007), pp. 258–279; Braun/Schonard, 德国与中国的新双边投资条约: 以国际公法中投资保护制度的发展为背景的述评, Chinese Journal of International Economic Law (2009).

[10]After China (approximately 120 concluded bilateral investment treaties): Egypt (approximately 100), Republic of Korea (approximately 80); UNCTAD, *World Investment Report 2008*, 2008, p. 15, fig. I.11; UNCTAD, South-South Investments Agreements Proliferating, IIA Monitor No. 3 (2007), pp. 1 et seq.

[11]Braun, Home-State Assisted Negotiations—an Alternative to Mediation?, in: Rovine (ed.), *Contemporary Issues in International Arbitration and Mediation: Fordham Papers 2009*, 2010; Wegen/Raible, Unterschätzt die deutsche Wirtschaft die Wirksamkeit des völkerrechtlichen Investitionsschutzes?, SchiedsVZ (2006), p. 225 (226); Schöbener, Der Rechtsrahmen des

protection treaties could, therefore, be understood – not only from the viewpoint of the companies – to be the creation of a stable legal framework which is familiar to all parties, upon which the protagonists can rely and whose enforcement mechanisms do not necessarily have to be put in motion.

The "internationalization of the rule of law" and the legally binding nature of economic actions resulting from bilateral investment treaties and investor–state arbitral proceedings do not solely serve the interests of investors. They also equally serve the interests of the states and the international community as a whole in providing a basis for legal settlements in investment disputes between the host state and the investor, as well as in the enforcement of international law.

Moreover, reaching beyond any specific case, international investment law fulfils an *ordering function* for international investment relations. The legal implementation of international investment law can itself be described as a *global public good*.[12] Bilateral investment treaties and investor–state arbitration as an institutionalized form of an "investment law culture" remain committed to the common aim of promoting international economic exchange and development through the rule of law. The treaty states such as Germany – as well as the arbitral tribunals themselves[13] – bear the responsibility for ensuring a sensible form and functionality of this system of international investment arbitration.

Second Thesis: It would appear that there is no final consensus agreed by all participants concerning the exact extent of the future investment competence of the European Union [according to Art. 207 of the Treaty on the Functioning of the European Union (TFEU)]. However, it is likely that future investment treaties or investment chapters of the European Union could, in general, be described as *mixed treaties*.[14]

Internationalen Investitionsrechts: Ein Überblick zu den bilateralen Investitionsschutzabkommen, WiVerw 2009, p. 3 (18).

[12]Classically, see Samuelson, The pure theory of public expenditure, Review of Economics and Statistics 36 (1954), p. 387; Kaul/Grunberg/Stern, *Global Public Goods. International Cooperation in the 21st Century*, 1999; referring to international economic law: Tietje, Begriff, Geschichte und Grundlagen des Internationalen Wirtschaftssystems und Wirtschaftsrechts, in: Tietje (ed.), *Internationales Wirtschaftsrecht*, 2009, p. 58; Meessen, Economic Law as an Economic Good, in: Meessen/Bungenberg/Puttler, *Economic Law as an Economic Good*, 2009, p. 3.

[13]*MCI Power Group and New Turbine v Republic of Ecuador*, Decision on Annulment, 19 October 2009, http://ita.law.uvic.ca/documents/MCI-Annulment.pdf, Para. 24: "(. . .) The responsibility for ensuring consistency in the jurisprudence and for building a coherent body of law rests primarily with the investment tribunals."; and Para. 25: "(. . .) Although there is no hierarchy of international tribunals, as acknowledged in SGS v. Philippines, the Committee considers it appropriate to take those decisions into consideration, because their reasoning and conclusions may provide guidance to the Committee in settling similar issues arising in these annulment proceedings and help to ensure consistency and legal certainty of the ICSID annulment mechanism, thereby contributing to ensuring trust in the ICSID dispute settlement system and predictability for governments and investors."

[14]See also the Energy Charter Treaty: http://www.encharter.org.

European Union agreements which would sensibly include both direct investment *and* portfolio investment would have to be concluded jointly by the European Union and its 27 member states and the respective third state.[15] Furthermore, future European investment treaties would also normally have to formulate standards of treatment for areas for which the internal market of the European Union would probably not be competent even "after Lisbon," such as tax law and the systems of property ownership of the member states.[16]

This means, in practice, that European Union investment treaties could be concluded as *mixed treaties*, i.e. with the involvement of the member states, if and when their content can meaningfully "exceed the sphere of competence of the European Union and reaches into the area of competence of the member states."[17] Therefore, in the case of European investment protection, the member states and the European Commission depend upon each other.

Third Thesis: What does this mean for the formulation of European investment protection? What are the consequences for the implementation of the Lisbon Treaty, for the consideration of possible conflicts of interest and for the interplay between existing investment treaties of the member states, on the one hand, and the future competence of the European Union, on the other hand?[18]

From a foreign trade perspective,[19] a guiding principle should be the maintenance and linking of the undisputed advantages of both systems for the benefit of the European Union and its member states. So far, more than 1,500 bilateral investment treaties with third states in existence in Europe – above all those of capital-exporting countries such as the UK, France, Italy, the Netherlands, Belgium, Luxembourg and Germany – have fulfilled their task well. Against this background, it should, therefore, *also* be in the interest of the *European Union* to continue to guarantee existing foreign investments through these investment treaties.

These treaties should remain in place to preserve the advantages of their tried-and-tested protection standards and arbitration mechanisms. This also corresponds to the investors' and third countries' desire for legal certainty as investment treaties actually guarantee a higher degree of legal certainty than customary international

[15] Tietje, Die Außenwirtschaftsverfassung der EU nach dem Vertrag von Lissabon, in: Tietje/Kraft (eds.), *Beiträge zum Transnationalen Wirtschaftsrecht, Heft 83*, 2009, p. 16.

[16] Art. 345 TFEU; see also the "harmonization precept," Art. 207 Para. 6; Art. 113, 114 Para. 2 TFEU.

[17] Nettesheim, Kompetenzen, in: v. Bogdandy (ed.), *Europäisches Verfassungsrecht, Theoretische und dogmatische Grundzüge*, 2009, (2nd edition) p. 415 (432 et seq.).

[18] In general, see Ceyssens, Towards a Common Foreign Investment Policy?–Foreign Investment in the European Constitution, Legal Issues of Economic Integration 32 (2005) 3, pp. 259–291; Karl, The Competence for Foreign Direct Investment–New Powers for the European Union?, 5 The Journal of World Investment & Trade 5 (2004) 3, pp. 413–448; Shan, Towards a Common European Community Policy on Investment Issues, Journal of World Investment 2 (2001) 3, pp. 603–625; Griebel, Überlegungen zur Wahrnehmung der neuen EU-Kompetenz für ausländische Direktinvestitionen nach Inkrafttreten des Vertrages von Lissabon, RIW (2009), p. 469.

[19] German companies alone have invested a total of approximately €800 billion abroad.

law. After all, the legal situation according to European Union law may not influence the existing effectiveness in international law of these treaties of the member states.[20] The ongoing existence in international law of bilateral investment treaties should, therefore, be maintained as long as no adequate subsequent system exists.[21]

Fourth Thesis: Within the framework of new competences "after Lisbon" the member states, together with the Commission, need to vigorously support the negotiation of European investment treaties or substantial investment chapters within free-trade agreements. In addition to appropriate standards of protection,[22] improving access to foreign markets for European investors ("*pre-establishment*" and "*market access*") should be an important aim of these negotiations.

This is all the more important against the background of an apparent change in attitude towards the protection of investment in certain parts of the world. The long and extensive experience of member states in international investment protection

[20]In detail, see Johannsen, Die Kompetenz der Europäischen Union für ausländische Direktinvestitionen nach dem Vertrag von Lissabon, in: Tiejte/Kraft/Lehmann (eds.), *Beiträge zum Transnationalen Wirtschaftsrecht, Heft 90*, 2009, p. 22, with further references.

[21]For an express approval of the Council regarding the continuance of the investment treaties of the member states see the German Federal Constitutional Court Ruling of June 30, 2009, Paras. 377–380: "The continued legal existence of the agreements already concluded is not endangered. International agreements of the Member States that were concluded before 1st January 1958 shall in principle not be affected by the Treaty establishing the European Community (Art. 307.1 TEC; Art. 351.1 TFEU). In many cases, this provision is not directly applicable because bilateral investment protection agreements have, as a general rule, been concluded more recently, but the legal concept exists that a situation in the Member States which qualifies as a legal fact will in principle not be impaired by a later step of integration (see Bernhardt, Die Europäische Gemeinschaft als neuer Rechtsträger im Geflecht der traditionellen zwischenstaatlichen Beziehungen, EuR (1983), p. 199 (205); Schmalenbach, in: Calliess/Ruffert, TEU/TEC, 3rd ed. 2007, Art. 307 TEC, Margin no. 5). With a view to the mixed competence in investment issues, the existing investment protection agreements must be authorized by the European Union (see Council Decision of 15 November 2001 Authorising the Automatic Renewal or Continuation in Force of Provisions Governing Matters Covered by the Common Commercial Policy Contained in the Friendship, Trade and Navigation Treaties and Trade Agreements Concluded between Member States and Third Countries, OJEU 2001 L 320/13). This corresponds to the current practice, expressly declared or tacitly practiced, concerning the continued validity of international agreements concluded by the Member States." The legal view, which can be understood from Art. 351 Para. 1 TFEU (ex Art. 307 Para. 1 Treaty of Rome), is that a legal situation in the member states would not, in principle, be affected by a later step towards integration, cf. Tietje, Die Außenwirtschaftsverfassung der EU nach dem Vertrag von Lissabon, in: Tietje/Kraft (eds.), *Beiträge zum Transnationalen Wirtschaftsrecht, Heft 83*, 2009, p. 18.

[22]Such as the principle of non-discrimination or the basis of fair and just treatment. Higher standards of protection, similar to those provided by the German bilateral investment treaties, will in all likelihood not be included in the negotiating mandate owing to maintenance of the principle of consensus as there is a possible conflict of interests amongst the 27 European Union member states between capital-exporting and capital-importing states.

can be utilized profitably within the framework of such negotiations and the conclusion of treaties.

In this context the following considerations, which have their precursors in the development of Community law, should be examined[23]: One possible form could involve the European Union concluding a framework investment treaty with third states, leaving the details of the investment protection guarantees to the member states, not least to take into account special political/historical factors within the relationship of the individual European Union state with third countries.[24] This graduated combination of treaties with various levels has already been described as the Commission's "*multi-level governance reflected in a multi-level conclusion of international agreements*,"[25] a description which is equally well suited to the introduction recommended here of complementary, European investment protection.

Fifth Thesis: The idea and principle of most-favoured treatment should apply concerning the relationship between existing treaties of the member states and future European investment treaties, as is already the case in European free-trade agreements or in various directives in European law. In the "*Minimum Platform on Investment*," which the Council adopted on 27 November 2007 and which was renewed on 6 March 2009, (even before the Lisbon Treaty came into effect), the member states had already expressly stated the following concerning existing and future investment protection treaties:

> Article ["Other Agreements"]: Nothing in this title shall be taken to limit the rights of investors of the Parties to benefit from any more favourable treatment provided for in any existing or future international agreement relating to investment to which a Member State of the Community and [a 'region' or country] are parties.[26]

---

[23]Burgstaller, European Law and Investment Treaties, Journal of International Arbitration 26 (2009) 2, p. 181 (215).

[24]Something similar was provided for in the investment chapters – this was, however, "before Lisbon": Art 21 No. 2 [Promoting Investment] of the EU-Chile Association Agreement: "Cooperation will cover in particular the following: (b) developing a legal framework for the Parties that favours investment, by conclusion, where appropriate, of bilateral agreements between the Member States and Chile to promote and protect investment and avoid dual taxation," http://trade.ec.europa.eu/doclib/docs/2004/november/tradoc_111620.pdf; Art. 50 of the Agreement Euro-Med Countries, http://trade.ec.europa.eu/doclib/docs/2006/march/tradoc_127986.pdf; Art. 21 Cotonou Agreement; Eilmansberger, Bilateral Investment Treaties and EC Law, Common Markets Law Review 46 (2009), p. 383 (393).

[25]Kuijper, Fifty years of EC/EU external relations: Continuity and the dialogue between judges and member states as constitutional legislators, Fordham Int'l L.J. 31 (2007–2008), p. 1571 (1597); regarding international trade policy: Petersmann, Multilevel Judicial Governance of International Trade Requires a Common Conception of Rule of Law and Justice, J. Int'l Econ. L. 10 (2007) 3, p. 529.

[26]Council of European Union, 15375 / 06 [unpublished], revised version of 6 March 2009; see also the suggested formulation by Karl, The Competence for Foreign Direct Investment–New Powers for the European Union?, The Journal of World Investment & Trade 5 (2004) 3, p. 413 (448) for an European Union investment protection treaty: "The parties to the treaty undertake to respect all other obligations to the other treaty partner regarding the investments of an investor. The EU can ensure that the member states observe their obligations to the parties to the treaty. This includes,

Thus, we would arrive at a complementary and interrelated European system of investment protection which would sensibly combine the benefits of both the existing investment treaties of the member states and the future free-trade agreements of the European Union. The new competences would generate further advantages if, for example, the European Commission succeeds in its negotiations with China and other large economic areas in its aim to achieve better, and mutual, *market access* for investors and thereby, in this respect, emulate the classic bilateral investment protection model of the USA.

Sixth Thesis: And finally, the following aspects have to be considered:

- An arbitration clause, at least regarding the *arbitral tribunals of the World Bank (ICSID)*, could not be included in a European Union investment treaty, so an investor from a third country could not initiate ICSID proceedings against the European Union following such an agreement. According to Art. 67 of the ICSID Convention, any new entrants have to be members of the World Bank (*"for signature on behalf of States member of the bank"*) or of the Statute of the International Court of Justice. The entry of a regional association such as the European Union is not possible.[27] Finally, Art. 66 of the ICSID Convention requires the *unanimous* agreement of all ICSID member states for any amendment to the ICSID Convention.
- "After Lisbon" a common trade policy will be much more strongly anchored in the principles and aims of the foreign trade policy of the European Union as a whole. With the reference in Art. 205 TFEU to Art. 21 Para. 2 TEU (Para. 3 Subsection 3, new version) the aims of economic liberalization contained in Art. 206 TFEU (Art. 131 Treaty of Rome) also result explicitly in the application and integration of these values in a common trade policy. The *values* anchored in the coherence policy regarding the international dealings of the European Union include "democracy, the rule of law, human rights, the principles of international law, the Charter of the United Nations, sustainable development, integration of developing nations in the world economy, protection of the environment and global governance."
- The *European Parliament* must be involved before any such agreement is concluded and, according to Art. 218 Para. 6 TFEU, the approval of the European Parliament is required in the case of new agreements. In any case, it has been apparent for some time that the European Parliament has been gaining in self-confidence in this area and has dedicated itself increasingly to technical questions concerning a common trade policy and has, thereby, clearly begun to prepare for the new legal situation following the entry into force of the Lisbon Treaty. This will require increased coordination

e.g. obligations arising from a BIT with individual member states or from other investment protection agreements with an investor of the other treaty partner."

[27] Art. 2 Para. 1 IBRD Articles of Agreement in conjunction with Art. II Agreement of the International Monetary Fund; Art. 34 Para. 1 ICJ Statute, Federal Law Gazette 1973 II, p. 505.

and harmonization from all parties involved – the member states, the Commission and the Council.

- Finally, it is necessary to clarify the question of *responsibility* and *liability* within the framework of mixed agreements. As in this case both the European Union and the member states are treaty partners in a mixed agreement, they bear joint liability. Within the framework of an investment agreement this liability would basically be linked to "reasonable" state behaviour.[28] Joint and several liabilities would only emerge in the case of a member state invoking European Union law as only then could *both* the European Union and the member state be considered as being potentially in breach of contract.

However, in the case of a mixed agreement, the member states and the European Union could only limit or divide their responsibility in international law amongst themselves by means of a specific declaration. Numerous treaties expressly require this: Annex IX Art. 4 of the United Nations Convention on the Law of the Sea (UNCLOS),[29] Art. 24 II and III of the Kyoto Protocol and, finally, in the ratification declaration to Art. 26 of the Energy Charter Treaty.[30]

Such a declaration concerning the limitation of responsibility would also be desirable in mixed investment agreements in order to avoid the duplication of legal action and to protect the member states from any duplication of liability owing to their being held responsible in international law for the execution of European Union law, thereby possibly infringing Community law due to the settlement of an arbitral ruling.

Seventh Thesis: It is high time, following the planned transfer of competences, for the cooperation between the member states and the Commission to be provided with an institutional framework – similar to that which exists in trade policy – and comparable with the previous Art. 133 and future Art. 207 committee on trade

[28]Fair and just treatment, no discrimination, observance of concluded treaties, etc.

[29]Annex IX Art. 4 UNCLOS: "1. The instrument of formal confirmation or of accession of an international organization shall contain an undertaking to accept the rights and obligations of States under this Convention in respect of matters relating to which competence has been transferred to it by its member States which are Parties to this Convention. 2. An international organization shall be a Party to this Convention to the extent that it has competence in accordance with the declarations, communications of information or notifications referred to in Article 5 of this Annex. 3. Such an international organization shall exercise the rights and perform the obligations which its member States which are Parties would otherwise have under this Convention, on matters relating to which competence has been transferred to it by those member States. The member States of that international organization shall not exercise competence which they have transferred to it."

[30]Regarding this, see Eilmansberger, Bilateral Investment Treaties and EC Law, Common Markets Law Review 46 (2009), p. 383 (396 fn. 70).

policy, in which all of these questions can be dealt with appropriately between those concerned.

The creation of such a complementary and correlated system of investment protection is demanding. It requires a prudent dialogue between those involved at European Union level in order to really enable advantage to be taken of the possibilities of such a system and the possible negotiating power of the European Union and, therefore, to engage in the competition between the legal systems[31] with other economic blocks also in this regard.

[31]Regarding this, see Bungenberg, Außenbeziehungen und Außenhandelspolitik, in: Schwarze/ Hatje (eds.), *Der Reforvertrag von Lissabon, EuR Beiheft 1*, 2009, p. 195.

Legal Arrangements for the Promotion and Protection of Foreign Investments Within the Framework of the EU Association Policy and European Neighbourhood Policy

Carsten Nowak*

Introduction

The progressing liberalisation of global trade has been accompanied by a constant rise and increased importance of foreign investments in recent decades. In this respect, foreign investments, particularly foreign direct investments, constitute indisputably an integral part of the increasing cross-linking of markets and form in their entirety an important element as well as an indicator of the so-called economic globalisation. Moreover, foreign investments are often described as an "engine of global economic growth".[1]This may be agreed with, as it has been evident for quite some time that foreign investments, or the inflow of foreign investments, make a great contribution to a positive economic development of a country and a national economy.[2]At the same time, they can be seen as an

---

[1]See, for example, Tietje, Die Beilegung internationaler Investitionsstreitigkeiten, in: Marauhn (ed.), *Streitbeilegung in den internationalen Wirtschaftsbeziehungen*, 2005, p. 47 (49 et seq.); for the tremendous increase of the volume of foreign direct investments in recent years see Easson, *Taxation of Foreign Direct Investment – An Introduction*, 1999, pp. 4 et seq.; Krajewski, *Wirtschaftsvölkerrecht*, 2006, pp. 167 et seq.; Moosa, *Foreign Direct Investment – Theory, Evidence and Practice*, 2002, pp. 16 et seq.; Shikata, *Legal Instruments of Foreign Investment: "The World Bank Guidelines"*, 1993, pp. 1 et seq.; UNCTAD, *Trends in International Investment Agreements: an Overview, 1999*, pp. 9 et seq.

[2]See, e.g., the report of the UNCTAD, *Economic Development in Africa – Rethinking the Role of Foreign Direct Investment*, 2006; Kehal, *Foreign Investment in Developing Countries*, 2004, pass.; Moran, *Does Foreign Investment promote development?*, 2005, pass.; Nieuwenhuys/Brus, Multilateral Regulation of Investment – Legal, Political and Economic Aspects, in: Nieuwenhuys/Brus (eds.), *Multilateral Regulation of Investment*, 2001, pp. 1 et seq.; Sauvant, Foreign direct investment and development, in: Sauvant/Weber (eds.), *International Investment Agreements: Key Issues*, 2005, Chap. 27.

*The author would like to thank his assistants, in particular Lena Borth and Caroline Slusarek, for very helpful support

C. Nowak*
Chair for public law, especially european law; furthermore, the author is the director for the Frankfurt Institute for European Law
Europa-Universität Viadrina, Große Scharrnstraße 59, 15230 Frankfurt (Oder), Germany
e-mail: cnowak@europa-uni.de

M. Bungenberg et al. (eds.), *International Investment Law and EU Law*, DOI 10.1007/978-3-642-14855-2_7, © Springer-Verlag Berlin Heidelberg 2011 important instrument for the creation and increase of economic welfare, for the reduction of poverty and thus in many cases for political and social stabilisation.[3]

Against this background it is hardly surprising that legal regulations and arrangements which serve the promotion and protection of foreign investments can mostly be found where the European Community (EC) and now the European Union (EU)[4] strives to make a significant contribution to the economic, political and/or social development of certain third states or regions. These efforts of the EU, which are not exclusively altruistic but essentially serve various selfish aims, for instance in the fields of energy, environment, trade, security, democracy and human rights, are shown, inter alia by the establishment and foundation of numerous "strategic", "strengthened" and "deepened partnerships" on the global and non-European level.[5] They can be found, for instance, in the relationships between the EU, of the one part, and the republics of Kazakhstan, Kyrgyzstan, Tajikistan, Turkmenistan and Uzbekistan, of the other part.[6] Within the framework of these partnerships, the European Communities and their Member States concluded in 1999 three bilateral "partnership and cooperation agreements" with the Republic of Kazakhstan,[7] the

---

[3]See for the largely uncontested (positive) effects of such investments Herdegen, *Internationales Wirtschaftsrecht*, (7th ed.) 2008, § 21 para. 1; Tietje, Die Beilegung internationaler Investitionsstreitigkeiten, in: Marauhn (ed.), *Streitbeilegung in den internationalen Wirtschaftsbeziehungen – Völkerrechtliche Einhegung ökonomischer Globalisierungsprozesse*, 2005, p. 47 (49 et seq.).

[4]For the EU as the legal successor of the EC see Art. 1(3)(3) TEU in the version of the Treaty of Lisbon amending the Treaty on European Union and the Treaty Establishing the European Community, signed at Lisbon, 13 December 2007, OJ 2007 C 306/1 et seq.; with further references see below fn. 19.

[5]See the Commission's Communication of 8 December 2005 to the Council and the European Parliament (EP) – "A stronger partnership between the European Union and Latin America", COM (2005) 636 final; the Commission's Communication of 16 June 2004 to the Council, the EP and the European Economic and Social Committee – "An EU-India Strategic Partnership", COM (2004) 430 final; the Commission's Communication of 24 October 2006 to the Council and the EP – "EU-China: Closer partners, growing responsibilities", COM (2006) 631 final; the Agreement in Partnership and Cooperation establishing a partnership between the European Communities and their Member States, of the one part, and the Russian Federation, of the other part (OJ 1997 L 327/3 et seq.); the Commission's Communication of 4 September 2001 to the Council – "Europe and Asia: A Strategic Framework for Enhanced Partnerships", COM (2001) 469 final; the Commission's Communication "A new partnership with South East Asia", COM (2003) 399 final; also see http://ec.europa.eu/development/geographical/regionscountries/euafrica_en.cfm#partnership for the new "Africa-EU Strategic Partnership: A Joint Africa-EU Strategy"; additionally see in this context the Interim Partnership Agreement between the European Community, of the one part, and the Pacific States, of the other part (OJ 2009 L 272/2 et seq.).

[6]For more on this see the booklet of the *Secretariat General of the Council*, European Union and Central Asia: Strategy for a New Partnership, October 2007 (available at http://www.consilium.europa.eu/uedocs/cms_data/librairie/PDF/EU_CtrlAsia_EN-RU.pdf); see also the "Joint Progress Report by the Council and the European Commission to the European Council on the implementation of the EU Central Asia Strategy" (available at http://ec.europa.eu/external_relations/central_asia/docs/progress_report_0608_en.pdf); as well as European Community, Regional Strategy Paper for Assistance to Central Asia for the period 2007–2013 (available at http://ec.europa.eu/external_relations/central _asia/rsp/07_13_en.pdf).

[7]OJ 1999 L 196/ 3 et seq.; hereinafter referred to as "PCA/Kazakhstan".

Kyrgyz Republic[8] and the Republic of Uzbekistan.[9] These were accompanied by the interim agreement on trade and trade-related matters between the EC and the European Atomic Energy Community, of the one part, and the Republic of Tajikistan, of the other part,[10] signed in 2004.

According to the object of the aforementioned partnership and cooperation agreements, they do not only serve the extension of the political relations, the lasting, environment-friendly and sustainable development of the national economies and the creation of a basis for cooperation in the fields of law-making, economics, social matters, finance, technology and culture,[11] but rather intend to extend trade and investment.[12] For this reason, they contain various statements and regulations, which relate to the development of trade and investments,[13] the improvement of investment conditions[14] as well as the guarantee of the free movement of capital in connection with direct and other investments.[15] Moreover, they contain articles,[16] captioned "Investment promotion and protection", that specify the investment-specific objectives of the said agreements in their second paragraph. The aims of cooperation are, in particular, the conclusion of agreements for the promotion and protection of investment, the conclusion of agreements to avoid double taxation, the creation of appropriate and favourable conditions for attracting foreign investments in the economy of the respective Central Asian partner, the exchange of information on statutes, regulations and administrative practices in the field of investment and the

[8]OJ 1999 L 196/48 et seq.; hereinafter referred to as "PCA/Kyrgyz".

[9]OJ 1999 L 229/3 et seq.; hereinafter referred to as "PCA/Uzbekistan".

[10]OJ 2004 L 340/2 et seq.

[11]To these varied aims see always Art. 1 of the three agreements mentioned above.

[12]E.g. Art. 1 (dash 2) PCA/Kazakhstan (fn. 7 above); Art. 1 (dash 3) PCA/Kyrgyz (fn. 8 above); Art. 1 (dash 4) PCA/Uzbekistan (fn. 9 above).

[13]See the preambles of PCA/Kazakhstan (fn. 7 above), of PCA/Kyrgyz (fn. 8 above) and of PCA/Uzbekistan (fn. 9 above), where it says: "[. . .] Convinced that this Agreement will create a new climate for economic relations between the Parties and in particular for the development of trade and investment, which are essential to economic restructuring and technological modernization [. . .]".

[14]See, for example, the preamble of PCA/Kazakhstan (fn. 7 above), where it says: "[. . .] Conscious of the need to improve conditions affecting business and investment, and conditions in areas such as the establishment of companies, labour, provision of services and capital movements, and of the desirability of moving towards granting of national treatment for each others companies [. . .]"; for very similar but shorter statements see the preambles of PCA/Kyrgyz (fn. 8 above) and of PCA/Uzbekistan (fn. 9 above).

[15]See Art. 41(2) PCA/Kazakhstan (fn. 7 above), Art. 42(2) PCA/Kyrgyz (fn. 8 above) and Art. 40(2) PCA/Uzbekistan (fn. 9 above), where it is stated: "With regard to transactions on the capital account of balance of payments, from entry into force of this Agreement, the free movement of capital relating to direct investments made in companies formed in accordance with the laws of the host country and investments made in accordance with the provisions of Chap. II, and the liquidation or repatriation of these investments and of any profit stemming therefrom shall be ensured".

[16]Art. 41(2) PCA/Kazakhstan (fn. 7 above), Art. 47(2) PCA/Kyrgyz (fn. 8 above); Art. 46(2) PCA/Uzbekistan (fn. 9 above).

exchange of information on investment opportunities in the form of, inter alia, trade fairs, exhibitions, trade weeks and other events.[17]

On a regional (European) level, which shall be prominently discussed in the following, the efforts of the EU and its Member States to make a positive contribution by public international investment-related regulations for the political stabilisation and economic development of numerous non-EU Member States in Europe is shown as well. On this level, the aforementioned efforts are especially embodied in the multitude of bilateral association, stabilisation, cooperation and/or partnership agreements concluded between the European Communities and their Member States, of the one part, and numerous states of eastern Europe, southeastern Europe, North Africa and the Middle East, of the other part. Although some of these agreements belong to the core elements of the so-called *Stabilisation and Association Process* (SAP) concerning the western Balkan countries, many others may be allocated to the so-called *European Neighbourhood Policy* (ENP), which applies to 16 direct neighbouring countries, namely Algeria, Armenia, Azerbaijan, Belarus, Egypt, Georgia, Israel, Jordan, Lebanon, Libya, Moldova, Morocco, Occupied Palestinian Territory, Syria, Tunisia and Ukraine.

As shall be shown in the following, those agreements, belonging to the bilateral core elements of the EU Association Policy and/or ENP,[18] contain multiple statements and regulations in regard to the promotion and the protection of foreign investments. Subsequently, it shall be addressed that the new *Eastern Partnership* created by a joint statement of the involved players on 7 May 2009 aims at the conclusion of new association agreements between the EU, of the one part, and Azerbaijan, Belarus, Georgia, Moldavia and the Ukraine, of the other part. Taking into consideration the exclusive competence of the EU for direct investment as provided by the Treaty of Lisbon,[19] it is particularly relevant whether the

[17]For these five single objectives (with rather similar formulations) see Art. 41(2) PCA/Kazakhstan (fn. 7 above), Art. 47(2) PCA/Kyrgyz (fn. 8 above) and Art. 46(2) PCA/Uzbekistan (fn. 9 above).

[18]For more on these multilateral and bilateral dimensions of the EU Association Policy and ENP see Nowak, Multilaterale und bilaterale Elemente der EU-Assoziations-, Partnerschafts- und Nachbarschaftspolitik, EuR (2010) 6, p. 746 et seq.

[19]See the Treaty of Lisbon (fn. 4 above) in conjunction with the consolidated versions of the Treaty on European Union and the Treaty on the Functioning of the European Union (OJ 2008 C115/13 et seq.). For more on the various reform potentials of the Treaty of Lisbon see the numerous articles, e.g. in Fastenrath/Nowak, *Der Lissabonner Reformvertrag – Änderungsimpulse in einzelnen Rechts- und Politikbereichen*, 2009; Hummer/Obwexer, *Der Vertrag von Lissabon*, 2009; Pernice, *Der Vertrag von Lissabon: Reform der EU ohne Verfassung?*, 2008; Schwarze/Hatje, *Der Reformvertrag von Lissabon, EuR Beiheft 1*, 2009; Weidenfeld, *Lissabon in der Analyse – Der Reformvertrag der Europäischen Union*, 2008; see also Fabbrini, Contesting the Lisbon Treaty: Structure and Implications of the Constitutional Division Within the European Union, EJLR 10 (2008) 4, pp. 457–476.; Harpaz/Herman, The Lisbon Reform Treaty: Internal and External Implications, EJLR 10 (2008) 4, pp. 431–436.; Hatje/Kindt, Der Vertrag von Lissabon – Europa endlich in guter Verfassung?, NJW (2008), pp. 1761–1768; Müller-Graff, Der Vertrag von Lissabon auf der Systemspur des Europäischen Primärrechts, Integration (2008), pp. 123 et seq.; Oppermann, Die Europäische Union von Lissabon, DVBl. (2008), pp. 473 et seq.; Pache/Rösch, Der Vertrag von Lissabon, NVwZ (2008), pp. 473–480; Streinz/Ohler/Herrmann, *Der Vertrag von*

contracting parties ought to be geared to provisions regarding investment law in other agreements, such as the Energy Charter Treaty[20] and the CARIFORUM Economic Partnership Agreement.[21] This might be the case, since they are, in view of the protection of foreign investments, considerably richer in content than association, stabilisation, cooperation and/or partnership agreements concluded within the framework of the EU Association Policy and ENP.

Present arrangements for the promotion and protection of investments within the framework of the EU Association Policy and ENP

The following appraisal of the present arrangements for the promotion and protection of foreign investments within the framework of the EU Association Policy and the ENP begins with an overview of the legal basis of investment promotion and protection concerning the relationship between the EU and the associated countries of the western Balkans. This will subsequently be contrasted with the legal arrangements for the promotion and protection of investments within the framework of the ENP. The ENP, established as an independent policy field in 2003–2004,[22] is a serious offer for the creation and development of privileged relationships regarding exclusively Algeria, Armenia, Azerbaijan, Belarus, Egypt, Georgia, Israel, Jordan, Lebanon, Libya, Moldova, Morocco, Palestinian National Authority, Syria, Tunisia and Ukraine.[23]

Lissabon zur Reform der EU, (3rd ed.) 2010, pp. 1 et seq.; Terhechte, Der Vertrag von Lissabon: Grundlegende Verfassungsurkunde der europäischen Rechtsgemeinschaft oder technischer Änderungsvertrag?, EuR (2008), pp. 143 et seq.

[20]OJEC 1998 L 69/26 et seq.; came into force on 16 April 1998.

[21]OJ 2008 L 289/3 et seq.; came into force on 15 April 2008.

[22]See especially the Commission's Communication of 12 May 2004 "European Neighbourhood Policy – Strategy Paper", COM (2004), 373 final.

[23]For the voluminous literature on the ENP see, for example, Balfour/Rotta, Beyond Enlargement – The European Neighbourhood Policy and its Tools, The International Spectator 40 (2005) 1, pp. 7 et seq.; Duta, European Neighbourhood Policy and Its Main Components, Romanian Journal of International Affairs 10 (2005), pp. 229 et seq.; Edwards, The Construction of Ambiguity and the Limits of Attraction: Europe and its Neighbourhood Policy, Journal of European Integration 30 (2008), pp. 45 et seq.; Hummer, Die Union und ihre Nachbarn: Nachbarschaftspolitik vor und nach dem Verfassungsvertrag, Integration (2005), pp. 233 et seq.; Kempe, Zwischen Anspruch und Wirklichkeit – Die Europäische Nachbarschaftspolitik, Osteuropa (2007), pp. 57 et seq.; Lippert, Erweiterungsfragen und Nachbarschaftspolitik der Europäischen Union, insbesondere die Türkeifrage und ihre Implikationen, in: Müller-Graff (ed.), *Die Rolle der erweiterten Europäischen Union in der Welt*, 2006, pp. 175 et seq.; Magen, The Shadow of Enlargement: Can the European Neighbourhood Policy Achieve Compliance, Columbia Journal of European Law (2006), pp. 383 et seq.; O'Donnell/Whitman, Das Phantom-Zuckerbrot – Die Konstruktionsfehler der ENP, Osteuropa (2007), pp. 95 et seq.; Parmentier, The reception of EU neighbourhood policy, in: Laïdi (ed.), *EU Foreign Policy in a Globalized World – Normative power and social preferences*, 2008, pp. 103 et seq.; Sasse, The European Neighbourhood Policy: Conditionality Revisited for the EU's Eastern Neighbours, Europa-Asia Studies 60 (2008), pp. 295 et seq.; Smits, The

The primary aim of the relatively young ENP is to prevent the emergence of new dividing lines between the EU, which due to the eastern European expansion is now enlarged to 27 Member States, and the aforementioned EU neighbours, and to rather strengthen prosperity, stability and security of the involved players.[24] Core elements of the ENP are numerous association, cooperation and/or partnership agreements, whose bilateral regulatory approach has recently been enhanced by two new forms of multilateral cooperation. In addition to the *Union for the Mediterranean*,[25] founded on 13 July 2008, having developed from the traditional EU Mediterranean Policy[26] and the Euro-Mediterranean Partnership,[27] respectively, the *Eastern Partnership*,[28] created on 7 May 2009, is addressed here. They show more clearly than ever before that, within the framework of the ENP, there is

Outsiders: The European Neighbourhood Policy, International Affairs 81 (2005), pp. 757 et seq.; Van Vooren, A case study of "soft law" in EU external relations: The European Neighbourhood Policy, ELRev. 34 (2009), pp. 696 et seq.

[24]For more on the backgrounds and objectives of the ENP see the Commission's Communication of 12 May 2004 "European Neighbourhood Policy – Strategy Paper", COM (2004), 373 final; the Commission's Communication of 5 December 2007 "A Strong European Neighbourhood Policy", COM (2007) 774 final; see also B. Lippert, Teilhabe statt Mitgliedschaft? – Die EU und ihre Nachbarn im Osten, Osteuropa (2007), pp. 69 et seq.

[25]See the Communication from the Commission of 20 May 2008 to the EP and the Council "Barcelona Process: Union for the Mediterranean", COM (2008) 319 final; and Nowak, Multilaterale und bilaterale Elemente der EU-Assoziations-, Partnerschafts- und Nachbarschaftspolitik, EuR (2010) 6, p. (forthcoming).

[26]See, in particular, Bretherton/Vogler, *The European Union as a Global Actor*, (2nd ed.) 2006, pp. 154 et seq.; Jünemann, Europas Mittelmeerpolitik im regionalen und globalen Wandel: Interessen und Zielkonflikte, in: Zippel (ed.), *Die Mittelmeerpolitik der EU*, 1999, pp. 29 et seq.; Martinez, European Union's exportation of democratic norms – The Case of North Africa, in: Laïdi (ed.), *EU Foreign Policy in a Globalized World – Normative power and social preferences*, 2008, pp. 118 et seq.; Schlotter, Die Europäische Union als außenpolitischer Akteur?: Zur Kohärenz der EU-Mittelmeerpolitik und zur Rolle der Kommission, Integration (2005), pp. 316 et seq.; Pace, The Ugly duckling of Europe: The Mediterranean in the Foreign Policy of the European Union, Journal of European Area Studies 10 (2002), pp. 189 et seq.; Youngs, European Approaches to Security in the Mediterranean, Middle East Journal 57 (2003), pp. 414 et seq.

[27]For more on this see Bicchi, "Our size fits all": normative power Europe and the Mediterranean, JEPP 13 (2006), pp. 286 et seq.; Jünemann, Ein Raum des Friedens, der Stabilität und des gemeinsamen Wohlstands – Die Euro-Mediterrane Partnerschaft zwischen Anspruch und Wirklichkeit, in: Harders/Jünemann (eds.), *Zehn Jahre Euro-Mediterrane Partnerschaft: Bilanz und Perspektiven*, Sonderheft Orient 46 (2005) 3, pp. 360 et seq.; Tzifakis, EU's region-building and boundary-drawing policies: the European approach to the Southern Mediterranean and the Western Balkans, Journal of Southern Europe and the Balkans 9 (2007), pp. 47 et seq.

[28]For more on this, with further references, see Böttger, Im Osten nichts Neues? Ziele, Inhalte und erste Ergebnisse der Östlichen Partnerschaft, Integration (2009), pp. 372 et seq.; Nowak, Multilaterale und bilaterale Elemente der EU-Assoziations-, Partnerschafts- und Nachbarschaftspolitik, EuR (2010) 6, p. 746 et seq.; Tiede/Schirmer, Die Östliche Partnerschaft der Europäischen Union im Rahmen des Gemeinschaftsrechts, Osteuropa-Recht 55 (2009), pp. 184 et seq.; for the development and motives of this partnership see Pop, Balkan's model to underpin EU's "Eastern Partnership", EUobserver (available at: http://euobserver.com/15/26766?print=1); see also Schäfer, The Eastern Partnership – "ENP plus" for Europe's Eastern neighbours, C·A·Perspectives (2009) 4, pp. 1 et seq.

differentiation between a southern dimension of the ENP (relating to Algeria, Morocco, Tunisia, Libya, Egypt, Jordan, Lebanon, Israel, the Palestinian National Authority and Syria) and an eastern ENP dimension relating to Armenia, Azerbaijan, Belarus, Georgia, Ukraine and Moldavia.[29]

The ENP's southern dimension has hitherto been substantially characterised by several bilateral *Euro-Mediterranean agreements*, concluded in the period from 1998 to 2005 between the European Communities and their Member States, of the one part, and Tunisia, Morocco, Israel, Jordan, Egypt, Algeria and the Lebanese Republic, of the other part, that contain various regulations relating to the promotion and protection of foreign investments. The eastern dimension of the ENP, on the other hand, is substantially characterised by the bilateral *partnership and cooperation agreements*, concluded in the period from 1998 to 1999 between the European Communities and their Member States, of the one part, and Ukraine, Moldova, Georgia, Armenia and Azerbaijan, of the other part, that contain numerous regulations regarding both aspects of the promotion and protection of investments as well.

Bilateral arrangements for the promotion and the protection of investments between the EU and the associated countries of the western Balkans

The relationship between the EU and the countries of the western Balkans is essentially characterised by the SAP, running for approximately 10 years[30] and the *Stability Pact for South Eastern Europe*, regarding Croatia, Macedonia, Albania, Bosnia and Herzegovina, Montenegro, Serbia and Kosovo as defined the resolution 1244 of the UN Security Council.[31] These countries are connected to the EU by

[29]For more details regarding these two ENP dimensions see Nowak, Multilaterale und bilaterale Elemente der EU-Assoziations-, Partnerschafts- und Nachbarschaftspolitik, EuR (2010) 6, p. 746 et seq.

[30]See, in particular, the fundamental Communication from the Commission of 26 May 1999 to the EP and the Council on the Stabilisation and Association process for South Eastern Europe, COM (1999) 235 final.

[31]In more detail and with further references see Bartlett/Samardžija, The Reconstruction of South East Europe, the Stability Pact and the Role of the EU: an Overview, MOCT-Most 10 (2000) 2, pp. 245 et seq.; Bretherton/Vogler, *The European Union as a Global Actor*, (2nd ed.) 2006, pp. 144 et seq.; Busek, South Eastern Europe: On the Way to Political and Economic Integration within the EU, The Analyst – Central and Eastern European Review (2007) 4, pp. 5 et seq. (available at: http://www.ceeol.com); Calic, EU Enlargement and Common Foreign and Security Policy in the Western Balkans, Südosteuropa Mitteilungen (2007), pp. 12 et seq.; Cameron/Kintis, Southeastern Europe and the European Union, Journal of Southeast European and Black Sea Studies 1 (2001) 2, p. 94 (99 et seq.); Chandler, The EU's promotion of democracy in the Balkans, in: Laïdi (ed.), *EU Foreign Policy in a Globalized World – Normative power and social preferences*, 2008, pp. 68 et seq.; Friis/Murphy, Turbo-charged negotiations: the EU and the Stability Pact for South Eastern Europe, JEPP (2000), pp. 767 et seq.; Hoffmeister, Die Beziehungen der Europäischen Union zu den

individual "accession partnerships"[32] or "European partnerships"[33] which are based on Council Regulation (EC) No 533/2004 of 22 March 2004 on the establishment of European partnerships in the framework of the SAP.[34] They show in their entirety that the perspectives of the respective SAP countries for future accession to the EU still differ, especially in terms of time.[35] In addition, certain interim agreements on trade and trade-related issues, in particular different bilateral stabilisation and association agreements, in which various statements and regulations with regard to the aspect of investment promotion and partly with regard to aspects of investment protection can be found, belong to the core elements of the aforementioned partnerships.

Bilateral contractual relationships between the EU and its Member States, of the one part, and individual countries of the western Balkans, of the other part

Within the framework of the SAP, bilateral relationships of association between the EU and its Member States, of the one part, and the countries of the western Balkans, of the other part, are realised by stabilisation and association agreements under international law, as far as possible. In the case of legal or actual obstacles opposing

Staaten des Westbalkans, in: Kadelbach (ed.), *Die Außenbeziehungen der Europäischen Union*, 2006, pp. 125 et seq.; Nowak, Multilaterale und bilaterale Elemente der EU-Assoziations-, Partnerschafts- und Nachbarschaftspolitik, EuR (2010) 6, p. (forthcoming); Stewart, EU Democracy Promotion in the Western Balkans, in: Jünemann/Knodt (eds.), *Externe Demokratieförderung durch die Europäische Union/European External Democracy Promotion*, 2007, pp. 231 et seq.

[32]See Council Decision 2008/119/EC of 12 February 2008 on the principles, priorities and conditions contained in the Accession Partnership with Croatia and repealing Decision 2006/145/EC (OJ 2008 L 42/51 et seq.); and Council Decision 2008/212/EC of 18 February 2008 on the principles, priorities and conditions contained in the Accession Partnership with the former Yugoslav Republic of Macedonia and repealing Decision 2006/57/EC (OJ 2008 L 80/32 et seq.).

[33]See Council Decision 2008/210/EC of 18 February 2008 on the principles, priorities and conditions contained in the European Partnership with Albania and repealing Decision 2006/54/EG (OJ 2008 L 80/1 et seq.); Council Decision 2008/211/EC of 18 February 2008 on the principles, priorities and conditions contained in the European Partnership with Bosnia and Herzegovina and repealing Decision 2006/55/EG (OJ 2008 L 80/18 et seq.); Council Decision 2008/213/EC of 18 February 2008 on the principles, priorities and conditions contained in the European Partnership with Serbia including Kosovo as defined by resolution 1244 of United Nations Security Council of 10 June 1999 and repealing Decision 2006/56/EG (OJ 2008 L 80/46 et seq.); and Council Decision 2007/49/EC of 22 January 2007 on the principles, priorities and conditions contained in the European Partnership with Montenegro (OJ 2007 L 20/16 et seq.).

[34]OJ 2004 L 86/1 et seq.; amended by Council Regulation (EC) No 269/2006 (OJ 2006 L 47/1 et seq.).

[35]See, in particular, the Communication from the Commission of 5 March 2008 to the EP and the Council "Western Balkans: Enhancing the European perspective", COM (2008) 127 final; and Elbasani, EU enlargement in the Western Balkans: strategies of borrowing and inventing, Journal of Southern Europe and the Balkans 10 (2008) 3, pp. 293 et seq.; Priebe, Beitrittsperspektive und Verfassungsreformen in den Ländern des Westlichen Balkans, EuR (2008) 3, pp. 301 et seq.

the conclusion or entry into force of such an agreement, preparatory interim agreements can be concluded beforehand. Currently, these agreements exist in the relationship between the EU and Bosnia and Herzegovina, officially called "European partnership".[36] In this context, a stabilisation and association agreement was signed on 16 June 2008, but has not yet entered into force.[37] Furthermore, a trade-related interim agreement between the EC and Montenegro[38] entered into force on 1 January 2008. It may be regarded as the core element of this particular European partnership.[39] Moreover, Serbia and Kosovo are currently integrated in a "European partnership"[40] which resulted in the conclusion of a trade-related interim agreement, signed in Luxembourg on 29 April 2008, as well as a stabilisation and association agreement, which has not yet entered into force.

However, the bilateral relations between the European Communities and their Member States, of the one part, and Macedonia, Croatia and Albania, of the other part, are entirely different. As an instrument of the SAP, the "accession partnership" of the EU with the former Yugoslav Republic of Macedonia, is based on the respective EC regulation.[41] This accession partnership is characterised by certain principles, priorities and conditions, which are updated regularly.[42] The stabilisation and

[36]Interim Agreement on trade and trade-related matters between the European Community, of the one part, and Bosnia and Herzegovina, of the other part (OJ 2008 L 233/6 et seq.), in conjunction with Council Decision 2008/474/EC of 16 June 2008 concerning the signing and conclusion of the Interim Agreement on trade and trade-related matters between the European Community, of the one part, and Bosnia and Herzegovina, of the other part (OJ 2008 L 233/5), in conjunction with Council Decision 2008/211/EC of 18 February 2008 on the principles, priorities and conditions contained in the European Partnership with Bosnia and Herzegovina and repealing Decision 2006/55/EC (OJ 2008 L 80/18 et seq.).

[37]See, in particular, Council Regulation (EC) No 594/2008 of 16 June 2008 on certain procedures for applying the Stabilisation and Association Agreement between the European Communities and their Member States, of the one part, and Bosnia and Herzegovina, of the other part, and for applying the Interim Agreement on trade and trade-related matters between the European Community, of the one part, and Bosnia and Herzegovina, of the other part (OJ 2008 L 169/1 et seq.).

[38]Interim Agreement on trade and trade-related matters between the European Community, of the one part, and the Republic of Montenegro, of the other part (OJ 2007 L 345/2 et seq.), in conjunction with Council Decision 2007/855/EC of 15 October 2007 concerning the signing and conclusion of the Interim Agreement on trade and trade-related matters between the European Community, of the one part, and the Republic of Montenegro, of the other part (OJ 2007 L 345/1).

[39]See, in particular, Council Decision 2007/49/EC (fn. 33 above).

[40]See Council Decision 2008/213/EC (fn. 33 above).

[41]Council Regulation (EC) No 533/2004 of 22 March 2004 on the establishment of European Partnerships in the framework of the stabilisation and association process (OJ 2004 L 86/1 et seq.); amended by Council Regulation (EC) No 269/2006 (OJ 2006 L 47/7).

[42]See Council Decision 2006/57/EC of 30 January 2006 on the principles, priorities and conditions contained in the European Partnership with the former Yugoslav Republic of Macedonia and repealing Decision 2004/518/EC (OJ 2006 L 35/57 et seq.) in conjunction with Council Decision 2008/212/EC (fn. 32 above).

association agreement,[43] concluded after the Council and Commission Decision,[44] forms a core element of this accession partnership. It entered into force on 1 April 2004 and is based on Article 310 TEC in conjunction with Article 300 (2 and 3) TEC (now Articles 217 and 218 of the Treaty on the Functioning of the European Union[45]). The same applies to the relationship between the EU and Croatia, constituting an "accession partnership"[46] as well. Again, the stabilisation and association agreement,[47] concluded following the Council and Commission Decision[48] and which came into force on 1 February 2005, forms the core element. Finally, the stabilisation and association agreement between the European Communities and their Member States, of the one part, and the Republic of Albania, of the other part,[49] can be assigned to the SAP as well. Subsequent to a trade-related interim agreement[50] that had also been concluded within the framework of this particular European partnership,[51] the stabilisation and association agreement was signed on 12 June 2006 and entered into force on 1 April 2009, following the respective Council and Commission Decision.[52] According to the objectives laid down in Article 1(2) SAA/Albania, which differ considerably from the objectives of the

[43]Stabilisation and Association Agreement between the European Communities and their Member States, of the one part, and the former Yugoslav Republic of Macedonia, of the other part, OJ 2004 L 84/13 et seq. (hereinafter referred to as "SAA/Macedonia"), in conjunction with the Agreement in the form of an Exchange of Letters concerning the conclusion of the Stabilisation and Association Agreement between the European Communities and their Member States, of the one part, and the former Yugoslav Republic of Macedonia, of the other part (OJ 2004 L 84/3).

[44]See the Council and Commission Decision of 23 February 2004 concerning the conclusion of the Stabilisation and Association Agreement between the European Communities and their Member States, of the one part, and the former Yugoslav Republic of Macedonia, of the other part (OJ 2004 L 84/1 et seq.).

[45]Consolidated version of this treaty in OJ 2008 C 115/47 et seq.

[46]See Council Decision 2008/119/EC of 12 February 2008 (fn. 32 above).

[47]Stabilisation and Association Agreement between the European Communities and their Member States, of the one part, and the Republic of Croatia, of the one part, of the other part (OJ 2005 L 26/3 et seq.; hereinafter referred to as "SAA/Croatia").

[48]See Council and Commission Decision (2005/40/EC, Euratom) of 13 December 2004 concerning the conclusion of the Stabilisation and Association Agreement between the European Communities and their Member States, of the one part, and the Republic of Croatia, of the other part (OJ 2005 L 26/1 et seq.).

[49]Stabilisation and Association Agreement between the European Communities and their Member States, of the one part, and the Republic of Albania, of the other part (OJ 2009 L 107/166 et seq.; hereinafter referred to as "SAA/Albania").

[50]Interim Agreement on trade and trade-related matters between the European Community, of the one part, and the Republic of Albania, of the other part (OJ 2006 L 239/2 et seq.) in conjunction with Council Decision 2006/580/EC of 12 June 2006 (OJ 2006 L 239/1).

[51]See, in particular, Council Decision 2008/210/EC of 18 February 2008 (fn. 33 above).

[52]See Council and Commission Decision of 26 February 2009 concerning the conclusion of the Stabilisation and Association Agreement between the European Communities and their Member States, of the one part, and the Republic of Albania, of the other part (OJ 2009 L 107/165).

stabilisation and association agreements with Macedonia and Croatia, the aims of this association are:

- to support the efforts of Albania to strengthen democracy and the rule of law;
- to contribute to political, economic and institutional stability in Albania, as well as to the stabilisation of the region;
- to provide an appropriate framework for political dialogue, allowing the development of close political relations between the Parties.

Article 1(2) SAA/Croatia and Article 1(2) SAA/Macedonia differ insofar as they formulate the identical aims of these associations established on the agreements as follows:

- [. . .] to provide an appropriate framework for political dialogue, allowing the development of close political relations between the Parties;
- to support the efforts of Croatia and the former Yugoslav Republic of Macedonia to develop their economic and international cooperation, also through the approximation of its legislation to that of the Community;
- to support the efforts t*o complete the transition into a market economy*, to promote harmonious economic relations and develop gradually a free trade area between the Community and Croatia[53];
- to foster regional cooperation in all the fields covered by this Agreement.

Apart from the aforementioned differences regarding the objectives, the three stabilisation and association agreements with Macedonia, Croatia and Albania share significant structural similarities. According to the general principles, respect for the democratic principles and human rights, respect for international law principles and the rule of law as well as the principles of a market economy shall constitute essential elements of the aforementioned agreements.[54] Furthermore, they always contain titles and provisions regarding "political dialogue", "regional cooperation", "free movement of goods", "movement of workers, establishment", "supply of services", "current payments and movement of capital", "approximation of laws and law enforcement", "competition", and "justice and home affairs", partly "cooperation policies", and "financial cooperation" as well as some "institutional, general and final provisions".

Investment promotion and investment protection within the scope of the aforementioned association and stabilisation agreements

Those three stabilisation and association agreements, connecting the European Communities or the EU and its Member States with Macedonia, Croatia and Albania, contain several investment-related statements and regulations, which are

[53]The words printed in italics are missing in SAA/Macedonia (fn. 43 above).

[54]Art. 2 SAA/Macedonia (fn. 43 above); Art. 2 SAA/Croatia (fn. 47 above); Art. 2 SAA/Albania (fn. 49 above).

partly nearly identical and partly divergent. Identical investment-related statements can be found in the preamble of the three aforementioned agreements, expressing the conviction that

> the Stabilisation and Association Agreement will create a new climate for economic relations between them and above all for the development of trade and investment, factors crucial to economic restructuring and modernisation.

With regard to transactions on the capital account of balance of payments, from the date of entry into force of the agreement, the parties shall ensure, subject to limitations justified on grounds of public policy, public security or public health,[55] the free movement of capital relating to direct investments made in companies, which are formed in accordance with the laws of the host country, and investments, which are made in accordance with the provisions of Chapter II, and the liquidation or repatriation of these investments and of any profit resulting therefrom.[56] According to the second paragraph in each case, the parties shall also ensure, at a later date, free movement of capital relating to portfolio investment and financial loans and credits with a duration of less than 1 year.[57] These provisions serve the investment promotion, manifesting itself mainly in guaranteeing the freedom of establishment and free movement of capital.

As an additional safeguard of the aforementioned freedoms, the contracting parties are obliged to provide legal protection as laid down in the last title of the three aforementioned stabilisation and association agreements.[58] According to this provision, which remarkably is not included in the already mentioned partnership and cooperation agreement between the EC/EU and its Member States, of the one part, and several Central Asian states, of the other part,[59] each party shall ensure that natural and legal persons of the other party have access, free of discrimination in relation to its own nationals, to the courts having jurisdiction and the competent administrative organs of the parties to defend their individual rights and their property rights, including intellectual and industrial property rights.[60] Whereas it is not entirely clear what legal consequences arise from a breach of this obligation, it seems relatively clear that the internal market freedoms, especially in the shape of the freedom of establishment and the free movement of capital, also belong to the aforementioned rights guaranteed by these agreements. Also, it seems clear that disputes connected with the

---

[55]See Art. 61(1) SAA/Macedonia (fn. 43 above); Art. 62(1) SAA/Croatia (fn. 47 above); Art. 63(1) SAA/Albania (fn. 49 above).

[56]See Art. 59(1)(2) SAA/Macedonia (fn. 43 above); Art. 60(1) SAA/Croatia (fn. 47 above); Art. 61 (1) SAA/Albania (fn. 49 above).

[57]With different formulations and time periods see 59(2)(2) SAA/Macedonia (fn. 43 above), Art. 60(4) SAA/Croatia (fn. 47 above); Art. 61(2)(subpara. 3) SAA/Albania (fn. 49 above).

[58]See Art. 117 SAA/Croatia (fn. 47 above); Art. 115 SAA/Macedonia (fn. 43 above); Art. 123 SAA/Albania (fn. 49 above).

[59]For these agreements see "Introduction" above.

[60]See Art. 117 SAA/Croatia (fn. 47 above); Art. 115 SAA/Macedonia (fn. 43 above); Art. 123 SAA/Albania (fn. 49 above); the supplements printed in italics are only to be found in SAA/ Macedonia (fn. 43 above).

aforementioned obligations belong to "disputes relating to the application or interpretation of this agreement" that can be referred by each party to the respective stabilisation and association council.[61,62] Established to supervise the application and implementation of the respective agreement, the stabilisation and association councils may settle the dispute by means of a binding decision.[63]

Beyond that, another article, appearing in all three aforementioned stabilisation and association agreements and captioned "Investment promotion and protection", states that the aim of the associations based on these agreements is to bring about a favourable climate for private investment, both domestic and foreign.[64] Additionally, Article 91 SAA/Albania states that such a climate is "essential to economic and industrial revitalisation in Albania". In the two stabilisation and association agreements relating to Macedonia and Croatia, following directly the aforementioned provision, the nearly identical "particular aims" of these cooperations, established in both of these agreements, are listed as follows:

- for the former Yugoslav Republic of Macedonia and for Croatia to improve a legal framework which favours and protects investment;
- the conclusion, where appropriate, with Member States of bilateral agreements for the promotion and protection of investment;
- the improvement of investment protection.[65]

The aforementioned provisions, which entered into force in 2004 with regard to Macedonia and in 2005 with regard to Croatia,[66] show that the contracting parties hitherto assumed that the legal protection of foreign investment was not so much a subject matter of the stabilisation and association agreements, but rather a concern of the EU Member States. These states have already concluded hundreds of bilateral treaties regarding investment promotion and protection with third states.[67]

---

[61]See the first sentences of Art. 111 SAA/Macedonia (fn. 43 above), Art. 113 SAA/Croatia (fn. 47 above) and Art. 119 SAA/Albania (fn. 49 above).

[62]For the installation of the Councils, their tasks and compositions see Art. 108 et seq. SAA/ Macedonia (fn. 43 above), Art. 110 et seq. SAA/Croatia (fn. 47 above) and Art. 116 et seq. SAA/ Albania (fn. 49 above).

[63]See the second sentences of Art. 111 SAA/Macedonia (fn. 43 above), Art. 113 SAA/Croatia (fn. 47 above) and Art. 119 SAA/Albania (fn. 49 above).

[64]See Art. 84(1) SAA/Macedonia (fn. 43 above); Art. 85(1) SAA/Croatia (fn. 47 above).

[65]For these single objectives see Art. 85(2) SAA/Croatia (fn. 47 above). Art. 84(2) SAA/Macedonia (fn. 43 above) deviates by listing a further (fourth) special objective of cooperation ("implementation of suitable arrangements for the transfer of capital"); no special objectives are mentioned in Art. 91 SAA/Albania (fn. 49 above).

[66]For more on this see the paragraph above concerning the bilateral contractual relationships between the EU and its Member States, of the one part, and individual countries of the western Balkan, of the other part.

[67]For more on this see Schöbener, Der Rechtsrahmen des Internationalen Investitionsrechts: ein Überblick zu den bilateralen Investitionsschutzabkommen, WiVerw (2009) 1, pp. 3 et seq.; Perkams/Secomb, Der Schutz deutscher Auslandsinvestitionen in Lateinamerika, WiVerw (2009) 1, pp. 31 et seq.

They can be found, inter alia, between Germany and Croatia,[68] as well as between Germany and Macedonia.[69] The same applies for the relationship between Germany and Albania.[70] Interestingly, however, there is no explicit reference in the stabilisation and association agreement concluded between the European Communities and their Member States, of the one part, and the Republic of Albania, of the other part,[71] having entered into force on 1 April 2009, that the specific arrangements of legal protection of foreign investment must be an imperative or primarily bilateral concern of the EU Member States. In view of the transfer of competences by the Treaty of Lisbon[72] in the field of direct investment in favour of the EU, this might not be regarded as a coincidence.

Bilateral arrangements for investment promotion and protection within the framework of the southern dimension of the ENP

With regard to the multilateral aspect, the southern dimension of the ENP is currently characterised by the Union for the Mediterranean, founded on 13 July 2008. The bilateral aspect is shaped by various agreements,[73] namely numerous trade-related interim, association and/or so called Euro-Mediterranean agreements, which partly contain multifaceted statements and regulations concerning the promotion and protection of foreign investment.

Bilateral contractual relationships between the EU and several neighbouring states within the framework of the southern ENP dimension

EU neighbours participating in the Union for the Mediterranean and associated with the EU and its Member States by trade-related interim, association and/or so called Euro-Mediterranean agreements are Algeria, Egypt, Israel, Jordan, Lebanon, Morocco, the Palestinian National Authority, Syria and Tunisia. The aforementioned Euro-Mediterranean agreements, which were concluded and entered into

---

[68] The relevant act of assent is published in BGBl 2000 II, p. 653; it came into force on 28 September 2000.

[69] The relevant act of assent is published in BGBl 2000 II, p. 646; it came into force on 17 September 2000.

[70] The relevant act of assent is published in BGBl 1994 II, p. 3720; it came into force on 18 August 1995.

[71] SAA-EC/Albania (fn. 49 above).

[72] With further references see fn. 19 above.

[73] For the complementary relation between the bilateral Euro-Mediterranean agreements and the multilateral Union for the Mediterranean see Nowak, Multilaterale und bilaterale Elemente der EU-Assoziations-, Partnerschafts- und Nachbarschaftspolitik, EuR (2010) 6, p. 746 et seq.

force in the period from 1998 to 2005, constitute bilateral association agreements of the "new generation", since they replaced the agreements of the "first generation". Those had already been concluded in the 1970s between the European Economic Community (EEC) and individual states of North Africa and the Middle East.[74] Only the cooperation agreement between the EEC and Syria[75] still remains a relevant agreement of the first generation, as there has not been a replacement of the old cooperation agreement by a newer Euro-Mediterranean agreement within the framework of this particular neighbourly relation yet. Apart from that, such a Euro-Mediterranean agreement does not exist in the relationship between the EU and the Palestinian Authority either, whose connection simply consists of an interim association agreement,[76] which entered into force in 1997.

The first North African state to succeed in concluding a Euro-Mediterranean agreement of the new generation with the EC, or rather the European Communities and their Member States, was Tunisia.[77] Morocco[78] and Israel[79] followed subsequently in 2000. Further Euro-Mediterranean association agreements were "signed and sealed" thereafter with Jordan in 2002,[80] with Egypt in

[74]See OJEC 1978 L 263/1 et seq. (Algeria); OJEC 1978 L 266/1 et seq. (Egypt); OJEC 1978 L 267/1 et seq. (Lebanon); OJEC 1978 L 268/1 et seq. (Jordan).

[75]Cooperation Agreement between the European Economic Community and the Syrian Arab Republic, OJEC 1978 L 269/2 et seq.

[76]Euro-Mediterranean Interim Association Agreement on trade and cooperation between the European Community, of the one part, and the Palestine Liberation Organization (PLO) for the benefit of the Palestinian Authority of the West Bank and the Gaza Strip, of the other part (OJEC 1997 L 187/3 et seq.).

[77]Euro-Mediterranean Agreement establishing an association between the European Communities and their Member States, of the one part, and the Republic of Tunisia, of the other part (OJEC 1998 L 97/2 et seq.; hereinafter referred to as "EMA/Tunisia"), in conjunction with Decision 98/238/EC of the Council and the Commission of 26 January 1998 (OJEC 1998 L 97/1).

[78]Euro-Mediterranean Agreement establishing an association between the European Communities and their Member States, of the one part, and the Kingdom of Morocco, of the other part (OJEC 2000 L 70/2 et seq.; hereinafter referred to as "EMA/Morroco"), in conjunction with Council and Commission Decision 2000/204/EC of 24 January 2000 (OJEC 2000 L 70/1; with amendments in OJEC 2000 L 138/31).

[79]Euro-Mediterranean Agreement establishing an association between the European Communities and their Member States, of the one part, and the State of Israel, of the other part (OJEC 2000 L 147/3 et seq.; hereinafter referred to as "EMA/Israel"), in conjunction with Council and Commission Decision 2000/384/EC, ECSC, of 19 April 2000 (OJEC 2000 L 147/1 et seq.), in conjunction with the Protocol to the Euro-Mediterranean Agreement establishing an Association between the European Communities and their Member States, of the one part, and the State of Israel, of the other part, part, on a framework Agreement between the European Community and the State of Israel on the general principles governing the State of Israel's participation in Community programmes (OJ 2008 L 129/40 et seq.).

[80]Euro-Mediterranean Agreement establishing an Association between the European Communities and their Member States, of the one part, and the Hashemite Kingdom of Jordan, of the other part (OJEC 2002 L 129/3 et seq.; hereinafter referred to as "EMA/Jordan"), in conjunction with Council and Commission Decision 2002/357/EC, ECSC, of 26 March 2002 (OJEC 2002 L 129/1 et seq.).

2004,[81] with Algeria in 2005[82] and finally with the Lebanese Republic in 2006.[83] According to the objectives contained in those Euro-Mediterranean agreements, the aims of the associations, established by these agreements, are:

- to provide an appropriate framework for political dialogue, allowing the development of close political relations between the Parties,[84] respectively the consolidation, strengthening and development of their relations and their cooperation in all areas they consider relevant to such dialogue;[85]
- to promote trade;[86]
- to promote the expansion of harmonious economic and social relations between the parties[87] or to foster the development of such relations through dialogue and cooperation;[88]
- through the expansion, inter alia, of trade in goods and services, the reciprocal liberalisation of the right of establishment, the further progressive liberalisation of public procurement, the free movement of capital and the intensification of cooperation in science and technology to promote the harmonious development of economic relations between the Community [and the respective party] and thus to foster in the Community and in [the respective party] the advance of economic activity, the improvement of living and employment conditions, and increased productivity and financial stability;[89]

---

[81]Euro-Mediterranean Agreement establishing an Association between the European Communities and their Member States, of the one part, and the Arab Republic of Egypt, of the other part (OJ 2004 L 304/39 et seq.; hereinafter referred to as "EMA/Egypt"), in conjunction with Council Decision 2004/635/EC of 21 April 2004 (OJ 2004 L 304/38).

[82]Euro-Mediterranean Agreement establishing an Association between the European Community and its Member States, of the one part, and the People's Democratic Republic of Algeria, of the other part (OJ 2005 L 265/2 et seq.; hereinafter referred to as "EMA/Algeria"), in conjunction with Council Decision 2005/690/EC of 18 July 2005 (OJ 2005 L 265/1).

[83]Euro-Mediterranean Agreement establishing an Association between the European Community and its Member States, of the one part, and the Republic of Lebanon, of the other part (OJ 2006 L 143/2 et seq.; hereinafter referred to as "EMA/Lebanon"), in conjunction with Council Decision 2006/356/EC of 14 February 2006 (OJ 2006 L 143/1).

[84]See Art. 1(2)(dash 1) EMA/Egypt (fn. 81 above); Art. 1(2)(dash 1) EMA/Israel (fn. 79 above); Art. 1(2)(dash 1) EMA/Jordan (fn. 80 above).

[85]See Art. 1(2)(dash 1) EMA/Tunisia (fn. 77 above); Art. 1(2)(dash 1) EMA/Morocco (fn. 78 above); Art. 1(2)(dash 1) EMA/Algeria (fn. 82 above); Art. 1(2)(lit. a) EMA/Lebanon (fn. 83 above).

[86]See Art. 1(2)(dash 2) EMA/Algeria (fn. 82 above); Art. 1(2)(dash 3) EMA/Tunisia (fn. 77 above); Art. 1(2)(dash 3) EMA/Morocco (fn. 78 above).

[87]See Art. 1(2)(dash 2) EMA/Algeria (fn. 82 above).

[88]See Art. 1(2)(dash 3) EMA/Jordan (fn. 80 above); Art. 1(2)(dash 3) EMA-EC/Egypt (fn. 81 above); very similar see Art. 1(2)(lit. c) EMA/Lebanon (fn. 83 above); Art. 1(2)(dash 3) EMA/Tunisia (fn. 77 above); Art. 1(2)(dash 3) EMA/Morocco (fn. 78 above).

[89]See Art. 1(2)(dash 2) EMA/Israel (fn. 79 above); very similar, but shorter, see Art. 1(2)(dash 4) EMA/Jordan (fn. 80 above), where only the improvement of living and employment conditions as well as the enhancement of productivity and financial stability are mentioned.

- to contribute to the economic and social development of the state having concluded an agreement with the EC and its Member States;[90]
- to establish the conditions for the gradual, respectively progressive liberalisation of trade in goods, services and capital;[91]
- to facilitate human exchanges, particularly in the context of administrative procedures;[92]
- to encourage integration of the Maghreb countries by promoting trade and cooperation within the Maghreb group and between it and the Community and its Member States;[93]
- to encourage regional cooperation with a view to the consolidation of peaceful coexistence and economic and political stability;[94]
- to promote economic, social, cultural and financial cooperation[95] and/or to promote cooperation in other areas which are of reciprocal interest[96] or of mutual interest.[97]

Apart from the aforementioned divergences regarding the respective objectives, the Euro-Mediterranean agreements share significant structural similarities. Firstly, according to the general principles, included in all agreements, respect for democratic principles and human rights, which guides their internal and international policy, shall constitute essential parts or elements of these agreements.[98] Secondly, all the following titles and provisions of these agreements basically relate to the same subject matter, only differing slightly in order and wording. The subject matter includes political

[90]See Art. 1(2)(dash 4) EMA/Egypt (fn. 81 above).

[91]See Art. 1(2)(dash 2) EMA/Algeria (fn. 82 above); Art. 1(2)(dash 2) EMA/Egypt (fn. 81 above); Art. 1(2)(dash 2) EMA/Jordan (fn. 80 above); Art. 1(2)(lit. b) EMA/Lebanon (fn. 83 above); Art. 1 (2)(dash 2) EMA/Tunisia (fn. 77 above); Art. 1(2)(dash 2) EMA/Morocco (fn. 78 above).

[92]See Art. 1(2)(dash 3) EMA/Algeria (fn. 82 above).

[93]See Art. 1(2)(dash 4) EMA/Algeria (fn. 82 above); similarly Art. 1(2)(dash 4) EMA/Tunisia (fn. 77 above) and Art. 1(2)(dash 4) EMA Morocco (fn. 78 above).

[94]See Art. 1(2)(dash 5) EMA/Egypt (fn. 81 above); Art. 1(2)(dash 3) EMA/Israel (fn. 79 above); Art. 1(2)(dash 5) EMA/Jordan (fn. 80 above).

[95]See Art. 1(2)(dash 5) EMA/Tunisia (fn. 77 above); Art. 1(2)(dash 5) EMA/Algeria (fn. 82 above); Art. 1(2)(dash 5) EMA/Morocco (fn. 78 above); including "monetary cooperation" see Art. 1(2)(lit. d) EMA/Lebanon (fn. 83 above).

[96]See Art. 1(2)(dash 4) EMA/Israel (fn. 79 above); Art. 1(2)(dash 6) EMA/Jordan (fn. 80 above).

[97]See Art. 1(2)(dash 6) EMA/Egypt (fn. 81 above); Art. 1(2)(lit. e) EMA/Lebanon (fn. 83 above).

[98]See Art. 2 EMA/Algeria (fn. 82 above); Art. 2 EMA/Egypt (fn. 81 above); Art. 2 EMA/Israel (fn. 79 above); Art. 2 EMA/Jordan (fn. 80 above); Art. 2 EMA/Lebanon (fn. 83 above); very similar, but less substantial, see Art. 2 EMA/Tunisia (fn. 77 above) and Art. 2 EMA/Morocco (fn. 78 above).

dialogue,[99] free movement of goods,[100] trade in services[101] or rather the right of establishment and supply of services,[102] the fields of payment, capital and competition provisions,[103] economic cooperation,[104] social and cultural cooperation[105] and cooperation in numerous other fields,[106] financial cooperation,[107] cooperation in the field of justice and home affairs[108] as well as institutional and general provisions.[109]

Investment promotion and investment protection within the scope of the Euro-Mediterranean agreements

The aforementioned *Euro-Mediterranean agreements* contain several, in many instances identical, investment-related statements and regulations, which share many common features with the investment-relevant provisions[110] in the

[99]See Arts. 3–5 EMA/Algeria (fn. 82 above); Arts. 3–5 EMA/Egypt (fn. 81 above); Arts. 3–5 EMA/Israel (fn. 79 above); Arts. 3–5 EMA/Jordan (fn. 80 above); Arts. 3–5 EMA/Lebanon (fn. 83 above); Arts. 3–5 EMA/Morocco (fn. 78 above); Arts. 3–5 EMA/Tunisia (fn. 77 above).

[100]See Arts. 6–29 EMA/Algeria (fn. 82 above); Arts. 6–28 EMA/Egypt (fn. 81 above); Arts. 6–28 EMA/Israel (fn. 79 above); Arts. 6–29 EMA/Jordan (fn. 80 above); Arts. 6–29 EMA/Lebanon (fn. 83 above); Arts. 6–18 EMA/Morocco (fn. 78 above); Arts. 6–30 EMA/Tunisia (fn. 77 above).

[101]See Arts. 30–37 EMA/Algeria (fn. 82 above).

[102]See Arts. 29 and 30. EMA/Egypt (fn. 81 above); Arts. 29 and 30 EMA/Israel (fn. 79 above); Arts. 30–47 EMA/Jordan (fn. 80 above); Art. 30 EMA/Lebanon (fn. 83 above); Arts. 31 and 32 EMA/Morocco (fn. 78 above); Arts. 31 and 32 EMA/Tunisia (fn. 77 above).

[103]See Arts. 38–46 EMA/Algeria (fn. 82 above); Arts. 31–38 EMA/Egypt (fn. 81 above); Arts. 31–39 EMA/Israel (fn. 79 above); Arts. 48–58 EMA/Jordan (fn. 80 above); Arts. 31–39 EMA/Lebanon (fn. 83 above); Arts. 33–41 EMA/Morocco (fn. 78 above); Arts. 33–41 EMA/Tunisia (fn. 77 above).

[104]See Arts. 47–66 EMA/Algeria (fn. 82 above); Arts. 39–61 EMA/Egypt (fn. 81 above); Arts. 59–79 EMA/Jordan (fn. 80 above); Arts. 42–63 EMA/Morocco (fn. 78 above); Arts. 42–63 EMA/Tunisia (fn. 77 above); including the cooperation related to audiovisual issues see Arts. 58–66 EMA/Israel (fn. 79 above).

[105]See Arts. 67–78 EMA/Algeria (fn. 82 above); Arts. 62–71 EMA/Egypt (fn. 81 above); Arts. 80–85 EMA/Jordan (fn. 80 above); Arts. 63–70 EMA/Lebanon (fn. 83 above); Arts. 64–74 EMA/Morocco (fn. 78 above); Arts. 64–74 EMA/Tunisia (fn. 77 above); similarly, but including technological cooperation, see Arts. 40–57 EMA/Israel (fn. 79 above).

[106]See Arts. 40–62 EMA/Lebanon (fn. 83 above).

[107]Arts. 79–81 EMA/Algeria (fn. 82 above); Arts. 72 and 73 EMA/Egypt (fn. 81 above); Arts. 86–88 EMA/Jordan (fn. 80 above); Arts. 71–73 EMA/Lebanon (fn. 83 above); Arts. 75–77 EMA/Morocco (fn. 78 above); Arts. 75–77 EMA/Tunisia (fn. 77 above).

[108]See Arts. 82–91 EMA/Algeria (fn. 82 above).

[109]See Arts. 92–110 EMA/Algeria (fn. 82 above); Arts. 74–92 EMA/Egypt (fn. 81 above); Arts. 67–85 EMA/Israel (fn. 79 above); Arts. 89–107 EMA/Jordan (fn. 80 above); Arts. 74–93 EMA/Lebanon (fn. 83 above); Arts. 78–96 EMA/Morocco (fn. 78 above); Arts. 78–96 EMA/Tunisia (fn. 77 above).

[110]For the investment-related statements and regulations of the stabilisation and association agreements, see the paragraphs above concerning the bilateral agreements for the promotion and the protection of investments between the EU and Macedonia, Croatia and Albania, respectively).

afore-discussed stabilisation and association agreements. Identical investment-related statements can be found in the respective preambles of these seven Euro-Mediterranean agreements, expressing with nearly identical wording either the "desire" of enhancing the development of trade and investment[111] or the "conviction" that the Euro-Mediterranean agreement in question

> will create a new climate for their economic relations and in particular for the development of trade, investment and economic and technological cooperation",[112] or "provides a suitable framework for the development of a partnership based on private initiative, and that it will create a climate conducive to economic, trade and investment relations between the Parties, a consideration which offers vital backing for economic restructuring and technological modernisation.[113]

In the Euro-Mediterranean agreement relating to Jordan, several provisions addressing certain types of investment in direct connection with the free movement of capital follow the aforementioned provisions. Article 49 (1) EMA/Jordan determines that within the framework of the provisions of the agreement, there generally shall be "no restrictions on the movement of capital from the Community to Jordan involving direct investment from Jordan to the Community".[114] Moreover, Article 50 EMA/Jordan clarifies that the provisions of Article 49 shall be without prejudice to the application of any restrictions which exist between the parties on the date of entry into force of the agreement, in respect of the movement of capital between them involving direct investment, including real estate and establishment. Furthermore, the transfer of investment made in Jordan by EC residents or in the EC by Jordanian residents and of any profits abroad stemming therefrom shall not be affected.[115]

In several other Euro-Mediterranean agreements it is stated that the contracting parties will ensure, from the entry into force of the agreement, the free circulation of capital for direct investments made in companies formed in accordance with the laws of the host country, and the liquidation or repatriation of these investments and of any profit stemming therefrom.[116] In the Euro-Mediterranean agreements the parties renounced the addendum, being included in a further paragraph of the stabilisation and association agreements discussed above, which contain the

---

[111]See the preamble of EMA/Egypt (fn. 81 above).

[112]In this sense see the penultimate sentences of the preambles of EMA/Israel (fn. 79 above) and of EMA/Jordan (fn. 80 above); very similar is the penultimate sentence of the preamble of EMA/Tunisia (fn. 77 above), where it says: "In the convincement, that the Agreement will accomplish a positive effect of expansion of their economic relations, trade and investments, which are indispensable for their economic transformation and technology modernization [...]", similarly see the penultimate sentence of the preamble of EMA/Lebanon (fn. 83 above).

[113]In this sense see the penultimate sentences of the preamble of EMA/Algeria (fn. 82 above) and of EMA/Morocco (fn. 78 above).

[114]Additionally, Art. 49(2) EMA/Jordan (fn. 80 above) clarifies that the "outflow of Jordanian capital to the Community, other than direct investment, shall be subject to the prevailing laws in Jordan".

[115]In this sense see Art. 33(2) EMA/Lebanon (fn. 83 above).

[116]See Art. 34(1) EMA/Tunisia (fn. 77 above); Art. 32(1) EMA/Egypt (fn. 81 above); similarly Art. 39(1) EMA/Algeria (fn. 82 above) and Art. 34(1) EMA/Morocco (fn. 78 above).

obligation of the parties to ensure, at a later date, free movement of capital relating to portfolio investment and financial loans and credit with a duration of less than 1 year.[117] Remarkably, the same applies to the obligation of each party, laid down in the aforementioned stabilisation and association agreements and aimed at the creation of a recourse to a court, within the scope of the agreement, to undertake to ensure that natural and legal persons of the other party have access free of discrimination in relation to its own nationals to the courts having jurisdiction and the competent administrative organs of the parties to defend their individual rights and their property rights.[118] Similarities between the stabilisation and association agreements and the Euro-Mediterranean agreements exist, however, regarding legal protection and dispute settlement. Within the scope of application of the latter agreements, each party may refer any dispute relating to the application or interpretation of the respective agreement[119] to the respective association council,[120] which may then settle the dispute by means of a decision.[121]

With regard to investment law, it is interesting to note that all Euro-Mediterranean agreements, except for EMA/Israel, contain either an article captioned "Investment promotion and protection"[122] or an article captioned "Investments and promotion of investments".[123] With minor deviations, such an article can also be found in the initially addressed partnership and cooperation agreements between the EC in its Member States, of the one part, and several Central Asian states, of the other part,[124] as well as in the stabilisation and association agreements discussed before.[125] According to this article included in almost all Euro-Mediterranean agreements but

[117]See, with further references, the paragraphs above concerning the bilateral agreements for the promotion and the protection of investments between the EU and Macedonia, Croatia and Albania, respectively.

[118]See, with further references, the paragraphs above concerning the bilateral agreements for the promotion and the protection of investments between the EU and Macedonia, Croatia and Albania, respectively.

[119]See Art. 86(1) EM/Tunisia (fn. 77 above); Art. 86(1) EMA/Morocco (fn. 78 above); Art. 100(1) EMA/Algeria (fn. 82 above); Art. 82(1) EMA/Egypt (fn. 81 above); Art. 75(1) EMA/Israel (fn. 79 above); Art. 97(1) EMA/Jordan (fn. 80 above); Art. 82(1) EMA/Lebanon (fn. 83 above).

[120]For the installation of these councils, their tasks and compositions see Art. 78 et seq. EMA/Tunisia (fn. 77 above); Art. 78 et seq. EMA/Morocco (fn. 78 above); Art. 92 et seq. EMA/Algeria (fn. 82 above), Art. 74 et seq. EMA/Egypt (fn. 81 above); Art. 67 et seq. EMA/Israel (fn. 79 above); Art. 89 et seq. EMA/Jordan (fn. 80 above); Art. 74 et seq. EMA/Lebanon (fn. 83 above).

[121]See Art. 86(2) EMA/Tunisia (fn. 77 above); Art. 86(2) EMA/Morocco (fn. 78 above); Art. 100 (2) EMA/Algeria (fn. 82 above); Art. 82(2) EMA/Egypt (fn. 81 above); Art. 75(2) EMA/Israel (fn. 79 above); Art. 97(2) EMA/Jordan (fn. 80 above); Art. 82(2) EMA/Lebanon (fn. 83 above).

[122]See Art. 50 EMA/Tunisia (fn. 77 above); Art. 50 EMA/Morocco (fn. 78 above); Art. 54 EMA/Algeria (fn. 82 above); Art. 47 EMA/Lebanon (fn. 83 above).

[123]See Art. 46 EMA/Egypt (fn. 81 above) and Art. 67 EMA/Jordan (fn. 80 above).

[124]For these Agreements see, with further references, "Introduction" above.

[125]See above the paragraphs above concerning the bilateral contractual agreements for the promotion and the protection of investments between the EU and the associated countries of the western Balkan.

not generally phrased identically, the aim of cooperation shall be "to create a favourable climate for investment flows", in particular by means of the following:

- the establishment of harmonised and simplified procedures, co-investment machinery (especially to link small and medium-sized enterprises) and methods of identifying and providing information on investment opportunities;[126]
- the establishment, where appropriate, of a legal framework to promote investment, chiefly through the conclusion by the individual North African or Middle Eastern state and the Member States investment protection agreements and agreements preventing double taxation;[127]
- technical assistance to schemes to promote and guarantee national and foreign investments.[128]

In the Euro-Mediterranean agreement relating to Jordan, this article differs in content and is slightly more extensive. As stated in Article 67, first sentence, "the objective of cooperation will be the creation of a favourable and stable environment for investment in Jordan". According to the second sentence of the aforementioned provision, this cooperation will entail the development of:

- harmonised and simplified administrative procedures; co-investment machinery, especially for small and medium-sized enterprises of both parties; and information channels and means of identifying investment opportunities;
- a legal environment conducive to investment between the two Parties, where appropriate through the conclusion by the Member States and Jordan of investment protection agreements and agreements to prevent double taxation;
- access to the capital market for the financing of productive investments;
- joint ventures between Jordanian and Community business.

Again different and quantitatively even more extensive are Article 46, captioned "Investments and promotion of investments" of the Euro-Mediterranean agreement relating to Egypt, and Article 47, captioned "Promotion and protection of investment" of the Euro-Mediterranean agreement relating to the Lebanese Republic. In both agreements it is stated that the cooperation shall aim at increasing the flow of capital, expertise and technology to Egypt and Lebanon through, inter alia,

- appropriate means of identifying investment opportunities and information channels on investment regulations;
- providing information on European investment regimes (such as technical assistance, direct financial support, fiscal incentives and investment insurance) related to outward investments and enhancing the possibility for Egypt, respectively Lebanon to benefit from them;

[126]See Art. 54 lit. a) EMA/Algeria (fn. 82 above); Art. 50 lit. a) EMA/Tunisia (fn. 77 above); Art. 50 lit. a) EMA/Morocco (fn. 78 above).

[127]See Art. 50 lit. b) EMA/Tunisia (fn. 77 above); Art. 50 lit. b) EMA/Morocco (fn. 78 above); Art. 54 lit. b) EMA/Algeria (fn. 82 above).

[128]See Art. 54 lit. c) EMA/Algeria (fn. 82 above).

- a legal environment conducive to investment between the two Parties, where appropriate through the conclusion by the Member States and Egypt, respectively Lebanon of investment protection agreements, and agreements to prevent double taxation;
- examining the creation of joint ventures, especially for SMEs and, when appropriate, the conclusion of agreements between the Member States and Egypt, respectively Lebanon;
- establishing mechanisms for encouraging and promoting investments.

The aforementioned provisions, primarily aimed at the promotion of investment, show rather clearly that, despite the existing differences between them, the contracting parties hitherto assumed that the legal protection of foreign investment was not so much subject matter of the Euro-Mediterranean agreements, but rather a concern of the EU Member States to be organised bilaterally. Consistently, the EU Member States have already concluded hundreds of bilateral treaties concerning investment promotion and protection with third states.[129] Counted among those are the bilateral treaties concerning investment promotion and protection which were concluded in recent years and decades between Germany and states included in the Euro-Mediterranean agreements, namely Tunisia,[130] Morocco,[131] Israel,[132] Jordan,[133] Egypt,[134] Algeria[135] and the Lebanese Republic.[136]

Bilateral arrangements for investment promotion and protection within the framework of the eastern dimension of the ENP

With regard to the multilateral aspect, the eastern dimension of the ENP is characterised by the Eastern Partnership,[137] established on 7 May 2009. The bilateral

[129] In more detail see Schöbener, Der Rechtsrahmen des Internationalen Investitionsrechts: ein Überblick zu den bilateralen Investitionsschutzabkommen, WiVerw (2009) 1, pp. 3 et seq.

[130] The relevant act of assent is published in BGBl 1965 II, p. 1377; it came into force on 6 February 1966.

[131] The relevant act of assent is published in BGBl 2004 II, p. 333; it came into force on 12 April 2008.

[132] The relevant act of assent is published in BGBl 1978 II, p. 209; signed on 24 June 1976.

[133] The relevant act of assent is published in BGBl 1975 II, p. 1254; it came into force on 10 October 1997; for the new contract – signed on 13 November 2007, but not yet in effect – see BGBl. 2009 II, 469.

[134] The relevant act of assent is published in BGBl 1977 II, p. 1145; it came into force on 22 July 1978; for the new contract – signed on 16 June 2005, but not yet in effect – see BGBl. 2007 II, 94.

[135] The relevant act of assent is published in BGBl 2002 II, p. 268; it came into force on 30 May 2002.

[136] The relevant act of assent is published in BGBl 1998 II, p. 1439; it came into force on 25 March 1999.

[137] With further references to this Eastern Partnership see fn. 28 above.

aspect is shaped by several partnership and cooperation agreements. Those partnership and cooperation agreements, concluded in the period from 1998 to 1999, between the European Communities and their Member States, of the one part, and Ukraine, the Republic of Moldova, Georgia, Armenia and Azerbaijan, of the other part, contain in different parts partly identical and partly divergent statements and regulations regarding the promotion and protection of foreign investments.

Bilateral contractual relationships between the EU and several neighbouring countries within the framework of the eastern ENP dimension

Bilateral contractual relationships existing between the EU and its Member States, of the one part, and partner countries participating in the Eastern Partnership, of the other part, have developed gradually. The two *partnership and cooperation agreements* concluded in 1998 between the European Communities and their Member States, of the one part, and Ukraine[138] and the Republic of Moldova,[139] of the other part, were preludes. In 1999, they were followed by three additional partnership and cooperation agreements concluded between the European Communities and their Member States, of the one part, and Georgia,[140] Armenia[141] and Azerbaijan,[142] of the other part. According to the objectives laid down in the five aforementioned partnership and cooperation agreements, the aim of the partnerships established by these agreements is

- to provide an appropriate framework for the political dialogue between the Parties allowing the development of (close) political relations;[143]

[138]Partnership and Cooperation Agreement establishing a partnership between the European Communities and their Member States, of the one part, and Ukraine, of the other part (OJEC 1998 L 49/3 et seq.; hereinafter referred to as "PCA/Ukraine").

[139]Partnership and Cooperation Agreement establishing a partnership between the European Communities and their Member States, of the one part, and the Republic of Moldova, of the other part (OJEC 1998 L 181/3 et seq.; hereinafter referred to as "PCA/Moldavia").

[140]Partnership and Cooperation Agreement establishing a partnership between the European Communities and their Member States, of the one part, and Georgia, of the other part (OJEC 1999 L 205/3 et seq.; hereinafter referred to as "PCA/Georgia").

[141]Partnership and Cooperation Agreement establishing a partnership between the European Communities and their Member States, of the one part, and the Republic of Armenia, of the other part (OJEC 1999 L 239/3 et seq.; hereinafter referred to as "PCA/Armenia").

[142]Partnership and Cooperation Agreement establishing a partnership between the European Communities and their Member States, of the one part, and the Republic of Azerbaijan, of the other part (OJEC 1999 L 246/3 et seq.; hereinafter referred to as "PCA/Azerbaijan").

[143]See Art. 1 (dash 1) PCA/Ukraine (fn. 138 above); Art. 1 (dash 1) PCA/Moldavia (fn. 139 above); Art. 1 (dash 1) APZ/Georgia (fn. 140 above); Art. 1 (dash 1) PCA/Armenia (fn. 141 above); Art. 1 (dash 1) PCA/Azerbaijan (fn. 142 above).

- to promote trade and investment and harmonious economic relations between the Parties and so to foster their sustainable economic development;[144]
- to provide a basis for legislative, economic, social, financial, civil scientific, technological and cultural cooperation;[145]
- to support the efforts [of the respective eastern partner country] to consolidate its democracy and to develop its economy and to complete the transition into a market economy.[146]

Apart from the aforementioned differences regarding the objectives, the five partnership and cooperation agreements share significant structural similarities. Firstly, according to the general principles included in all those agreements, respect for democracy, for the principles of international law and human rights as well as for the principles of a market economy underpin the internal and external policies of the parties and constitute essential elements of partnerships, established by these agreements.[147] Secondly, these are followed in all of the aforementioned agreements by further titles and provisions relating essentially to political dialogue,[148] trade in goods,[149] provisions affecting business and investment,[150] current payments and capital,[151] certain aspects regarding competition, intellectual, industrial

[144]See Art. 1 (dash 3) PCA/Georgia (fn. 140 above); Art. 1 (dash 2) PCA/Moldavia (fn. 139 above); Art. 1 (dash 3) PCA/Armenia (fn. 141 above); Art. 1 (dash 3) PCA/Azerbaijan (fn. 142 above); similarly, but only talking about "sustainable development" see Art. 1 (dash 2) PCA/ Ukraine (fn. 140 above).

[145]See Art. 1 (dash 4) PCA/Armenia (fn. 141 above); Art. 1 (dash 4) PCA/Azerbaijan (fn. 142 above); Art. 1 (dash 4) PCA/Georgia (fn. 140 above); similarly, but without "civil scientific and technological cooperation", see Art. 1 (dash 3) PCA/Moldavia (fn. 139 above); also very similar, but without "legislative cooperation", see Art. 1 (dash 3) PCA/Ukraine (fn. 138 above).

[146]See Art. 1 (dash 4) PCA/Ukraine (fn. 138 above); Art. 1 (dash 4) PCA/Moldavia (fn. 139 above); Art. 1 (dash 2) PCA/Georgia (fn. 140 above); Art. 1 (dash 2) PCA/Armenia (fn. 141 above); Art. 1 (dash 2) PCA/Azerbaijan (fn. 142 above).

[147]Insofar as provided for in Art. 2 of the partnership and cooperation agreements concerning Moldavia, Georgia, Armenia and Azerbaijan; in Art. 2 PCA/Ukraine (fn. 138 above) the "principles of international law" are missing.

[148]See Arts. 6–9 PCA/Ukraine (fn. 139 above); Arts. 6–9 PCA/Moldavia (fn. 139 above); Arts. 5–8 PCA/Georgia (fn. 140 above); Arts. 5–8 PCA/Armenia (fn. 141 above); Arts. 5–8 PCA/Azerbaijan (fn. 142 above).

[149]See Arts. 10–23 PCA/Ukraine (fn. 138 above); Arts. 10–22 PCA/Moldavia (fn. 139 above); Arts. 9–19 PCA/Georgia (fn. 140 above); Arts. 9–19 PCA/Armenia (fn. 141 above); Arts. 9–19 PCA/Azerbaijan (fn. 142 above).

[150]See Arts. 24–47 PCA/Ukraine (fn. 138 above); Arts. 23–46 PCA/Moldavia (fn. 139 above); Arts. 20–40 PCA/Georgia (fn. 140 above); Arts. 20–40 PCA/Armenia (fn. 141 above); Arts. 20–40 PCA/Azerbaijan (fn. 142 above).

[151]See Art. 48 PCA/Ukraine (fn. 138 above); Art. 47 PCA/Moldavia (fn. 139 above); Arts. 41 and 42 PCA/Georgia (fn. 140 above); Art. 41 PCA/Armenia (fn. 141 above); Art. 41 PCA/Azerbaijan (fn. 142 above).

and commercial property protection and legislative cooperation[152] or solely legislative cooperation,[153] economic, cultural and financial cooperation[154] as well as those closely connected to some final provisions relating to several important institutional and legal aspects.[155] Additionally, provisions dealing with cooperation on matters relating to democracy and human rights as well as cooperation on prevention of illegal activities and the prevention and control of illegal immigration can be found in some of these agreements.[156]

Common characteristics regarding legal protection are ultimately exhibited by the partnership and cooperation agreements in question, as they all contain a provision, remarkably not found in the Euro-Mediterranean agreements[157] discussed above, obliging each party to ensure, within the scope of the respective agreement, that natural and legal persons of the other party have access free of discrimination in relation to its own nationals to the courts having jurisdiction and the competent administrative organs of the parties to defend their individual rights and their property rights, including those concerning intellectual, industrial and commercial property.[158] Apart from that, the contracting parties may settle disputes relating to the application or interpretation of the respective agreement by referring[159] them to the Cooperation Council,[160] established to supervise the

[152]Arts. 49–51 PCA/Ukraine (fn. 138 above); Arts. 48–50 PCA/Moldavia (fn. 139 above); aspects of competition are neither mentioned in Arts. 42 and 43 PCA/Armenia (fn. 141 above) nor in Arts. 42 and 43 PCA/Azerbaijan (fn. 142 above).

[153]See Arts. 43 and 44 PCA/Georgia (fn. 140 above).

[154]See Arts. 52–84 PCA/Ukraine (fn. 138 above); Arts. 51–81 PCA/Moldavia (fn. 139 above), Arts. 45–80 PCA/Georgia (fn. 140 above); Arts. 44–77 PCA/Armenia (fn. 141 above); Arts. 44–80 PCA/Azerbaijan (fn. 142 above).

[155]See Arts. 85–109 PCA/Ukraine (fn. 138 above); Arts. 82–106 PCA/Moldavia (fn. 139 above); Arts. 81–105 PCA/Georgia (fn. 140 above); Arts. 78–102 PCA/Armenia (fn. 141 above); Arts. 81–105 PCA/Azerbaijan (fn. 142 above).

[156]See Arts. 71–75 PCA/Georgia (fn. 140 above); Arts. 68–72 PCA/Armenia (fn. 141 above); Arts. 71–75 PCA/Azerbaijan (fn. 142 above).

[157]For these agreements see, with further references, the paragraphs above concerning the bilateral arrangements for the promotion and the protection of investments between the EU and the associated countries of the western Balkans.

[158]See Art. 93(1) PCA/Ukraine (fn. 138 above); Art. 90(1) PCA/Moldavia (fn. 139 above); Art. 89 (1) PCA/Georgia (fn. 140 above); Art. 86(1) PCA/Armenia (fn. 141 above); Art. 89(1) PCA/Azerbaijan (fn. 142 above).

[159]See Art. 96(1) PCA/Ukraine (fn. 138 above); Art. 93(1) PCA/Moldavia (fn. 139 above); Art. 92 (1) PCA/Georgia (fn. 140 above); Art. 89(1) PCA/Armenia (fn. 141 above); Art. 92(1) PCA/Azerbaijan (fn. 142 above).

[160]For the installation of these councils, their tasks and compositions see Art. 85 et seq. PCA/Ukraine (fn. 138 above); Art. 82 et seq. PCA/Moldavia (fn. 139 above); Art. 81 et seq. PCA/Georgia (fn. 140 above); Art. 78 et seq. PCA/Armenia (fn. 141 above); Art. 81 et seq. PCA/Azerbaijan (fn. 142 above).

implementation of the agreement in question. The Cooperation Council may then settle the dispute by means of a recommendation.[161]

Investment promotion and investment protection within the scope of the aforementioned partnership and cooperation agreements

The partnership and cooperation agreements, concluded in the period from 1998 to 1999 between the European Communities and their Member States, of the one part, and the Ukraine, the Republic of Moldova, Georgia, Armenia and Azerbaijan, of the other part, contain in different parts partly identical and partly divergent statements and regulations regarding the promotion and protection of foreign investments. Identical statements relating to investments can be found in the preambles of these five partnership and cooperation agreements, where investments are addressed not only once, as is the case in the preambles of the afore-discussed stabilisation and association agreements, but twice and sometimes even three times:

> [...] CONSIDERING the necessity of promoting investment in [the respective eastern partner country], including in the energy sector[162] [...] CONSCIOUS of the need to improve conditions affecting business and investment, and conditions in areas such as establishment of companies, labour, provision of services and capital movements[163] [...] CONVINCED that these Agreements will create a new climate for economic relations between the parties and in particular for the development of trade and investment, which are essential to economic restructuring and technological modernization[164] [...].

In other passages of these five partnership and cooperation agreements it is stated that the parties shall ensure, subject to limitations justified on grounds of public policy, public security or public health,[165] with regard to transactions on the capital account of balance of payments, from entry into force of the agreement, the free movement of capital relating to direct investments made in companies formed in accordance with the laws of the host country and investments made in accordance with the provisions of Chapter II, and the liquidation or repatriation of these

[161]See Art. 96(2) PCA/Ukraine (fn. 138 above); Art. 93(2) PCA/Moldavia (fn. 139 above); Art. 92 (2) PCA/Georgia (fn. 140 above); Art. 89(2) PCA/Armenia (fn. 141 above); Art. 92(2) PCA/ Azerbaijan (fn. 142 above).

[162]See the preambles of PCA/Georgia (fn. 140 above), PCA/Armenia (fn. 141 above) and PCA/ Azerbaijan (fn. 142 above).

[163]See the preambles of PCA/Ukraine (fn. 138 above), PCA/Moldavia (fn. 139 above), PCA/ Georgia (fn. 140 above), PCA/Armenia (fn. 141 above) and PCA/Azerbaijan (fn. 142 above).

[164]See the preambles of PCA/Ukraine (fn. 138 above), PCA/Moldavia (fn. 139 above), PCA/ Georgia (fn. 140 above), PCA/Armenia (fn. 141 above) and of PCA/Azerbaijan (fn. 142 above).

[165]See Art. 41(1) PCA/Ukraine (fn. 138 above); Art. 40(1) PCA/Moldavia (fn. 139 above); Art. 34 (1) PCA/Georgia (fn. 140 above); Art. 34(1) PCA/Armenia (fn. 141 above); Art. 34(1) PCA/ Azerbaijan (fn. 142 above).

investments and of any profit stemming therefrom.[166] Those provisions serve the promotion of investments, manifesting itself primarily in the guarantee of the freedom of establishment and free movement of capital in favour of the respective investors. Above all, these freedoms are additionally safeguarded by an obligation relating to legal protection of the respective contractual parties, laid down in a provision always included in the last title of the respective agreement.[167] According to these provisions, remarkably appearing neither in the initially addressed partnership and cooperation agreements between the EC and its Member States, of the one part, and several Central Asian states, of the other part,[168] nor in the afore-discussed Euro-Mediterranean agreements,[169] the parties undertake to ensure, within the scope of the respective agreement, that natural and legal persons of the other party have access free of discrimination in relation to their own nationals to the courts having jurisdiction and the competent administrative organs of the parties to defend their individual rights and their property rights, including those concerning intellectual, industrial and commercial property.[170] Whereas it is not entirely clear what legal consequences arise from a breach of this obligation, it seems relatively clear that the internal market freedoms, for instance in the form of the freedom of services and establishment and the free movement of capital, also belong to the aforementioned rights guaranteed by these agreements. Also, it seems clear that disputes connected with the aforementioned obligations belong to "disputes relating to the application or interpretation of this agreement", which can be referred by each party[171] to the respective Cooperation Council[172] which has been established

[166]See Art. 48(2) PCA/Ukraine (fn. 138 above); Art. 47(2) PCA/Moldavia (fn. 139 above); Art. 41 (2) PCA/Georgia (fn. 140 above); Art. 41(2) APZ/Armenia (fn. 141 above); Art. 41(2) PCA/ Azerbaijan (fn. 142 above).

[167]See Art. 93(1) PCA/Ukraine (fn. 138 above); Art. 90(1) PCA/Moldavia (fn. 139 above); Art. 89 (1) PCA/Georgia (fn. 140 above); Art. 86(1) PCA/Armenia (fn. 141 above); Art. 89(1) PCA/ Azerbaijan (fn. 142 above).

[168]For these agreements see, with further references, "Introduction" above.

[169]For these agreements see, with further references, the paragraphs above concerning the bilateral arrangements for the promotion and the protection of investments between the EU and the associated countries of the western Balkans.

[170]See Art. 93(1) PCA/Ukraine (fn. 138 above); Art. 90(1) PCA/Moldavia (fn. 139 above); Art. 89 (1) PCA/Georgia (fn. 140 above); Art. 86(1) PCA/Armenia (fn. 141 above); Art. 89(1) PCA/ Azerbaijan (fn. 142 above).

[171]See Art. 96(1) PCA/Ukraine (fn. 138 above); Art. 93(1) PCA/Moldavia (fn. 139 above); Art. 92 (1) PCA/Georgia (fn. 140 above); Art. 89(1) PCA/Armenia (fn. 141 above); Art. 92(1) PCA/ Azerbaijan (fn. 142 above).

[172]For the installation of these Councils, their tasks and compositions see Art. 85 et seq. PCA/ Ukraine (fn. 138 above); Art. 82 et seq. PCA/Moldavia (fn. 139 above); Art. 81 et seq. PCA/ Georgia (fn. 140 above); Art. 78 et seq. PCA/Armenia (fn. 141 above); Art. 81 et seq. PCA/ Azerbaijan (fn. 142 above).

to supervise the application and implementation of the respective agreement and may settle the dispute by means of a recommendation.[173]

Moreover, an additional article, captioned "Investment promotion and protection" can be found in all five partnership and cooperation agreements.[174] With minor deviations, it can also be found in the afore-addressed partnership and cooperation agreements,[175] in the stabilisation and association agreements[176] as well as in the Euro-Mediterranean agreements.[177] According to this article, the partnerships established by these agreements aim to establish a favourable climate for investment, both domestic and foreign, especially through better conditions for investment protection, the transfer of capital and the exchange of information on investment opportunities, bearing in mind the respective powers and competences of the EC or rather the EU and the Member States.[178] Subsequent to this provision, the objectives of the "cooperation" guaranteed by the agreements in question are listed non-exhaustively ("in particular") as follows:

- the conclusion, where appropriate, between the Member States and [the respective eastern partner country) of agreements for the promotion and protection of investment;[179]
- the conclusion, where appropriate, between the Member States and [the respective eastern partner country) of agreements to avoid double taxation;[180]

[173]See Art. 96(2) PCA/Ukraine (fn. 138 above); Art. 93(2) PCA/Moldavia (fn. 139 above); Art. 92 (2) PCA/Georgia (fn. 140 above); Art. 89(2) PCA/Armenia (fn. 141 above); Art. 92(2) PCA/ Azerbaijan (fn. 142 above).

[174]See Art. 54(1) PCA/Ukraine (fn. 138 above); Art. 53(1) PCA/Moldavia (fn. 139 above); Art. 49 (1) PCA/Georgia (fn. 140 above); Art. 47(1) PCA/Armenia (fn. 141 above); Art. 48(1) PCA/ Azerbaijan (fn. 142 above).

[175]For these agreements see, with further references, "Introduction" above.

[176]For these agreements see, with further references, the paragraphs above concerning the bilateral arrangements for the promotion and the protection of investments between the EU and the associated countries of the western Balkans.

[177]For these agreements see, with further references, the paragraphs above concerning the bilateral arrangements for the promotion and the protection of investments between the EU and the associated countries of the western Balkans.

[178]See Art. 54(1) PCA/Ukraine (fn. 138 above); Art. 53(1) PCA/Moldavia (fn. 139 above); Art. 49 (1) PCA/Georgia (fn. 140 above); Art. 47(1) PCA/Armenia (fn. 141 above); Art. 48(1) PCA/ Azerbaijan (fn. 142 above).

[179]See Art. 54(2) (dash 1) PCA/Ukraine (fn. 138 above); Art. 53(2) (dash 1) PCA/Moldavia (fn. 139 above); Art. 49(2) (dash 1) PCA/Georgia (fn. 140 above); Art. 47(2) (dash 1) PCA/Armenia (fn. 141 above); Art. 48(2) (dash 1) PCA/Azerbaijan (fn. 142 above).

[180]See Art. 54(2) (dash 2) PCA/Ukraine (fn. 138 above); Art. 53(2) (dash 2) PCA/Moldavia (fn. 139 above); Art. 49(2) (dash 2) PCA/Georgia (fn. 140 above); Art. 47(2) (dash 2) PCA/Armenia (fn. 141 above); Art. 48(2) (dash 2) PCA/ Azerbaijan (fn. 142 above).

- the creation of favourable conditions for attracting foreign investments into the [...] economy [of the respective eastern partner country);[181]
- to establish stable and adequate business law and conditions, and to exchange information on laws, regulations and administrative practices in the field of investment;[182]
- to exchange information on investment opportunities in the form of, inter alia, trade fairs, exhibitions, trade weeks and other events.[183]

The aforementioned provisions, primarily aimed at the promotion of investment, show rather clearly that, despite the existing differences between, the contracting parties hitherto assumed that the legal protection of foreign investment was not so much subject matter of the partnership and cooperation agreements, but rather a concern of the EU Member States to be organised bilaterally. Consistently, the EU Member States have already concluded hundreds of bilateral treaties concerning investment promotion and protection with third states.[184] These include, for example, bilateral treaties concerning investment promotion and protection which were concluded in recent years and decades between Germany and states covered by the partnership and cooperation agreements, namely Ukraine,[185] the Republic of Moldavia,[186] Georgia,[187] Armenia[188] and Azerbaijan.[189]

[181]See Art. 54(2) (dash 3) PCA/Ukraine (fn. 138 above); Art. 53(2) (dash 3) PCA/Moldavia (fn. 139 above); Art. 49(2) (dash 3) PCA/Georgia (fn. 140 above); Art. 47(2) (dash 3) PCA/Armenia (fn. 141 above); Art. 48(2) (dash 3) PCA/Azerbaijan (fn. 142 above).

[182]See Art. 54(2) (dash 4) PCA/Ukraine (fn. 138 above); Art. 53(2) (dash 4) PCA/Moldavia (fn. 139 above); Art. 49(2) (dash 4) PCA/Georgia (fn. 140 above); Art. 47(2) (dash 4) PCA/Armenia (fn. 141 above); Art. 48(2) (dash 4) PCA/Azerbaijan (fn. 142 above).

[183]See Art. 54(2) (dash 5) PCA/Ukraine (fn. 138 above); Art. 53(2) (dash 5) PCA/Moldavia (fn. 139 above); Art. 49(2) (dash 5) PCA/Georgia (fn. 140 above); Art. 47(2) (dash 5) PCA/Armenia (fn. 141 above); Art. 48(2) (dash 5) PCA/Azerbaijan (fn. 142 above).

[184]For more on this see Schöbener, Der Rechtsrahmen des Internationalen Investitionsrechts: ein Überblick zu den bilateralen Investitionsschutzabkommen, WiVerw (2009) 1, pp. 3 et seq.

[185]The relevant act of assent is published in BGBl 1996 II, p. 75; it came into force on 29 June 1996.

[186]The relevant act of assent is published in BGBl 1997 II, p. 2072; it came into force on 15 June 2006; for relevant amendments see the protocol published in BGBl. 2005 II, p. 523, in force since 15 June 2006.

[187]The relevant act of assent is published in BGBl 1998 II, p. 576; it came into force on 27 September 1998.

[188]The relevant act of assent is published in BGBl 2000 II, p. 46; it came into force on 4 August 2000.

[189]The relevant act of assent is published in BGBl 1998 II, p. 567; it came into force on 29 July 1998.

Conclusion and perspectives

The stabilisation and association agreements connecting the EU and its Member States with the three countries of the western Balkans[190] contain numerous provisions for the *promotion* of foreign investments.[191] The *protection* of foreign investments, however, only touched upon in these agreements, is in substance left to the EU Member States,[192] which have concluded bilateral treaties relating to investment protection with the countries of the western Balkans.[193] A very similar approach is pursued by the Euro-Mediterranean agreements, belonging to the southern ENP dimension.[194] Also these agreements contain various provisions for the *promotion* of foreign investments,[195] whereas the conclusion of treaties relating to investment *protection* is handed over to the EU Member States.[196] Apart from that, a comparable approach is pursued by the partnership and cooperation agreements,[197] equally containing various provisions for the *promotion* of foreign investment[198] but with regard to the conclusion of bilateral treaties relating to investment *protection* consistently referring to the EU Member States.[199]

The aforementioned provisions assigning the conclusion of bilateral treaties relating to investment protection to the area of responsibility of the EU Member States require a revision, since the Treaty of Lisbon[200] intends for there to be an

---

[190]In more detail see the paragraph above concerning bilateral contractual relationships between the EU and its Member States, of the one part, and individual countries of the western Balkans, of the other part.

[191]In more detail see the paragraph above concerning investment promotion and investment protection within the scope of the aforementioned association and stabilisation agreements.

[192]See Art. 84(2) SAA/Macedonia (fn. 43 above) and Art. 85(2) SAA/Croatia (fn. 46 above).

[193]In more detail see the paragraph above concerning investment promotion and investment protection within the scope of the aforementioned association and stabilisation agreements.

[194]In more detail see the paragraph above concerning bilateral contractual relationships between the EU and several neighbouring states within the framework of the southern ENP dimension.

[195]In more detail see the paragraph above concerning investment promotion and investment protection within the scope of the Euro-Mediterranean agreements.

[196]See Art. 50 lit. b) EMA/Tunisia (fn. 77 above); Art. 50 lit. b) EMA/Morocco (fn. 78 above); Art. 54 lit. b) EMA/Algeria (fn. 82 above); Art. 67 (first sentence) EMA/Jordan (fn. 80 above); Art. 47 (1) EMA/Lebanon (fn. 83 above); Art. 46 (first sentence) EMA/Egypt (fn. 81 above).

[197]In more detail see the paragraph above concerning bilateral contractual relationships between the EU and several neighbouring countries within the framework of the eastern ENP dimension.

[198]In more detail see the paragraph above concerning investment promotion and investment protection within the scope of the aforementioned partnership and cooperation agreements.

[199]See Art. 54(2) (dash 2) PCA/Ukraine (fn. 138 above); Art. 53(2) (dash 2) APZ/Moldavia (fn. 139 above); Art. 49(2) (dash 2) PCA/Georgia (fn. 140 above); Art. 47(2) (dash 2) PCA/Armenia (fn. 141 above); Art. 48(2) (dash 2) PCA/Azerbaijan (fn. 142 above).

[200]With further references see fn. 19 above.

exclusive competence for the EU in the field of foreign direct investment.[201] The partnership and cooperation agreements, attributed to the eastern ENP dimension, currently lend themselves to such a revision since they apparently shall be replaced by new bilateral association agreements. This assessment is particularly based on the *Joint Declaration* of the Prague Eastern Partnership summit of 7 May 2009,[202] where it is pointed out that, inter alia, the bilateral cooperation under the Eastern Partnership umbrella should provide the foundation for association agreements between the EU and those partner countries which are willing and able to comply with the resulting commitments. When revising provisions within this framework, which have so far entrusted the conclusion of bilateral treaties relating to investment protection to the EU Member States, the contracting parties may by all means follow the model of the stabilisation and association agreement between the European Communities and their Member States, of the one part, and the Republic of Albania, of the other part.[203] Already, this stabilisation and association agreement no longer contains a reference that the specific arrangements of legal protection of foreign investment must be or should stay imperatively or primarily a bilateral concern of the EU, in contrast to those stabilisation and association agreements relating to Macedonia and Croatia.[204]

The conclusion of new association agreements, provided within the framework of the Eastern Partnership, raises primarily the question whether, when creating new bilateral association agreements, further investment-related subject matters of the existing partnership and cooperation agreements require modifying or altering too.

---

[201] In more detail see Bungenberg, Außenbeziehungen und Außenhandelspolitik, in: Schwarze/Hatje, Der Reformvertrag von Lissabon, *EuR Beiheft 1*, 2009, p. 195 (207 et seq.); Griebel, Überlegungen zur Wahrnehmung der neuen EU-Kompetenz für ausländische Direktinvestitionen nach Inkrafttreten des Vertrags von Lissabon, RIW (2009), pp. 469 et seq.; Tietje, Die Gemeinsame Handelspolitik der EU im System des Welthandelsrechts: Ein Spannungsverhältnis zwischen fortschreitender Liberalisierung und zunehmendem Protektionismus, in: Pache/Schorkopf (eds.), *Die Europäische Union nach Lissabon – Beiträge zu Organisation, Außenbeziehungen und Stellung im Welthandelsrecht*, 2009, pp. 48 et seq.; this exclusive EU-competence in the area of direct investments was also intended by the Treaty establishing a Constitution for Europe from 2004, for more on this see Hummer, in: Vedder/Heintschel v. Heinegg (eds), *Europäischer Verfassungsvertrag – Handkommentar*, 2007, Art. III-315 paras. 9 et seq.; Krajewski, Demokratische Kontrolle der Gemeinsamen Handelspolitik, in: Bruha/Nowak (eds.), *Die Europäische Union: Innere Verfasstheit und globale Handlungsfähigkeit*, 2006, pp. 249 et seq.

[202] For more on this Declaration see Nowak, Multilaterale und bilaterale Elemente der EU-Assoziations-, Partnerschafts- und Nachbarschaftspolitik, EuR (2010) 6, p. 746 et seq.; Tiede/Schirmer Die Östliche Partnerschaft der Europäischen Union im Rahmen des Gemeinschaftsrechts, Osteuropa-Recht 55 (2009), pp. 184 et seq.

[203] For this agreement, which entered into force on 1 April 2009, see the paragraph above concerning bilateral contractual relationships between the EU and its Member States, of the one part, and individual countries of the western Balkans, of the other part.

[204] In detail see the paragraph above concerning investment promotion and investment protection within the scope of the aforementioned association and stabilisation agreements.

In this context and especially in view of the exclusive competence for the EU in the field of foreign direct investments, provided by the Treaty of Lisbon,[205] it will be necessary to discuss more intensively in the future whether the regulations for the protection of foreign investment, hitherto included in bilateral treaties relating to investment protection between the EU Member States and third states,[206] have to be integrated from now on in the new association agreements, since the EU, having already set up a so-called *Minimum Platform on Investment* after all,[207] has exclusive competence in the field of direct investment. The thereby accomplished overcoming of the hitherto existing separation of individual provisions for the *promotion* of foreign investments in the afore-discussed association agreements and individual provisions for the *protection* of foreign investments in numerous bilateral treaties relating to investment protection would indeed be welcomed for reasons of transparency, unilateral application of law and coherency. The consolidation of provisions promoting and protecting investments on a supranational level would not constitute a true novelty, however. For one thing, it is already shown by the so-called CARIFORUM Economic Partnership Agreement, i.e. the economic partnership agreement between Antigua, Barbados, Haiti, Jamaica, Trinidad and some other CARIFORUM states, of the one part, and the EC and its Member States, of the other part,[208] which is closely related to the older *Cotonou Partnership Agreement*.[209] In this agreement, the aspects of investment promotion being addressed in the objectives three times,[210] an abundance of quite progressive investment-related regulations that would also fit well in European SAP and ENP agreements can be

---

[205]For further references see fn. 201 above.

[206]For the controversial effects of the above-mentioned transfer of powers in the area of foreign direct investments on current and future planed bilateral contracts on investment protection of the Member States see in detail Raith, The Common Commercial Policy and the Lisbon judgement of the German Constitutional Court of 30 June 2009, ZEuS 2009, p. 613 (620 et seq.); Tietje, Außenwirtschaftsrechtliche Dimensionen der europäischen Wirtschaftsverfassung, in: Fastenrath/Nowak, *Der Lissabonner Reformvertrag – Änderungsimpulse in einzelnen Rechts- und Politikbereichen*, 2009, p. 237 (246 et seq.); see further the "Lisbon"-Decision of the German Federal Constitutional Court of 30 June 2009 (2 BvE 2/08), EuGRZ 2009, p. 339 (383).

[207]For more details see Bungenberg, Außenbeziehungen und Außenhandelspolitik, in: Schwarze/Hatje, Der Reformvertrag von Lissabon, *EuR Beiheft 1*, 2009, p. 195 (208); Burgstaller, European Law and Investment Treaties, J.Int.Arb. 26 (2009), p. 181 (204 et seq.); Maydell, The European Community's Minimum Platform on Investment or the Trojan Horse of Investment Competence, in: Reinisch/Knahr (eds.), *International Investment Law in Context*, 2007, pp. 73 et seq.; Klamert/Maydell, Lost in Exclusivity: Implied Non-exclusive External Competences in Community Law, European Foreign Affairs Review 13 (2008), p. 493 (511 et seq.); for the revisited version of the Minimum Platform on Investment see Council Document 7242/09 (Limite) of 6 March 2009.

[208]Economic Partnership Agreement between the CARIFORUM States, of the one part, and the European Community and its Member States, of the other part (OJ 2008 L 289/3 et seq.).

[209]For more on this see B. Friesen, Das Abkommen von Cotonou unter besonderer Berücksichtigung des neuen Handelsregimes, ZEuS 2009, pp. 419 et seq.

[210]See Art. 1 lit. b), e) and f) of this economic partnership agreement (fn. 208 above).

found. In this regard, the principles concerning market access for investors, equal treatment with nationals and most-favoured-nation treatment,[211] contained in these economic partnership agreements, as well as Article 72 of the CARIFORUM Economic Partnership Agreement, which lays down several rules of behaviour for investors, prohibiting them, inter alia, from generating advantages by means of corruption or not acting in accordance with core labour standards, is exemplarily pointed out. Furthermore, the Energy Charter Treaty,[212] which entered into force on 16 April 1998, is pointed out in this context. It contains numerous instructive regulations relating to the protection of foreign investments,[213] among them different provisions on investment promotion and protection,[214] compensation for losses,[215] expropriation[216] and transfer related to investments.[217]

Moreover, the Energy Charter Treaty contains extensive regulations on settlement of disputes between an investor and a contracting party,[218] as well as on settlement of disputes between the contracting parties, which refer, inter alia, to the ICSID Convention on the Settlement of Investment Disputes between States and Nationals of other States and to the so-called Arbitration Rules of UNCITRAL.[219] Many of these rules on investment protection of the CARIFORUM

---

[211]See Arts. 67, 68 and 70 of this economic partnership agreement (fn. 208 above); see also Westcott, The Cariforum-EU Economic Partnership Agreement and Interim Agreements between Other ACP Regions and the EU: Investment Provisions and Commitments, in: GTZ (ed.), *Cariforum EPA and beyond: Recommendations and negotiations on Services and Trade related Issues in EPAs*, 2008 (available at: http://www.gtz.de/en/themen/laendliche-entwicklung/24568.htm).

[212]German translation published in OJEC 1998 L 69/26 et seq. (hereinafter referred to as "the Energy Charter Treaty"); for important additional information see the final act of the European Energy Charta Conference (OJEC 1998 L 69/5 et seq.); for more details regarding the Energy Charter Treaty see Nowak, Multilaterale und bilaterale Elemente der EU-Assoziations-, Partnerschafts- und Nachbarschaftspolitik, EuR (2010) 6, p. (forthcoming).

[213]In more detail see Burgstaller, European Law and Investment Treaties, J. Int. Arb. 26 (2009), p. 181 (206 et seq.); Tietje Die Beilegung internationaler Investitionsstreitigkeiten, in: Marauhn (ed.), *Streitbeilegung in den internationalen Wirtschaftsbeziehungen*, 2005, p. 47 (56 et seq.).

[214]See Art. 10 of the Energy Charter Treaty (fn. 212 above).

[215]See Art. 12 of the Energy Charter Treaty (fn. 212 above).

[216]See Art. 13 of the Energy Charter Treaty (fn. 212 above).

[217]See Art. 14 of the Energy Charter Treaty (fn. 212 above).

[218]See Art. 26 of the Energy Charter Treaty (fn. 212 above).

[219]See Art. 26(4) lit. a) and b) as well as Art. 27(3) lit. f) of the Energy Charter Treaty (fn. 212 above); for the Settlement of Investment Disputes according to the ICSID-System see Broches, *Selected Essays: World Bank, ICSID, and Other Subjects of Public and Private International Law*, 1995, pp. 161 et seq.; Comeaux/Kinsella, *Protecting Foreign Investment under International Law: Legal Aspects of Political Risk*, 1997, pp. 195 et seq.; Hirsch, *The Arbitration Mechanism of the International Center for the Settlement of Investment Disputes*, 1993, pp. 9 et seq.; Hobe/Müller, Die Schiedsgerichtsbarkeit des International Centre for Settlement of Investment Disputes (ICSID), WiVerw (2009) 1, pp. 65 et seq.; Krajewski, *Wirtschaftsvölkerrecht*, 2006, pp. 208 et seq.; Reinisch, Die Beilegung von Investitionsstreitigkeiten, in: Tietje (ed.), *Internationales Wirtschaftsrecht*, 2009, pp. 809 et seq.; Sornarajah, *The Settlement of Foreign Investment Disputes*, 2000, pp. 151 et seq.; Vinuesa, Jurisdictional Objections to ICSID Arbitration under

Economic Partnership Agreement and the Energy Charter Treaty would, after the successful entry into force of the Treaty of Lisbon on 1 December 2009, fit in well with the bilateral core elements of the EU Association Policy and ENP, that is in the stabilisation and association agreements, in the Euro-Mediterranean agreements as well as in the partnership and cooperation agreements, as long as other, more extensive reform considerations, for instance directed at the creation of a multilateral *EU-based open investment treaty*,[220] cannot be put into practice.

Bilateral Investment Treaties, in: Bröhmer/Bieber/Calliess/Langenfeld/Weber/Wolf (eds.), *Internationale Gemeinschaft und Menschenrechte – Festschrift für G. Ress*, 2005, pp. 331 et seq.

[220]For more on this see Griebel, Überlegungen zur Wahrnehmung der neuen EU-Kompetenz für ausländische Direktinvestitionen nach Inkrafttreten des Vertrags von Lissabon, RIW (2009), pp. 469 et seq.

The New Great Challenge After the Entry Into Force of the Treaty of Lisbon: Bringing About a Multilateral EU-Investment Treaty

Jörn Griebel

Apart from the destiny of the bilateral investment treaties (BITs) of the Member States, the great challenge posed by the Treaty of Lisbon concerns the future use of the new EU competence over foreign direct investments.

The EU will be faced with several different possibilities. The EU may proceed with or without the involvement of the Member States. It may follow the dominant approach and seek to conclude BITs with third countries on its own. Alternatively, the EU may take on the thus far unsuccessful challenge of a multilateral treaty. Finally, the EU may consider the appropriateness of combining trade- and investment-related issues within one document or adhering to the classical investment treaty approach.

Further, after the EU chooses its approach towards foreign direct investment, many issues will arise regarding the substance of the new rules. Regarding content, the EU could adhere to the dominant approach of the EU Member States' model BITs. Alternatively, the EU could use the approach of states such as the USA, the current model BIT of which, although five times more extensive and accordingly also more sophisticated that the European ones, often provides lesser strength regarding investment protection. A connected issue is that the investor–state dispute resolution mechanism will be questioned.

How will these questions be met considering the EU Commission's main expertise lies in the field of trade? The rapid developments of international investment law especially during the past 6–10 years will not be familiar to all decision-makers and negotiators within the EU.

Unfortunately, the time to meet this challenge is short. The current investment protection systems of the Member States are remarkably divergent: two thirds of all Member States have only concluded at most 70 BITs, and some have only concluded 20. At the same time, as of January 2010, 127 of Germany's BITs were currently in force. Accordingly, the major problem lies in the fact that, owing to a lack of investment treaties, some Member States are by far less attractive for

J. Griebel
International Investment Law Centre Cologne, University of Cologne, Germany
e-mail: joern.griebel@uni-koeln.de

M. Bungenberg et al. (eds.), *International Investment Law and EU Law*,
DOI 10.1007/978-3-642-14855-2_8,

foreign direct investments than others. This makes the situation particularly grave for the Member States within eastern Europe which are seeking foreign direct investments but lack existing investment treaties which would influence the willingness to invest within those states. Numerically speaking, if every Member State were to enjoy the same the number of BITs as Germany, an additional 2000 treaties would need to be concluded.

The EU must fill this existing vacuum of protection. And considering that – as indicated – there are many capital-importing countries within the EU which are in urgent need of investments, this should be done quickly. This is particularly true if one considers that the current investment flows move particularly towards emerging markets and not the EU.

Against this background it seems by far more unreasonable to advise the EU to follow a bilateral approach than to consider a multilateral one. The former would require so much time that the competence would be rendered unusable.

Considering a multilateral approach seems prima facie daring. The last two attempts undertaken in this respect within the OECD and the WTO have failed. However, the situation for the EU is different. For third states, it is very attractive to conclude a treaty with 27 states at once rather than with each state individually. This gives the EU great bargaining power. The EU could invite third states to sign a treaty upon which the EU and its Member States have already agreed: a Europe-based open investment treaty. For the EU it seems a viable approach, especially considering that the alternative option of bilateral agreements is by no means excluded.

Regarding international investment law in its entirety, a multilateral agreement could bring about the needed legal certainty which has not been achieved thus far. For this reason, a multilateral option could prove to be an expedient solution to the problem of the lacking legal certainty and should seriously be considered. There have already been proposals on how such a solution could look. UNCTAD regards a multilateral solution as ideal. Perhaps policy-makers and government representatives – if permitted to express their personal views – would also feel the same. In fact, one might wonder why EU Member States such as Germany, France, the UK, and others should not have a major interest in investments being made also within the smaller partners, now that they have decided to share their economic fates with one another. The EU needs a reliable investment protection environment and the Treaty of Lisbon opens the window of opportunity to bring about such a system by way of a multilateral agreement.

Balancing Investors' and Host States' Rights – What Alternatives for Treaty-makers?

André von Walter

The quest for a viable balancing of investors' and host states' rights has always been the core issue of the law of foreign investment. Within the realm of customary international law, the opposition between concepts advocated by capital-exporting countries – such as the acquired-rights doctrine or the Hull formula – and those defended by capital-importing states – such as the Calvo doctrine or the concept of "new international economic order" – demonstrates the long history of the difficulties to find common ground on this fundamental question. Attempts to negotiate multilateral investment agreements have repeatedly been hampered by the opposition of those states who wish to obtain maximum investment protection and those who are concerned about their "policy space". The failed negotiations within the OECD in the 1960s and the 1990s, within the UN between the 1970s and the 1990s, and within the WTO at the beginning of the twenty-first century are striking examples of the difficulties in agreeing on clear-cut rules in this regard.

Nevertheless, two apparently asymmetrical evolutions have occurred in the past. First, although sometimes arguing for large policy space in multilateral forums, many capital-importing states – competing for foreign investments – concluded bilateral investment treaties (BITs) based on the Abs–Shawcross model with no explicit exceptions aimed at safeguarding the home-state's interests. Second, some capital-exporting-countries, such as the USA and Canada, have come to find themselves in the role of defendants in investment claims and, consequently, added policy-space exceptions to their BITs. Even though the opposition between capital-exporting and capital-importing states remains strong on these issues within most of the bilateral negotiations, one may wonder whether it still is as insurmountable as it was during the last century. The difficult question, however, is how to break down a compromise on the balance of the investor's and the host state's rights in black-letter law within an investment protection treaty. As with every exception

The views expressed are those of the author alone and do not necessarily reflect the position of the French government

A. von Walter
Ministry of Foreign and European Affaires, Paris, France
e-mail: andre.von-walter@diplomatie.gouv.fr

M. Bungenberg et al. (eds.), *International Investment Law and EU Law*,
DOI 10.1007/978-3-642-14855-2_9, © Springer-Verlag Berlin Heidelberg 2011

to a system of established rights to the benefit of one party, it must be ensured that the exception cannot be used or abused by the other party for purposes that would undermine the spirit of the treaty. So what can treaty-makers do to balance the investor's and the host state's rights in a way that would be satisfactory for all the parties concerned?

Should investment protection treaties stick to the time-tested Abs–Shawcross model and only grant investor's rights, while leaving it up to the national law of the host state to defend the state's public interest as long as this national law conforms to the terms of the treaty? This classic approach based on the interplay between national and international law could function well if doubt were not cast on it by diverging interpretations of the same facts and investment protection standards by different arbitral tribunals. It remains to be seen whether this problem can be solved by more stringent recourse to commonly accepted rules of interpretation by arbitral tribunals.

In the meantime, would it be beneficial to describe in more detail how the parties to an agreement understand the terms contained therein? For example, some recent treaties tie the fair and equitable treatment clause to the international minimum standard known in customary law or specify that the finding of an indirect expropriation requires a fact-by-fact inquiry which takes into account a number of listed factors, such as the character of the government action and the investor's expectations. Do such specifications make it really easier for arbitral tribunals to come to shared conclusions when striking the balance between the investor's and the state's interests in a specific case?

Alternatively, would it be sufficient to exclude some sectors deemed particularly important for the state from the scope of application of investment treaties or to rely on so-called emergency clauses to safeguard the state's essential interests? But what can states do when new sectors become particularly important owing to the evolution of public policy? Have emergency clauses been interpreted and applied in a satisfactory and harmonious manner by recent arbitral tribunals to safeguard the state's essential interests?

What about the inclusion of generally worded exception clauses such as those contained in some North American treaties or in the recently proposed Norwegian draft model BIT? Aren't these too circular to provide for clear answers when it comes to weighing the host state's interests against those of the investor? Would it make it easier for arbitral tribunals to rely on a GATT Article XX-style exception clause as is provided for by the ASEAN Framework Agreement on Investment or the latest Canadian Model BIT?

These are only some of the questions which treaty-makers face when it comes to organizing the trade-off between the investor's and the host state's rights within the terms of an investment protection agreement. They are discussed in more detail elsewhere in this volume.

It seems that all of the proposed alternatives have some advantages and some disadvantages. It appears, however, that the balancing of the investor's and the host state's interest can only partly be made in abstract terms and always depends on the specific facts of a given situation. The application of an abstract rule of law to such a factual situation then often implies the recourse to general legal principles, such as the rule of good faith, the respect of legitimate expectations and the principle of proportionality. This is where individual convictions and preferences can come into play, with the result of diverging jurisprudence depending on the appointment of different arbitrators. Until now, for the investment-law regime, the choice has been made to renounce to a WTO-like appeal system, which may be able to guarantee some coherence in the weighing of the host state's and the investor's interests by the development of compulsory methodological rules and an institutional memory. But even with a highly institutionalized dispute-settlement system, as in the area of world trade law, decisions implying a general concern such as the protection of the environment have led to sharp criticism from nearly all of the stakeholders involved. For the time being, investment-treaty negotiators will have to continue their quest for the best terms for striking a fair and predictable balance between the rights and interests of foreign investors and host states. Further academic research and discussion, such as in the chapter by Lars Markert, will be highly appreciated.

The Crucial Question of Future Investment Treaties: Balancing Investors' Rights and Regulatory Interests of Host States

Lars Markert

Introduction

When the Lisbon Treaty entered into force on December 1, 2009, competence over foreign direct investment passed to the European Union (EU).[1] Whether this gives the EU exclusive competence for the conclusion of future international investment agreements (IIAs) has yet to be clarified.[2] However, now more than ever the question arises of how protection of investors should be harmonized with the regulatory interests of the EU and its Member States. Pursuant to Article 205 TFEU and Article 21 EU Treaty, the principles and objectives encompassing the promotion of human rights, sustainable development, and the protection of the environment will have to be taken into account as part of the EU's Common Commercial Policy[3] and will influence the negotiation of future IIAs. Along with the intense debate as to whether the EU should retain investor–state dispute settlement provisions in future IIAs, the balance between investors' rights and

---

[1]Article 206 and Article 207(1) Treaty on the Functioning of the European Union (TFEU), OJEU, May 9, 2008, C115/47.

[2]See, e.g., Tietje, Die Außenwirtschaftsverfassung der EU nach dem Vertrag von Lissabon, Beiträge zum Transnationalen Wirtschaftsrecht (2009), Heft 83 p. 16, http://www.wirtschaftsrecht.uni-halle.de/Heft83.pdf.

[3]Bungenberg, Going Global? The EU Common Commercial Policy After Lisbon, in: Herrmann/Terhechte (eds.), *European Yearbook of International Economic Law 2010*, pp. 123 et seq. (128); Tietje, Die Außenwirtschaftsverfassung der EU nach dem Vertrag von Lissabon, Beiträge zum Transnationalen Wirtschaftsrecht (2009), Heft 83, p. 19, http://www.wirtschaftsrecht.uni-halle.de/Heft83.pdf. For possible implications, see Bungenberg, The Politics of the European Union's Investment Treaty Making, in: Broude/Porges (eds.), *The Politics of International Economic Law*, forthcoming 2010.

The author would like to thank the editors as well as, Martin Raible and Todd Fox, for helpful comments, and Elisa Freiburg and Luc Bigel for their research assistance. This article represents solely the author's views.

L. Markert
Gleiss Lutz, Maybachstraße 6, 70469 Stuttgart, Germany
e-mail: Lars.Markert@gleisslutz.com

M. Bungenberg et al. (eds.), *International Investment Law and EU Law*, 145
DOI 10.1007/978-3-642-14855-2_10, © Springer-Verlag Berlin Heidelberg 2011

state regulatory interests will surely constitute one of the crucial questions in the drafting of future IIAs.

This question is not easy to answer since the necessary balance of interests poses one of the classic dilemmas in international investment law. On the one hand, the investor desires legal certainty, the protection of its investment, and the realization of profit. This coincides to a large extent with the interests of the contracting states to an IIA in promoting foreign investment and depoliticizing potential investment disputes. On the other hand, the "host states" of the investments generally seek to retain the greatest regulatory flexibility in order to react to national or global challenges by means of appropriate state measures – an aim that falls under the slogan "sovereign freedom of action." Although IIAs do not legally limit such freedom of action, they contain obligations to pay compensation or damages in the case of a violation of the IIA. Thus, freedom of action and the right to regulate will come at a dissuasive cost, also called "regulatory chill."

This article intends to introduce some ideas on how the conflicting interests between investors' rights and regulatory freedom could be harmonized. Nowadays, it is no longer sufficient to insist that IIAs were created for the very purpose of preventing states from interfering with investments.[4] Many states have begun to realize that IIAs entail significant obligations[5] and that these obligations can be effectively enforced by investors through investor–state dispute settlement mechanisms. This has led to public criticism and backlashes[6] ranging from the lowering of protection standards[7] to the termination of IIAs[8] or membership of the ICSID

[4]See, e.g., ICSID, Case No. ARB/01/3, *Enron Corporation Ponderosa Assets L.P./Argentine Republic*, Award (May 22, 2007), para. 331. This and all subsequent decisions are available at http://ita.law.uvic.ca or http://www.investmentclaims.com, as long as no other source is indicated.

[5]This was recently admitted by the South African government in a policy paper: "*Prior to 1994, the RSA [Republic of South Africa] had no history of negotiating BITs and the risks posed by such treaties were not fully appreciated at that time. The Executive had not been fully apprised of all the possible consequences of BITs. While it was understood that the democratically elected government of the time had to demonstrate that the RSA was an investment friendly destination, the impact of BITs on future policies were not critically evaluated. As a result the Executive entered into agreements that were heavily stacked in favour of investors without the necessary safeguards to preserve flexibility in a number of critical policy areas.*" Bilateral Investment Treaty Policy Framework Review, 2009, p. 5, www.thedti.gov.za/ads/bi-lateral_policy.pdf.

[6]See C.H. Brower II, Obstacles and Pathways to Consideration of the Public Interest in Investment Treaty Disputes, in: Sauvant (ed.), *Yearbook on International Investment Law & Policy 2008-2009*, 2009, pp. 347 et seq. (357); Sornarajah, The Retreat of Neo-Liberalism in Investment Treaty Arbitration, in: Rogers/Alford (eds.), The Future of Investment Arbitration, 2009, pp. 273 et seq. (291).

[7]This tendency is apparent in the USA, see Schwebel, The United States 2004 Model Bilateral Investment Treaty: An Exercise in the Regressive Development of International Law, in: Aksen/Böckstiegel/Mustill/Patocchi/Whitesell (eds.), *Liber Amicorum Rober Briner*, 2005, pp. 815 et seq. (823); Alvarez, The Evolving BIT, TDM 7 (2010) 1, p. 8.

[8]Ecuador, e.g., terminated nine of its bilateral investment treaties (BITs) in 2008, Perkams/Secomb, Der Schutz deutscher Auslandsinvestitionen in Lateinamerika, WiVerw (2009) 1, pp. 31 et seq. (32); Cabrera Diaz, Ecuador Continues Exit from ICSID, Investment Treaty News (June 8, 2009),

Convention.[9] Interestingly, this tendency is not limited to a few Latin American states rediscovering the *Calvo* Doctrine. It can also be detected in various capital-exporting states and has influenced former "pioneers of investment protection" such as the USA.[10] The reactions are to some extent the result of the growing view that investment arbitral tribunals have not yet sufficiently taken into account states' regulatory interests.[11] This is attributed in part to the inconsistency of the arbitral awards dealing with regulatory interests,[12] and in part to a perceived bias in favor of the interests of investors.[13]

If states are to be prevented from weakening or completely abandoning the system of investment protection in the future, it will become necessary to find a balance between investors' rights and state regulatory interests. In undertaking this task, this article will first set out to delimit the regulatory interests that will be the focus of this study. In a second step, different ways of balancing investors' rights and state regulatory interests shall be examined. In so doing, a focus will be placed on the inclusion of the right to regulate in provisions of IIAs and possible issues associated with it. Finally, the question must be asked whether the inclusion of the right to regulate in provisions of IIAs can effectively establish an adequate balance between the interests of investors and those of host states.

Types of Regulatory Interests

The current uncertainty of how an adequate balance between investors' rights and regulatory interests of host states should be established might be due to the fact that the latter can be asserted in a multitude of ways. Depending on the factual and legal circumstances, regulatory interests do not necessarily belong to one and the same legal category.

---

http://www.investmenttreatynews.org/cms/news/archive/2009/06/05/ecuador-continues-exit-from-icsid.aspx.

[9]Bolivia declared its termination on May 2, 2007, whereas Ecuador declared its termination on July 5, 2009, http://icsid.worldbank.org/ICSID/ICSID/ViewNewsReleases.jsp.

[10]Alvarez, The Evolving BIT, TDM 7 (2010) 1, p. 14; Vandvelde, A Comparison of the 2004 and 1994 U.S. Model BITs, Rebalancing Investor and Host Country Interests, in: Sauvant (ed.), *Yearbook on International Investment Law & Policy 2008-2009*, 2009, pp. 283 et seq. (288).

[11]C.H. Brower II, Obstacles and Pathways to Consideration of the Public Interest in Investment Treaty Disputes, in: Sauvant (ed.), *Yearbook on International Investment Law & Policy 2008-2009*, 2009, pp. 347 et seq. (361).

[12]Kalderimis, Investment Treaties and Public Goods, TDM 7 (2010) 1, p. 10; Muchlinski, Trends in International Investment Agreements, Balancing Investor Rights and the Right to Regulate. The Issue of National Security, in: Sauvant (ed.), *Yearbook on International Investment Law & Policy 2008-2009*, 2009, pp. 35 et seq. (53).

[13]Kalderimis, Investment Treaties and Public Goods, TDM 7 (2010) 1, pp. 15, 18.

Case law and the legal literature seem to use the term "regulatory interests" in connection with the state of necessity,[14] measures for the protection of national security and public order,[15] environmental protection,[16] protection of health[17] and of social and labor standards,[18] cultural exceptions,[19] human rights,[20] and the regulation of the economy in times of financial crisis.[21] However, not all of these regulatory interests are recognized to the same extent and not all contain the same conditions for implementing regulatory measures.

State of Necessity and IIA Provisions for the Protection of National Security and Public Order

Regulatory interests and the right to regulate have been extensively discussed in investment arbitration cases dealing with Argentina's financial crisis in 2001 and its aftermath.[22] Two specific legal categories potentially granting a right to regulate

[14]E.g., ICSID, Case No. ARB/01/8, *CMS Gas Transmission Company/ Argentine Republic*, Award (May 12, 2005), para. 251.

[15]E.g., ICSID, Case No. ARB/02/1, *LG&E Energy Corp, LG&E Capital Corp, LG&E International Inc/Argentine Republic*, Decision on Liability (October 3, 2006), para. 205.

[16]E.g., ICSID, Case No. ARB/00/2, *Tecnicas Medioambientales Tecmed SA/United Mexican States*, Award (May 29, 2003), para. 121.

[17]E.g., NAFTA/UNCITRAL Tribunal, *Methanex Corporation/United States of America*, UNCITRAL (NAFTA), Award (August 3, 2005), Part IV Chapter D, para. 9.

[18]ICSID, Case No. ARB/02/1, *LG&E Energy Corp, LG&E Capital Corp, LG&E International Inc/ Argentine Republic*, Decision on Liability (October 3, 2006), para. 195.

[19]Article 10(6) Canadian Model BIT (2003).

[20]ICSID, Case No. ARB(AF)/07/1, *Piero Foresti, Laura de Carli and others/Republic of South Africa*, Award (August 4, 2010) Coleman/Williams, South Africa's Bilateral Investment Treaties, Black Economic Empowerment and Mining: A Fragmented Meeting? Business Law International 9 (2008) 1, pp. 56 et seq. (83); Peterson, Human Rights and Bilateral Investment Treaties: Mapping the Role of Human Rights Law Within Investor–State Arbitration, International Centre for Human Rights and Democratic Development, 2009, Volume 3 of Investing in Human Rights series, http://www.dd-rd.ca/site/_PDF/publications/globalization/HIRA-volume3-ENG.pdf.

[21]Van Aaken/Kurtz, The Global Financial Crisis: Will State Emergency Measures Trigger International Investment Disputes? Columbia FDI Perspectives, No. 3 (March 23, 2009), http://www.vcc.columbia.edu/documents/Perspective3-vanAakenandKurtz-FINAL.pdf; Subrate Bhattacharjee, National Security with a Canadian Twist, Columbia FDI Perspectives No. 10 (July 30, 2009), http://www.vcc.columbia.edu/pubs/documents/ICAPerspective-Final.pdf.

[22]Di Pietro, State of Necessity in Investment Arbitration, The European and Middle Eastern Arbitration Review 2009, pp. 25 et seq.; Aguirre Luzi, BITs & Economic Crises: Do States have *carte blanche?* in: Weiler (ed.), *Investment Treaty Arbitration and International Law – Volume 1*, 2008, pp. 188 et seq.; Bottini, Protection of Essential Interests in the BIT Era, in: Weiler (ed.), *Investment Treaty Arbitration and International Law – Volume 1*, 2008, pp. 147 et seq.; Kurtz, Adjudging the Exceptional at International Law: Security, Public Order and Financial Crisis, Jean Monnet Working Paper No. 6, 2008, http://centers.law.nyu.edu/jeanmonnet/papers/08/080601.html; Binder, Changed Circumstances in Investment Law: Interfaces between the Law

were invoked and analyzed: the state of necessity under customary international law and clauses in IIAs for the protection of national security and public order – also called nonprecluded measures clauses. The former may preclude the wrongfulness of the host state's regulation if it constitutes the only way for the host state to safeguard essential interests against grave and imminent peril and if the act does not seriously impair an essential interest of the state towards which the obligation exists.[23] The latter allow host states to take far-reaching regulatory measures as long as interests of national security and public order are concerned.[24] Both the scope of and the differences[25] between the two categories have already been debated at length and will not have to be addressed by this article.

Declaratory Right to Regulate

This article will also not engage in an analysis of what seems to be a mere declaratory right to regulate. Such a right can be found, for example, in Article 12 of the Norway Model BIT.[26] Article 12 essentially provides that the host state of

of Treaties and the Law of State Responsibility with a Special Focus on the Argentine Crisis, in: Binder/Kriebaum/Reinisch/Wittich (eds.), *International Investment Law for the 21st Century: Essays in Honour of Christoph Schreuer*, 2009, pp. 608 et seq.; Alvarez/Khamsi, The Argentinean Crisis and Foreign Investors: A Glimpse into the Heart of the Investment Regime, in: Sauvant (ed.), *Yearbook on International Investment Law & Policy 2008-2009*, 2009, pp. 379 et seq.; Bjorklund, Economic Security Defenses in International Investment Law, in: Sauvant (ed.), *Yearbook on International Investment Law & Policy 2008-2009*, 2009, pp. 479 et seq.; Burke-White/von Staden, Investment Protection in Extraordinary Times: The Interpretation and Application of Non-Precluded Measures Provisions in Bilateral Investment Treaties, Virginia Journal of International Law 48 (2008), pp. 307 et seq.

[23]See Article 25 ILC Draft Articles on the Responsibility of States for Internationally Wrongful Acts, International Law Commission, Draft Articles on Responsibility of States for Internationally Wrongful Acts, with Commentaries, Report of the Work of the ILC's 53rd session, A/56/10 (2001), Yearbook of the International Law Commission 2001 II, pp. 31 et seq. (80 et seq.); ICJ, *Gabčíkovo-Nagymaros Project (Hungary/Slovakia)*, Judgment (September 25, 1997), ICJ Reports 1997, pp. 7, 40, para. 52.

[24]See, e.g., Article 24(3) ECT; Article 11 Argentina-USA BIT; Article 18 Uruguay-USA BIT; Article 3(2) at the end of the German Model BIT (2009); Article 2102 NAFTA. Further references in Muchlinski, Trends in International Investment Agreements, Balancing Investor Rights and the Right to Regulate. The Issue of National Security, in: Sauvant (ed.), *Yearbook on International Investment Law & Policy 2008-2009*, 2009, pp. 35 et seq. (52), footnote 83.

[25]ICSID, Case No. ARB/01/8, *CMS Gas Transmission Company/Argentine Republic*, Decision on Annulment (September 25, 2007), para. 130; Binder, Changed Circumstances in Investment Law: Interfaces between the Law of Treaties and the Law of State Responsibility with a Special Focus on the Argentine Crisis, in: Binder/Kriebaum/Reinisch/Wittich (eds.), International Investment Law for the 21st Century, Essays in Honour of Christoph Schreuer, 2009, pp. 608, 613.

[26]Similar provisions can be found, for example, in Article 1114(1) NAFTA; Article 12(2) Rwanda-USA BIT.

the investment may freely regulate in the interest of health, safety, or environmental concerns as long as the host state's measures are consistent with the IIA.[27] The provision appears to be somewhat redundant since it does not provide the host state with additional regulatory freedom.[28] The host state is restricted – as it would be without Article 12 – to regulating the investment within the boundaries of the substantive standards of the Norway Model BIT.

Regulation in the Public Interest

Instead, the article will try to focus on a "regulation in the public interest" – or "general exceptions" as they are called in the GATT/GATS context. Such regulatory interests pursue legitimate public welfare objectives and include the preservation of life, health, the environment, and social standards as well as the promotion of sustainable development and social and ecological progress of the host state. Although such regulation is not triggered by a state of necessity or national security concerns, it may still impair the profitability of an investment and conflict with substantive provisions in IIA.

A classic example is the establishment of a natural preserve at the site of a foreign investment.[29] Even if the host state's regulation promotes the environment, is nondiscriminatory, and is in compliance with the minimum standards under customary international law, the host state might still be under the obligation to pay compensation in accordance with the expropriation provisions of an applicable IIA.[30] Although the host state's right to regulate is not affected, the host state might feel that the obligation to compensate the investor impedes its sovereign freedom of action. The obligation to compensate might come at such a high cost to the host state that it causes a "regulatory chill." Ultimately, this could lead to the

---

[27]See Article 12 Norway Model BIT (2007): "Nothing in this Agreement shall be construed to prevent a Party from adopting, maintaining or enforcing any measure otherwise consistent with this Agreement that it considers appropriate to ensure that investment activity is undertaken in a manner sensitive to health, safety or environmental concerns."

[28]See Newcombe/Paradell, *Law and Practice of Investment Treaties, Standards of Treatment*, 2009, p. 509; Muchlinski, Trends in International Investment Agreements, Balancing Investor Rights and the Right to Regulate. The Issue of National Security, in: Sauvant (ed.), *Yearbook on International Investment Law & Policy 2008-2009*, 2009, pp. 35 et seq. (45).

[29]See, e.g., ICSID, Case No. ARB/96/1, *Compañía del Desarrollo de Santa Elena/Costa Rica*, Final Award (February 17, 2000), paras. 17 and 18.

[30]Confirming an obligation to pay compensation or damages on the part of the host state based on environmental regulations of the host state, ICSID, Case No. ARB/96/1, *Compañía del Desarrollo de Santa Elena/Costa Rica*, Final Award (February 17, 2000), para. 72; ICSID, Case No. ARB/00/2, *Tecnicas Medioambientales Tecmed SA/United Mexican States*, Award (May 29, 2003), paras. 151, 195; ICSID, Case No. ARB(AF)97/1, *Metalclad Corporation/United Mexican States*, Award (August 30, 2000), para. 111.

undesirable result that host states lower or abolish substantive standards of protection in future IIAs.

Up to now, the balancing between investors' rights and the "regulation in the public interest" by host states has received little attention. Therefore, an analysis of the problems associated with a balancing of interests could lead to useful conclusions. In what follows, the article will analyze various concepts that might be useful in resolving the described conflict between investors' rights and state regulatory interests.

Concepts of Achieving a Balance of Interests

Possible ideas for a balance of interests can be derived from a critical analysis of the status quo, as well as from considerations *de lege ferenda*. The former will show that substantive provisions in IIAs and rules of customary international law allow host states to implement regulatory interests to a considerable, yet still unsatisfactory, extent. *De lege ferenda* considerations therefore have to solve the question of how best to enshrine regulatory interests in IIAs.

Pursuing Host States' Regulatory Interests under the status quo

A closer look reveals that there exist various ways for host states to pursue regulatory interests despite their obligations toward investors under IIAs. Both substantive provisions of IIAs and customary international law seem to leave enough leeway for host states to take regulatory measures without violating provisions in IIAs. Yet, it remains to be examined whether these options are capable of achieving a balance of interests that is satisfactory for host states and investors alike.

Status quo of IIAs

IIAs contain various provisions that seem to allow a regulation in the public interest without compensation even if such regulation is not mentioned explicitly. As will be seen, among them are clauses governing the admission of investments, sector-specific exceptions, clauses allowing host states to influence investment disputes, limited dispute settlement clauses, and "relative" standards of protection.

The broadest regulatory freedom in IIAs can be found in clauses governing the admission of investments into the host state. The admission of investments must usually comply with the national legislation in force in the host state.[31] This gives

[31] See, e.g., Article 2(1) German Model BIT (2009).

the host state the possibility to regulate the admission of investments or the modalities thereof without breaching other substantive provisions of the IIA. Although, for example, Germany amended its Foreign Trade Act in 2009 with a view to restricting the market access of foreign sovereign wealth funds, it was generally not considered to be an infringement of the substantive standards of protection in German investment treaties.[32] Even states such as the USA and Canada, whose BITs and free trade agreements (FTAs) usually protect the admission of investments,[33] preserve the right to regulate admissions. Either the admission rights of potential investors are subject to extensive sector-specific exceptions or the right to initiate arbitration proceedings to enforce admission rights is excluded.[34] This – at least de facto – regulatory freedom is evidenced by Canada's tightening of the Investment Canada Act by introducing a broad national security test[35] and by the US Congress blocking investments of United Arab Emirates-based Dubai Ports World in US trade ports and investments of China National Offshore Oil Corporation in a US oil firm.[36] The weakness of the regulation of the admission of investment is that it only allows host states to preemptively block the entry of investments into the host state. It does not permit the balancing of interests with regard to investments that have already been made.

In contrast, other provisions in IIAs allow for an unrestricted regulation of investments already made. Among them are sector-specific exceptions for individual categories of state regulation. Some IIAs, for example, provide that their substantive protections do not extend to the regulation of taxation, state aid, or financial services.[37] Sector-specific exceptions can take the form of general clauses in IIAs or be included as part of individual protection provisions.[38] However, to

---

[32]But see Otto Sandrock, Staatsfonds und deutsche bilaterale Investitionsförderungs- und -Schutzverträge – Die Kontrolle von Staatsfonds ist mit diesen Verträgen nicht zu vereinbaren –, in: Grundmann/Kirchner/Raiser/Schwintowski/Weber/Windbichler (eds.), *Festschrift für Eberhard Schwark*, 2009, pp. 729 et seq.

[33]Muchlinski, Trends in International Investment Agreements, Balancing Investor Rights and the Right to Regulate. The Issue of National Security, in: Sauvant (ed.), *Yearbook on International Investment Law & Policy 2008-2009*, 2009, pp. 35 et seq. (40).

[34]Canadian Model BIT (2003), Annex IV; Article 1138 NAFTA and Annex 1138.2 NAFTA.

[35]Subrate Bhattacharjee, National Security with a Canadian Twist, Columbia FDI Perspectives No. 10 (July 30, 2009), http://www.vcc.columbia.edu/pubs/documents/ICAPerspective-Final.pdf.

[36]C.H. Brower II, Obstacles and Pathways to Consideration of the Public Interest in Investment Treaty Disputes, in: Sauvant (ed.), *Yearbook on International Investment Law & Policy 2008-2009*, 2009, pp. 347 et seq. (352, para. 30, 353, para. 31) with further supporting documentation; UNCTAD, The Protection of National Security in IIAs, UNCTAD/DIAE/IA/2008/5, 2009, p. 11, http://www.unctad.org/templates/Download.asp?docid=11891&lang=1&intItemID=2983 with additional examples.

[37]Article 20 (financial services), Article 21 (taxation) US Model BIT (2004); further examples in Newcombe/Paradell, *Law and Practice of Investment Treaties, Standards of Treatment*, 2009, pp. 506–508.

[38]The scope of protection afforded by most-favoured-nation clauses, for example, is often restricted regarding free trade zones or customs unions, see German Model BIT (2009), Article 3(3)-(5).

date such clauses are rare and usually restricted to very narrowly defined categories. Based on the status quo, these categories would not encompass a regulation in the public interest or allow the promotion of social or environmental goals.

In some cases, IIAs provide for a right of host states to influence investment disputes after they have arisen. For example, under North American treaty practice, the tax authorities of the contracting states may concur that their tax measures do not constitute an expropriation (so-called *joint tax veto*).[39] This would preclude a request for arbitration by investors.[40] Some IIAs also stipulate that the contracting states may interpret the IIA in a manner that is binding for arbitral tribunals.[41] This would allow contracting states to "interpret" standards of protection in such a way that gives them more regulatory discretion. Both mechanisms are rightly called into question, as they permit host states and their authorities to "judge their own cause" and to thereby compromise the legitimate expectations of investors.[42] This does not seem conducive to ensuring a fair balance of interests. At the same time, the scope of application (taxes) and the effect (an interpretation providing clarification) of the measures are too limited to guarantee host states extensive regulatory freedom in the public interest.

Another way for states to exercise de facto regulatory freedom consists in restricting the scope of investor–state dispute settlement clauses. Some next-generation FTAs and IIAs dispense with investor–state dispute settlement clauses altogether[43]; others exclude from their scope of application certain protection provisions, such as the admission of an investment.[44] As a result, state measures might possibly violate the protections provided for in the IIA. Yet, this may not necessarily lead to the enforcement of the investor's rights, as the affected investor would not be able to initiate arbitration proceedings against the host state. Whether the investor's home state would claim a violation of the IIA by way of diplomatic protection is questionable. Given the increased desire of states to regulate during tougher

[39]Article 21(2) US Model BIT (2004); Article 16(3) Canadian Model BIT (2003); Article 2103(6) NAFTA; Article 170(4) b Japan-Mexico FTA; similarly Article 21(5)(b) ECT; Kolo, Tax "Veto" as a Special Jurisdictional and Substantive Issue in Investor-State Arbitration: Need for Reassessment? Suffolk Transnational Law Review 32 (2009) 2, pp. 475 et seq.

[40]Not the case in the Energy Charter Treaty, see Article 21(5)(b)(iv) ECT.

[41]Article 1131 NAFTA; Article 30(3) US Model BIT (2004); Article 40(2) Canadian Model BIT (2003).

[42]Kolo, Tax "Veto" as a Special Jurisdictional and Substantive Issue in Investor-State Arbitration: Need for Reassessment? Suffolk Transnational Law Review 32 (2009) 2, pp. 475 et seq. (479); Weiler, Investment Arbitration and the Growth of International Economic Law, Business Law International 2 (2002) 2, pp. 158 et seq. (181–185); Whitsitt, NAFTA fifteen years later: the success, failures and future prospects of Chapter 11 (Interview with Todd Weiler) (February 16, 2009), http://www.investmenttreatynews.org/cms/news/archive/2009/02/17/nafta-fifteen-years-later-the-successes-failures-and-future-prospects-of-chapter-11.aspx.

[43]Article 11.16 Australia-US FTA; Article 107 Japan-Philippines FTA.

[44]Schedule Article 12 Mexico-Netherlands BIT; Canadian Model BIT (2003), Annex IV; Article 1138 NAFTA and Annex 1138.2.

economic times, it might be in the states' own interest to grant each other extensive regulatory freedom.

Expropriation provisions generally do not prevent states from pursuing regulatory interests. If an expropriation is nondiscriminatory and in the public interest, the host state's regulation is usually not considered to be illegal. However, expropriation clauses in IIAs usually provide that even a legal expropriation creates an obligation to pay compensation. Yet, some IIAs contain explicit exceptions from the duty to pay compensation in the case of indirect expropriations through nondiscriminatory regulations in the public interest.[45]

Finally, the terms of most provisions in IIAs are kept so general that, when interpreted, they seemingly allow for the accommodation of states' regulatory interests.[46] The wording of some provisions even permits the reading into them of implicit exceptions. The standards of national or most-favored-nation treatment, for example, are inherently relative and presuppose a comparison between the investor and another domestic or foreign investor. However, IIAs do not normally stipulate when "comparability" exists. This grants a rather broad discretion to host states and arbitral tribunals.[47] As long as no "comparability" exists, the host states are free to regulate without violating the national or most-favored-nation treatment provisions. Similarly, the broad wording of most fair and equitable treatment provisions[48] allows one to take into account whether a regulation occurred in the public interest when considering whether a treatment of an investor was fair or equitable. However, despite – or perhaps because of – the leeway certain provisions allow in their interpretation, the distinction between admissible regulations and violations of substantive protections remains a difficult one to make.[49]

As the status quo of IIAs shows, host states generally remain free to pursue regulatory interests without incurring an obligation to pay compensation – even in the absence of specific regulatory clauses in IIAs. However, the existing IIA provisions are too limited and diffuse to achieve a comprehensive balance of interests between investors and host states. For host states and investors alike,

---

[45]See Annex B.4(b) US Model BIT 2004; Article 13 Footnote 4 and Annex B(13)(1)(c) Canadian Model BIT (2003).

[46]McLachlan/Shore/Weiniger, *International Investment Arbitration, Substantive Principles*, 2007, para. 1.62.

[47]See Newcombe/Paradell, *Law and Practice of Investment Treaties, Standards of Treatment*, 2009, pp. 176–181, 504; Wilske/Raible, The Arbitrator as Guardian of International Public Policy? Should Arbitrators Go Beyond Solving Legal Issues? in: Rogers/Alford (eds.), *The Future of Investment Arbitration*, 2009, pp. 249 et seq. (268); Kalderimis, Investment Treaties and Public Goods, TDM 7 (2010) 1, p. 10.

[48]This might be different for clauses that are limited to the minimum standard of protection under international law, see Article 5(2) US Model BIT 2004.

[49]The same applies to incorporating the stage of development of a host state in the interpretation process, which could justify regulation in an individual case; see Article 15(d) ASEAN-Australia-New Zealand FTA; Gallus, The Influence of the Host State's Level of Development on International Investment Treaty Standards of Protection, Journal of World Investment & Trade 6 (2005) 5, pp. 711 et seq.

IIAs do not provide sufficient legal certainty when it comes to regulatory measures in the public interest. It remains to be examined whether public international law standards beyond IIAs will be able to create a more satisfactory balance.

Status quo in international law beyond IIAs

Public international law norms beyond IIAs might provide for a more consistent balance between investors' rights and the host states' regulatory interests.[50] It will be examined whether the application of Article 31(3)(c) of the Vienna Convention on the Law of Treaties of 1969 (VCLT) might achieve a homogenization of IIAs and other international law regimes by means of interpretation.[51] Also, a broader understanding of the state of necessity under international law or the taking into account of peremptory norms (*jus cogens*) could increase states' regulatory freedom in investment protection.

Pursuant to Article 31(3)(c) VCLT, "*any relevant rules of international law applicable in the relations between the parties*" must be taken into account when interpreting IIA clauses.[52] This rule of interpretation could serve as a "gateway" for conventions governing the protection of the environment, human rights, or other areas covered by state regulatory interests applicable in relations between state parties to an IIA.[53] For example, this could mean that discrimination provisions in IIAs may have to be interpreted narrowly if this were the only way of achieving the purpose of environmental obligations applicable between the parties to an IIA. The problem with such homogenization is that it presupposes a concrete link between the IIA provision and the international law norm to be taken into account. This can be derived from the wording of Article 31(3)(c) VCLT, which stipulates that (only) "*relevant*" provisions are to be taken into account.[54] Ignoring the important qualifier "*relevant*" could lead to an inadmissible modification of the relevant IIA

[50] See also Hirsch, Interactions between Investment and Non-Investment Obligations, in: Muchlinksi/Ortino/Schreuer (eds.), *The Oxford Handbook of International Investment Law*, 2008, pp.154 et seq.

[51] German Federal Law Gazette 1985 II, pp. 927 et seq.

[52] For a study of Article 31(3)(c) VCLT, see French, Treaty Interpretation and the Incorporation of Extraneous Legal Rules, International and Comparative Law Quarterly 55 (2006) 2, pp. 253 et seq.; McLachlan, The Principle of Systemic Integration and Article 31(3)(c) of the Vienna Convention, International and Comparative Law Quarterly 54 (2005) 2, pp. 279 et seq.

[53] For examples, see van Aaken, Fragmentation of International Law: The Case of International Investment Law, Finnish Yearbook of International Law 17 (2008), pp. 91 et seq. (117–121).

[54] See examples cited in Binder, Changed Circumstances in Investment Law: Interfaces between the Law of Treaties and the Law of State Responsibility with a Special Focus on the Argentine Crisis, in: Binder/Kriebaum/Reinisch/Wittich (eds.), *International Investment Law for the 21st Century: Essays in Honour of Christoph Schreuer*, 2009, pp. 608 et seq. (618).

provision instead of a clarification of its meaning by interpretation.[55] Whether a particular provision is indeed "*relevant*" can only be determined on the basis of the specific facts. So far, the mechanism of Article 31(3)(c) VCLT is largely untested and without real precedent regarding the interaction between IIA provisions and states' regulatory interests. As a result, there is – at least presently – a great deal of legal uncertainty as to whether Article 31(3)(c) VCLT can adequately balance states' regulatory interests and investors' rights under IIAs.

Another way of pursuing regulatory measures in the public interest under customary international law could be to invoke the state of necessity. Some argue that the protection of material interests of host states under the state of necessity can also include economic or environmental interests.[56] This reasoning was adopted by Argentina in arbitration proceedings resulting from the Argentine financial crisis, in which it cited "an economic state of necessity" in justification of its measures. Zimbabwe used similar legal reasoning. It justified the expropriation and subsequent seizure of farms by war veterans with the catastrophic living conditions in the country.[57] To date, this justification has usually failed owing to the narrowly defined requirements for invoking the state of necessity. The requirements presuppose that measures taken by a host state must represent the only way for the state to safeguard an essential interest against grave and imminent peril. Only in rare instances have host states managed to convince arbitral tribunals that they have met these prerequisites.[58] Moreover, necessity as defined under customary international law only represents a ground for justification of a regulatory measure and cannot remedy a violation of the IIA.[59] Article 27(b) of the Articles on the Responsibility of States for Internationally Wrongful Acts therefore prescribes an obligation on the part of the state to provide for compensation even in the event of a

---

[55]SCC, Case No. 079/2005, *RosInvestCo UK Ltd./Russian Federation*, Award on Jurisdiction, October 2007, para. 39.

[56]Aguirre Luzi, BITs & Economic Crises: Do States have *carte blanche?* in: Weiler (ed.), *Investment Treaty Arbitration and International Law – Volume 1*, 2008, pp. 165 et seq. (172); Muchlinski, Trends in International Investment Agreements, Balancing Investor Rights and the Right to Regulate. The Issue of National Security, in: Sauvant (ed.), *Yearbook on International Investment Law & Policy 2008-2009*, 2009, pp. 35 et seq. (57–58).

[57]ICSID, Case No. ARB/05/6, *Bernardus Henricus Funnekotter/Zimbabwe*, Award (April 22, 2009), paras. 102–107.

[58]See, e.g., ICSID, Case No. ARB/02/1, *LG&E Energy Corp, LG&E Capital Corp, LG&E International Inc/Argentine Republic*, Award (October 3, 2006), para. 239; ICSID, Case No. ARB/03/9, *Continental Casualty Company/Argentine Republic*, Award (September 5, 2008), para. 213.

[59]For a dogmatic underpinning see Kurtz, Adjudging the Exceptional at International Law: Security, Public Order and Financial Crisis, Jean Monnet Working Paper No. 6, 2008, p. 41, http://centers.law.nyu.edu/jeanmonnet/papers/08/080601.html; Binder, Changed Circumstances in Investment Law: Interfaces between the Law of Treaties and the Law of State Responsibility with a Special Focus on the Argentine Crisis, in: Binder/Kriebaum/Reinisch/Wittich (eds.), *International Investment Law for the 21st Century: Essays in Honour of Christoph Schreuer*, 2009, pp. 608 et seq. (615); ICSID, Case No. ARB/01/8, *CMS Gas Transmission Company/ Argentine Republic*, Decision on Annulment (September 25, 2007), para. 134.

state of necessity.[60] Thus, just like under most expropriation provisions, the host state might be free to regulate but has a duty to compensate. This might again lead to a "regulatory chill" for host states, which is precisely what the balancing of interests seeks to avoid.

Finally, the principles of *jus cogens* could be taken into consideration when host states pursue regulatory interests. In connection with the ICSID case of *Piero Foresti et al. v. Republic of South Africa*, for example, it was asserted that South Africa's active elimination of racial discrimination that prevailed under the apartheid regime could fall within the scope of *jus cogens*. It was argued that this had to be taken into account when reviewing a violation of the IIA.[61] This line of argument is based on the notion that measures taken by a host state to protect human rights should be covered by *jus cogens*. In this case, such measures would – according to the hierarchy of norms in public international law – take priority over obligations arising out of an IIA and displace such obligations pursuant to Article 53 VCLT. A regulatory measure could thus not lead to a claim for compensation or damages. Although it is doubtful whether norms of *jus cogens* can trigger an obligation of "*affirmative action*" on the part of host states, the question ultimately remains irrelevant. In any case, states' regulatory interests would not generally and sufficiently be protected. First, it remains highly disputed as to precisely which rules form part of *jus cogens*,[62] causing a lack of legal certainty for future host states' regulation. Second, the few rules that are actually widely recognized as forming part of *jus cogens* (e.g., prohibition of slavery and genocide)[63] will likely never become relevant in an investment scenario.[64]

In conclusion, the standards of public international law may add to a certain degree to the regulatory freedom for host states. However, such freedom is paired with considerable legal uncertainty, only guaranteed in part, and does not lead to a more satisfactory balance of interests than under the IIA regime. Therefore, it is currently largely up to arbitral tribunals to decide whether, how, and in whose favor investors' rights under IIAs and host states' regulations in the public interest will be balanced.

---

[60]See also ICJ, *Gabčíkovo-Nagymaros Project (Hungary/Slovakia)*, Judgment (September 25, 1997), ICJ Reports 1997, pp. 7 et seq. (39, para. 48).

[61]*Amicus curiae* petition by the International Commission of Jurists, para. 25, http://www.investmenttreatynews.org/documents/p/215/download.aspx.

[62]ILC, Draft Articles on the Law of Treaties with Commentaries, Yearbook of the International Law Commission 1966 II, pp. 187 et seq. (248 para. 2).

[63]ICJ, *Barcelona Traction, Light and Power Company (Belgium/Spain)*, Judgment (February 5, 1970), ICJ Reports 1970, pp. 3, 32, para. 34; ILC, Draft Articles on the Law of Treaties with Commentaries, Yearbook of the International Law Commission 1966 II, pp. 187 et seq. (248 para. 3).

[64]C.H. Brower II, Obstacles and Pathways to Consideration of the Public Interest in Investment Treaty Disputes, in: Sauvant (ed.) *Yearbook on International Investment Law & Policy 2008-2009*, 2009, pp. 347 et seq. (372).

Role of tribunals under the status quo

Where host states pursue regulatory measures in the public interest which are not clearly justified under IIAs or other standards of international law, it is left to arbitral tribunals to assess whether the measures result in a violation of the IIAs and in the obligation to pay damages.

This ultimately leads to a shifting of responsibility to arbitral tribunals. Whether regulatory interests can be implemented – without incurring the obligation to pay compensation – largely depends on the tribunal's approach adopted with regard to interpreting IIAs. A predominantly teleological interpretation will frequently lead to recourse to the preamble of the IIA and the tipping of the balance in favor of the "protection of investments" prescribed therein.[65] As a result, the implementation of regulatory interests will usually be accompanied by a duty to pay compensation or damages in furtherance of investor protection.

The currently existing legal uncertainty is further compounded by the fact that arbitral awards do not establish precedents for future tribunals. As evidenced by the divergent case law on the state of necessity in the Argentine cases, arbitral tribunals are not bound by awards previously rendered. Case law is currently far from uniform, especially when it comes to balancing investors' rights and regulatory interests of host states. This situation is described by more pessimistic voices as the "legitimacy crisis" of investment law.[66] It is argued that IIAs – which are aimed at remedying the legal uncertainty of the customary international law governing aliens – fail to serve their purpose. This is not least due to the fact that arbitral case law has failed to provide IIAs with a uniform scope of application.

This view, however, fails to take into account that investment law is still in its infancy. Initial inconsistencies seem unavoidable given the abundance of novel legal problems and of differently worded IIAs. It can be expected that in the medium term the best legal solutions will prevail because of their persuasiveness – and not because any precedent has been set.[67] Against this background, the regulatory interests already recognized under the current status quo might in the long run lead to the development of case law establishing a proper balance of interests between investors and host states. As shown above, existing provisions in IIA as

[65]Dolzer/Schreuer, *Principles of International Investment Law*, 2008, p. 32; Van Aaken, Fragmentation of International Law: The Case of International Investment Law, Finnish Yearbook of International Law 17 (2008), pp. 91 et seq. (126); Kurtz, Adjudging the Exceptional at International Law: Security, Public Order and Financial Crisis, Jean Monnet Working Paper No. 6, 2008, p. 33, http://centers.law.nyu.edu/jeanmonnet/papers/08/080601.html.

[66]See Burke-White, The Argentine Financial Crisis: State Liability under BITs and the Legitimacy of the ICSID System, Asian Journal of WTO & International Health Law and Policy 3 (2008) 1, pp. 199 et seq. (221–223); Franck, The Legitimacy Crisis in Investment Treaty Arbitration: Privatizing Public International Law Through Inconsistent Decisions, Fordham Law Review 73 (2005), pp. 1521 et seq. (1557, 1582, footnote 303 with further references).

[67]Paulsson, International Arbitration and Generation of Legal Norms: Treaty Arbitration and International Law, TDM 3 (2006) 5, pp. 1 et seq. (4).

well as public international law standards already allow for some measure of regulatory discretion of host states.[68]

"Codifying" a right to regulate in the public interest in future IIAs would nevertheless make sense for three reasons. First, the issue of balancing investors' and host states' interests is currently perceived as a serious problem in international investment law. A gradual development of arbitral jurisprudence balancing the interests might possibly come too late. States might decide to significantly weaken or depart entirely from the current regime of investment protection before arbitral jurisprudence can be fully developed. Second, the incorporation of regulatory interests in IIAs would merely take up a process that has already been set in motion. States have become acutely aware of the need to incorporate regulatory freedoms in IIAs and many of the more recent IIAs address the problem, at least to some extent. Therefore, it presently makes sense to discuss and develop uniform concepts – particularly with a view to the new competences of the EU. Third, an incorporation of a right to regulate in IIAs will provide arbitral tribunals with better guidance on how to deal with regulatory measures of host states. It is not least the current legal uncertainty closely associated with the host states' regulation in the public interest that causes dissatisfaction with the status quo under IIAs and public international law. Of course, one might argue that provisions containing a right to regulate would themselves be subject to interpretation and thus a potential source of divergent awards. Yet, it can be safely assumed that an incorporation of the right to regulate in IIAs will produce consistent case law much more quickly than if it remained unclear as to when a host state's liability for a regulation in the public interest is triggered under an IIA.

Incorporating a Right to Regulate in the Public Interest in IIAs

There seem to be various alternatives of incorporating a right to regulate in IIAs. The regulatory interests could be made part of the preamble, of the respective standards of protection, or drafted as a clause dealing specifically with the right to regulate. These possibilities also exist for IIAs that so far do not contain a right to regulate. The contracting states to an IIA are in principle free to implement a right to regulate at any time. IIAs only limit a state's sovereign freedom of action insofar as the contracting states to an IIA have voluntarily restricted their sovereignty on the basis of contractual obligations. The contracting states can remove these restrictions by mutual consent.[69] IIAs provide investors with rights and protections only to the extent that these have been granted by the contracting states and have not

[68] For examples, see Newcombe, General Exceptions in International Investment Agreements, in: Cordonier Segger/Gehring/Newcombe (ed.), *Sustainable Development in International Investment Law*, forthcoming 2010.

[69] Alvarez/Khamsi, The Argentinean Crisis and Foreign Investors: A Glimpse into the Heart of the Investment Regime, in: Sauvant (ed.), *Yearbook on International Investment Law & Policy 2008-2009*, 2009, pp. 379 et seq. (478).

been subsequently rescinded or restricted. Which of the three possibilities seems preferable or most practical will be examined next.

Incorporating the Right to Regulate in the Preamble

The incorporation of regulatory interests in the preamble of an IIA would have the advantage that the typical structure of the IIA would be maintained. It would furthermore clarify that the regulatory interest must be taken into account when interpreting the substantive provisions of the IIA. The preamble could establish a balance between the goal of investment protection it already stipulates and a sufficient degree of regulatory freedom on the part of the host state.[70]

However, embedding regulatory interests in the preamble seems to have serious drawbacks. The right to regulate would not be of a binding nature. It could only be used to interpret the substantive protections in the IIA and would be of limited effectiveness. Since the host state's right to regulate without paying compensation and the protection of investments are often incompatible, the conflicting policy goals might plainly neutralize each other in the interpretation of IIA provisions. The main effect of inserting regulatory interests into the preamble might well be that it prevents arbitral tribunals from interpreting IIAs one-sidedly in favor of the investor by invoking the goal of investment protection contained in the preamble. However, the incorporation of the right to regulate would not guarantee that states' regulatory interests are unequivocally asserted.

Incorporating the Right to Regulate in the Respective Standards of Protection

It would also be possible to lay down the regulatory interests in the respective standards of protection of an IIA. States are already pursuing this option in their newer treaties. Article 3 of the German Model BIT (2009), for instance, provides for national and most-favored-nation treatment. At the same time, Article 3(2) of the German Model BIT (2009) stipulates that measures that have to be taken for reasons of public security and order will not be deemed treatment less favorable within the meaning of the article. The other standards of protection are not affected by this exception. Another possibility would be to exclude an obligation to pay compensation in the case of an expropriation for reasons of environmental protection,[71]

[70]See, e.g., the preamble of the Norway Model BIT (2007): "Desiring to achieve these objectives in a manner consistent with the protection of health, safety, and the environment, and the promotion of internationally recognized labour rights; (. . .)."

[71]See López/Ortiz, New BIT between Spain and Libya: Promoting investments while protecting the environment (November 5, 2009), http://arbitration.practicallaw.com/0-500-6695.

without abrogating the requirement of fair and equitable treatment or the prohibition of discrimination.

This option makes the protection provisions in IIAs more complex and entails the risk that investors will perceive a reduction in the level of substantive protection afforded by the IIA. It increases the probability that arbitral tribunals will come to different interpretations of such provisions and issue diverging awards. The upside for investors is, however, that the host state's regulatory freedom is restricted to the very provision with which it could come into conflict. Other provisions are not affected. This means greater protection for the investor than would be the case if the host state were to have general freedom to regulate. Therefore, this option seems to represent one feasible way of balancing investors' rights and states' regulatory interests. Given that the protection provisions in IIAs vary widely, it is, however, difficult to undertake a general assessment of how they would interact with regulatory provisions in a given case. A detailed case-by-case analysis of possible interactions would go beyond the scope of this article.[72] The following analysis of specific regulatory clauses could, however, to some extent be applied mutatis mutandis to a right to regulate which is incorporated in the respective standards of protection of an IIA.

Incorporating the Right to Regulate by Drafting Specific Regulatory Clauses

The third option of incorporating a right to regulate in IIAs would be to draft a specific clause dealing with the host states' right to undertake regulatory measures in the public interest.

There would appear to be three possible ways of embodying the state's regulatory interest in a specific provision of the IIA. One possibility would be for the contracting states to agree on a general clause granting the host state the unfettered freedom to regulate. Another possibility would be to draft a provision containing specific examples of public interests and rules on how they should be implemented. The third possibility would be to include provisions covering only very particular types of public interests.

The third solution is already being used in the area of environmental protection. The BIT between Libya and Spain which came into force in 2009 contains a clause in which the contracting states explicitly reserve the right to regulate environmental matters without being obliged to pay compensation.[73] The problem with provisions

[72]See the in-depth study by Ceyssens/Sekler, Bilaterale Investitionsabkommen (BITs) der Bundesrepublik Deutschland: Auswirkungen auf wirtschaftliche, soziale und ökologische Regulierung in Zielländern und Modelle zur Verankerung der Verantwortung transnationaler Konzerne, 2005.

[73]López/Ortiz, New BIT between Spain and Libya: Promoting investments while protecting the environment (November 5, 2009), http://arbitration.practicallaw.com/0-500-6695. Similar, but without dealing with the question of compensation, Article 10 of the El Salvador-Nicaragua

of this kind is that they do not take into account other public interests possibly colliding with IIA protections. The host state's freedom of regulation would be restricted to the particular type of public interest incorporated in the IIA.

The advantage of a general clause providing a universal right to regulate without a duty to compensate is that it gives the host state the greatest possible freedom in this regard. The downside of such a clause is, however, that it basically renders the IIA's protection provisions useless. The IIA no longer provides sufficient protection for investors' entrepreneurial interests and the profit from their investments. Whenever the investors' rights under the IIA are affected, the host state could claim that it has undertaken a regulatory measure within the meaning of the general clause. This could have significant adverse effects on the host state's investment climate. It is particularly true if the host state misuses the general clause to argue that arbitrary actions targeting the investors are no longer covered by the protection provisions in the IIA. Accordingly, general clauses providing for a right to regulate *in the public interest* do not seem to be used in IIA practice. However, IIA clauses allowing for host states' regulation in the interest of national security and public order often do take the form of general clauses and seem to be modeled after the "security exceptions" in Article XXI GATT/Article XIV GATS. One reason for the use of general clauses might be that the need to regulate is particularly politically sensitive and contracting states therefore insist on sufficient room to maneuver.[74] Another reason for using general clauses may be that the contracting states are relying on customary international law – such as the state of necessity – to fill in potential gaps left open by the general wording of the clauses.[75]

However, such considerations do not apply to a right to regulate in the public interest. Neither does customary international law seem suited to fill gaps in the regulation in the public interest, nor is such regulation necessarily as politically sensitive as a regulation in the interest of national security. Taking into account the criticism of general clauses just examined above, and in line with the sparse treaty

BIT. The Belgium/Luxembourg-Libya BIT lays down environmental protection provisions in Article 5 and provisions on labor standards in Article 6; likewise the US Model BIT (2004) in Articles 12 and 13.

[74]In treaty practice, the room to maneuver is also guaranteed by formulating clauses in such a way that they are "*self-judging*" [see, e.g., Article 18 US Model BIT (2004)] and, therefore, not subject to review by the courts. However, the measure should still be subject to review according to the principles of good faith, see UNCTAD, The Protection of National Security in IIAs, UNCTAD/DIAE/IA/2008/5, 2009, p. 60, http://www.unctad.org/templates/Download.asp?docid=11891&lang=1&intItemID=2983.

[75]See Schill, Auf zu Kalypso? Staatsnotstand und Internationales Investitionsschutzrecht – Anmerkungen zur Entscheidung LG&E Energy Corp/Argentina, SchiedsVZ (2007) 4, pp. 178 et seq. (184). It is, however, doubtful as to whether sufficient comparability exists to apply the principles of necessity mutatis mutandis to clauses aimed at protecting national security, see ICSID, Case No. ARB/01/3, *Enron Corporation Ponderosa Assets L.P./Argentine Republic*, Award (May 22, 2007), para. 334; but see Muchlinski, Trends in International Investment Agreements, Balancing Investor Rights and the Right to Regulate. The Issue of National Security, in: Sauvant (ed.) *Yearbook on International Investment Law & Policy 2008-2009*, 2009, pp. 35, 67.

practice,[76] one might better draft clauses allowing for a regulation in the public interest in the form of provisions containing specific examples of public interests and rules on how they should be implemented. Such drafting would be in line with the "general exceptions" clauses in Article XX GATT/Article XIV GATS. These clauses, despite being referred to as "general," do not provide a general or universal right to regulate, but instead lay down specific examples of public regulatory interests. This form of implementation increases legal certainty for investors and seems to be suited for an adequate balancing of interests in the case of regulations not justified by a state of necessity or by the protection of national security and public order.[77]

Article 10 of the Canadian Model BIT (2003) constitutes one of the few examples of specific clauses allowing for a regulation in the public interest[78]:

> 1. Subject to the requirement that such measures are not applied in a manner that would constitute arbitrary or unjustifiable discrimination between investments or between investors, or a disguised restriction on international trade or investment, nothing in this Agreement shall be construed to prevent a Party from adopting or enforcing measures necessary:
> (a) to protect human, animal or plant life or health;
> (b) to ensure compliance with laws and regulations that are not inconsistent with the provisions of this Agreement; or
> (c) for the conservation of living or non-living exhaustible natural resources.

Although the incorporation of specific regulatory clauses in IIAs seems suited to establish a balance between investors' rights and host states' regulatory interests, there remain a number of problems, and these will be considered in greater detail below.

---

[76]For examples of FTAs with investment chapters see Newcombe/Paradell, *Law and Practice of Investment Treaties, Standards of Treatment*, 2009, p. 490. "Security exceptions" and "general exceptions" are combined in Article 24 ECT. Article 24(1) and (2) ECT relates to public interest, whereas Article 24(3) ECT deals with the protection of national security and public order.

[77]*Newcombe* points out that the incorporation of specific regulatory clauses in IIAs might even prove beneficial for investors. Experience in WTO law has shown that a codification of regulatory clauses can limit the regulatory flexibility of host states. Host states might find themselves limited to a regulation of the particular public interests embodied in the specific regulatory clause. They would, however, be prevented from pursuing other kinds of public interests not contained in such a clause; see Newcombe, General Exceptions in International Investment Agreements, in: Cordonier Segger/Gehring/Newcombe (eds.), *Sustainable Development in International Investment Law*, forthcoming 2010. Thus, specific regulatory clauses seem to constitute an appropriate form of balancing investors' rights and host states' interests. The express confirmation of the regulatory freedom of host states through incorporation in an IIA is balanced by the increased legal certainty for investors as to what can be regulated.

[78]See also Article 24 Norway Model BIT (2007); Article 15(1)(c) Japan-Vietnam BIT. For additional examples see Newcombe, General Exceptions in International Investment Agreements, in: Cordonier Segger/Gehring/Newcombe (eds.), *Sustainable Development in International Investment Law*, forthcoming 2010.

Issues of Implementing the Balance of Interests

To actually *balance* the interests concerned when drafting a clause containing the right to regulate in the public interest, the legal nature of such a clause and the legal consequences associated with it have to be analyzed. One must also consider how regulatory clauses can be drafted in a way that sufficiently protects the investors' rights and prevents abuse by host states despite their greater regulatory freedom. If regulatory clauses are – in accordance with prevailing treaty practice – modeled on the provisions of the "general exceptions" of the GATT/GATS, one must also determine whether and how arbitral tribunals could draw on interpretative principles established in WTO case law dealing with "general exceptions."

Legal Nature and Legal Consequences of Regulatory Clauses

There seem to be two possible ways of incorporating a right to regulate in the public interest in IIAs. One would be to draft the regulatory clause as a true exception to the protections granted to investors in the IIA. The other would be to design the regulatory clause as a justification for the breach of IIA obligations. As both approaches are not free from criticism, a third way might be to focus on the legal consequences of regulatory clauses rather than on their legal nature.

Regulatory Clause as an Exception

Regulatory clauses that are drafted in the form of an exception to IIA obligations afford the contracting states ample freedom to act. If the clause applies, it excludes the operation of the substantive provisions of the IIA as well as the host state's obligation to pay compensation as a legal consequence of its regulatory measure.[79] The above-cited Article 10 of the Canadian Model BIT (2003) represents an example of such a type of clause.[80]

However, it is doubtful whether drafting regulatory clauses as exceptions to IIA obligations would establish an adequate balance of interests. With this type of clause, an investor could in some situations be worse off than he would be under the principles of customary international law governing the treatment of aliens.[81]

[79]ICSID, Case No. ARB/01/8, *CMS Gas Transmission Company/Argentina*, Decision on Annulment (September 25, 2007), para. 146.

[80]Similarly Article 24(2) ECT: "*The provisions of this Treaty (...) shall not preclude any Contracting Party from adopting or enforcing any measure (...).*"

[81]Newcombe/Paradell, *Law and Practice of Investment Treaties, Standards of Treatment*, 2009, pp. 505, 506.

Should the regulatory clause permit measures to protect the environment and should the investor's property be expropriated on account of the establishment of a natural preserve, he would not receive any compensation.[82] Because of the clause's legal nature as an exception, the application of the expropriation provision in the IIA would be excluded.

It could be argued that drafting regulatory clauses as veritable exceptions might run counter to the IIAs' aim of protecting and promoting investments. If instead of pursuing a balance of interests only the host state's interests are promoted, the host state's investment climate might deteriorate and the promotion of investments could be frustrated. One might object that this only applies to the specific regulatory interests that are contained in the regulatory clause. However, very much will depend on the drafting of the clause and the breadth of regulatory interests it encompasses.

Regulatory Clause as Justification

Another dogmatic possibility would be to draft the regulatory clause as a justification for the breach of obligations. It could be modeled after Article 25 ILC of the Articles on the Responsibility of States for Internationally Wrongful Acts and provide that a regulation in the public interest precludes the wrongfulness of a regulatory measure not in conformity with substantive IIA obligations. If this consequently precluded the host state's duty to pay compensation, it would actually not make much of a difference which legal nature the regulatory clause is given.

If, however, the justification entailed that, similarly to Article 27(b) of the Articles on the Responsibility of States for Internationally Wrongful Acts, the host state remained liable to pay compensation to the investor, other problems emerge. Such a regulatory clause would seem to be of little use because host states under the current system are already free to regulate – as long as they accept that the breach of the IIA leads to a duty to pay compensation or damages. Also, such a regulatory clause might not increase the regulatory freedom for host states because the host state's obligation to pay compensation could cause a "regulatory chill."[83]

[82]Therefore, even when framing the regulatory clause as an exception, the drafters of the regulatory clause should ensure that the duty to pay compensation in the case of an expropriation remains. Otherwise, the very principles of investment protection would be eroded. See also Newcombe, General Exceptions in International Investment Agreements, in: Cordonier Segger/ Gehring/Newcombe (eds.), *Sustainable Development in International Investment Law*, forthcoming 2010.

[83]This also applies to the concept of regulatory freedom as laid down in Article 24 ECT. Although the clause is effectively designed as an exception in Article 24(2) ECT, Article 24(1) ECT provides that the exception is not to be applied to compensation in the case of expropriation. Despite the freedom to regulate contained in Article 24(2) ECT, the host state would therefore still be obliged to pay compensation in the case of expropriation. See also Article 15 Japan-Vietnam BIT.

Focus on Legal Consequences of Regulatory Clauses

As the preceding discussion has shown, it is not so much the legal nature of regulatory clauses but much more their legal consequences – compensation/damages or not – which create a dilemma when trying to balance investors' rights and state regulatory interests.

This could call for a moving away from the current "all-or-nothing" model for compensation. Instead, a solution in accordance with the principle of proportionality[84] should be found which takes into consideration the importance of the host state's regulatory interest. The more the host state's regulation promotes the public interest and the less it impairs the investor or its investment, the lower the compensation payable would be. Conversely, the lesser the effect on the public interest and the greater the impairment of the investor's interests, the higher the compensation payable. Working out the specifics of such a balanced model for compensation would go beyond the scope of this article. That said, it should be pointed out that *Kriebaum* has already done the basic groundwork on the "proportionality of compensation" in connection with a study on expropriation in international law.[85] Her findings could be used as a basis for the balancing of interests when it comes to a right to regulate in the public interest. When the findings are transferred to the case of regulation in the public interest, it will be necessary to balance the impact of the regulatory measure and the justified expectations of the investor against the relevance of the measure for the regulatory objective[86] and the relevance of the public interests protected or pursued by the measure and the particular interest of the host state in paying reduced compensation.

Preconditions of a Regulation in the Public Interest

Besides focusing on the legal consequences of regulatory measures, the drafting of particular conditions for the exercise of a right to regulate could also lead to a reasonable balance of interests.

[84]On the principle of proportionality in international law, see van Aaken, Defragmentation of Public International Law Through Interpretation: A Methodological Proposal, Indiana Journal of Global Legal Studies 16 (2009) 2, pp. 483 et seq.

[85]Ursula Kriebaum, *Eigentumsschutz im Völkerrecht – Eine vergleichende Untersuchung zum internationalen Investitionsrecht sowie zum Menschenrechtsschutz*, 2008, p. 554; similarly Hirsch, Interactions between Investment and Non-Investment Obligations, in: Muchlinksi/Ortino/Schreuer (eds.), *The Oxford Handbook of International Investment Law 2008*, pp. 154 et seq. (177).

[86]Whether the regulation was necessary to achieve the desired effects will often have already been examined when the chapeau of the regulatory provision was reviewed, see, e.g., Article 10 Canadian Model BIT (2003) ("*necessary*").

In a study on the implementation of states' regulatory interests in the area of national security, the Organization for Economic Cooperation and Development (OECD) has prepared guidelines to be followed by host states when taking regulatory measures.[87] For example, it is suggested that the investor and the public should be notified and consulted in good time with regard to planned state measures and the related objectives pursued by such measures. The guidelines also call for effective and objective judicial and official reviewability as well as involvement of high government levels in the event of restrictive investment policy measures. These guidelines could be applied to a regulation in the public interest and appear suitable for taking into account the investor's interests in the case of regulatory measures. Although incorporating the entire guidelines into a regulatory clause of an IIA would likely exceed the scope of such a clause, a reference to the OECD guidelines might constitute a possibility.

The GATT/GATS-like Article 10 of the Canadian Model BIT (2003) contains a different kind of precondition for the exercise of a right to regulate. Its introductory clause ("*chapeau*") stipulates that the regulatory measure may not constitute arbitrary or unjustifiable discrimination or a disguised restriction on investment. In addition, such a measure must be necessary to achieve the regulatory objectives pursued. The final part of Article 24(2) Energy Charter Treaty sets forth a very similar provision. Both of these clauses embody the principle of good faith and the prohibition of the abuse of rights[88]: A host state that regulates in the public interest must safeguard the rights of the other contracting state – and therefore, indirectly, the rights of the investor. If this is not done, the right to regulate is precluded.

It is remarkable that "chapeau clauses" or similar clauses[89] seem to reintroduce through the "back door" some of the substantive IIA provisions – such as discrimination and fair and equitable treatment provisions – which the regulatory clauses are meant to exclude or justify. The *chapeau* contains standards similar to those of IIAs: The host states' *chapeau* obligations contained in Article 10 of the Canadian Model BIT (2003), the final part of Article 24(2) Energy Charter Treaty, or Article 4 (2)(a)-(c) Azerbaijan-Belgium/Luxembourg BIT can be found in a nearly identical form in the substantive IIA provision prohibiting discrimination and requiring fair and equitable treatment. If a just balancing of interests only appears possible by including typical substantive IIA standards in *chapeau* clauses, the question arises why explicit clauses for regulation of public interests should be included in IIAs at all. This question will be taken up again in the summary of this article.

[87]OECD, Building Trust and Confidence in International Investment, 2009, p. 17, http://www.oecd.org/dataoecd/18/47/42446942.pdf.

[88]Newcombe/Paradell, *Law and Practice of Investment Treaties, Standards of Treatment*, 2009, p. 504.

[89]See, e.g., Article 4(2) Azerbaijan-Belgium/Luxembourg BIT, which, however, only applies to regulation aimed at protecting national security.

Using GATT/GATS and WTO Jurisprudence as a Basis for Arbitral Decisions

Most of the clauses that provide for a right to regulate in the public interest in IIAs are either based on the provisions of Article XX GATT/Article XIV GATS or make direct reference to them.[90] Despite the indisputable differences between investment law and WTO law,[91] it seems possible to use tried and tested regulatory clauses as a model.[92] Arbitral tribunals basing their interpretative process on established WTO principles might provide greater legal certainty for the parties to arbitration proceedings.

Newcombe and *Paradell* are explicitly in favor of investment arbitration tribunals referring to WTO case law when interpreting regulatory clauses in IIAs.[93] They point to already developed principles that would promote the balance of interests between the investor and the host state. For example, the burden of proof that a measure falls within the regulatory clause should rest on the state taking the regulatory measure.[94] Moreover, a multistage analysis of "general exceptions" has emerged. Transferred to an investment arbitration scenario, one would first have to check whether the state regulation falls under the scope of the regulatory clause and in a second step examine whether the regulation meets the requirements of the "*chapeau*." In particular with regard to the question of whether a regulatory measure was "necessary," a finely differentiated WTO jurisprudence with multiple weighing and balancing steps has developed[95] which could also be applied when interpreting regulatory clauses in IIAs.

However, it remains doubtful whether arbitral tribunals are willing to take into consideration the already developed WTO jurisprudence on "general exceptions" when interpreting clauses for the regulation in the public interest.[96] This might be

---

[90]E.g., Article 200 China-New Zealand FTA.

[91]Kalderimis, Investment Treaties and Public Goods, TDM 7 (2010) 1, p. 1; Kurtz, The MFN Standard and Foreign Investment – an Uneasy Fit? Journal of World Investment & Trade 5 (2004) 6, pp. 861 et seq. (866–872).

[92]See ICSID, Case No. ARB/03/9, *Continental Casualty Company/Argentine Republic*, Award (September 5, 2008), para. 192.

[93]Newcombe/Paradell, *Law and Practice of Investment Treaties, Standards of Treatment*, 2009, p. 504.

[94]For a differentiated distribution of the burden of proof in the case of regulation aimed at protecting national security, see Muchlinski, Trends in International Investment Agreements, Balancing Investor Rights and the Right to Regulate. The Issue of National Security, in: Sauvant (ed.), *Yearbook on International Investment Law & Policy 2008-2009*, 2009, pp. 35 et seq. (71).

[95]Newcombe/Paradell, *Law and Practice of Investment Treaties, Standards of Treatment*, 2009, p. 504.

[96]According to *Newcomb* and *Paradell*, arbitral tribunals display a good deal of skepticism toward using WTO case law in their interpretative process, Newcombe/Paradell, *Law and Practice of Investment Treaties, Standards of Treatment*, 2009, p. 503, with reference to NAFTA/UNCITRAL Tribunal, *Methanex Corporation/United States*, Final Award (August 3, 2005), Part IV para. 21.

due to the fact that it is unsettled as to how and to what extent arbitral tribunals should take into account such WTO jurisprudence. For this reason, contracting states to an IIA could agree on interpretative guidance in IIAs and refer arbitral tribunals to WTO jurisprudence on "general exceptions" in a subparagraph of the regulatory clause, in an annex to the IIA, or in the documented negotiation history of the IIA. Regulatory clauses which make direct reference to the GATT/GATS provisions[97] also seem to suggest that arbitral tribunals should take into consideration WTO jurisprudence on "general exceptions."

The use of WTO jurisprudence as a basis for the interpretation of regulatory clauses in IIAs could accelerate uniform case law with a view to new regulatory clauses. Therefore, such a trend should be welcomed as long as the regulatory clauses in IIAs are in fact sufficiently similar to Article XX GATT/ Article XIV GATS and arbitral tribunals sufficiently take into account the differences between WTO and investment law when interpreting the regulatory clauses.

Conclusion

The analysis has shown that host states can pursue different regulatory goals in different ways. The status quo under IIAs and public international law allows for a regulation in the public interest – the exercise of which, however, lacks the necessary legal certainty. Therefore, the incorporation in IIAs of a clause containing specific examples of regulatory interests – similar to Article 10 of the Canadian Model BIT (2003) – appears to be a feasible approach.

In the analysis of the possible drafting of such a clause, it emerged that an appropriate balancing of interests might have to be pursued through a "proportionality of compensation" and a *chapeau* similar to GATT/GATS provisions. The application and interpretation of these new concepts bears the risk that arbitral tribunals will once again reach divergent conclusions. The situation could be aggravated by the fact that the concepts do not correspond to the already known standards of protection in IIAs and a uniform jurisprudence will yet have to develop. It also seems possible that some arbitral tribunals follow principles of WTO jurisprudence with regard to regulation in the public interest and the *cheapeau*, whereas others will opt for an investment-law-specific interpretation. In such a case, the incorporation of the right to regulate in IIAs might not resolve but instead intensify what is sometimes perceived as the legitimacy crisis in investment law. Therefore, some might argue that the legal uncertainty surrounding regulatory

By contrast, the arbitral tribunal in ICSID, Case No. ARB/03/9, *Continental Casualty Company/ Argentine Republic*, Award (September 5, 2008), para. 192, was more open toward referencing WTO case law. This might be explained by the fact that the president of the arbitral tribunal, Professor Sacerdoti, was a member of the WTO Appellate Body from 2001 to 2009.

[97]Article 200 of the China-New Zealand FTA; Chapter 15 Article 1(2) of the ASEAN-Australia-New Zealand FTA.

interests should be dealt with by introducing an appellate mechanism[98] or an international investment court[99], and not by incorporating regulatory clauses in IIAs.

However, it currently seems that the insistence on such a "grand solution" fails to give proper consideration to practical realities. The introduction of completely new or additional dispute resolution mechanisms has become a distant prospect, particularly after ICSID withdrew its proposal on an appeals mechanism. A multilateral effort that would be necessary for such reforms cannot be expected, given the currently prevailing critical view of investment law taken by states.

By contrast, there is an emerging trend of incorporating regulatory interests in IIAs. This trend could be taken up in the sense of a "small solution." Even if the status quo already offers a certain amount of regulatory freedom, incorporating the right to regulate in IIAs promises to provide improved clarity and certainty on how to deal with regulations in the public interest. It would also signify a clear acknowledgement of the regulatory freedom of states and could help diminish the current criticism of the investment protection regime.

It will be the task of arbitral tribunals to give shape to such norms and to harmonize investors' rights and state regulatory interests by means of a consistent interpretation. The incorporation of regulatory clauses should ultimately make the tribunals' task easier[100]: Instead of having to selectively and implicitly read regulatory clauses into already existing standards of protection, arbitral tribunals could use a regulatory clause with examples of regulatory interests as a starting point. The clause might give arbitral tribunals useful guidance and prevent overly narrow or broad interpretations of standards of protection by reference to the preambles of IIAs.[101] Incorporating the right to regulate in a specific clause should aid in developing a uniform case law on regulatory interests more quickly. This could be further facilitated by taking into account the existing WTO jurisprudence on "general exceptions."

Therefore, it seems advisable to take up the emerging trend and give thought to how to incorporate regulatory interests in IIAs.[102] In so doing, an appropriate balancing of interests only seems possible if a possible abuse of regulatory clauses

---

[98]For a critical view, see Tams, An Appealing Option? The Debate about an ICSID Appellate Structure, Beiträge zum Transnationalen Wirtschaftsrecht Heft 57, 2006, p. 42, http://www.wirtschaftsrecht.uni-halle.de/Heft57.pdf.

[99]See, e.g., Van Harten, *Investment Treaty Arbitration and Public Law*, 2007, p. 180.

[100]See Wilske/Raible, The Arbitrator as Guardian of International Public Policy? Should Arbitrators Go Beyond Solving Legal Issues? in: Rogers/Alford (eds.), *The Future of Investment Arbitration*, 2009, p. 249 et seq. (270): "Arbitrators – like judges – can only be as good as the law they apply."

[101]Newcombe/Paradell, *Law and Practice of Investment Treaties, Standards of Treatment*, 2009, p. 504.

[102]Kalderimis, Investment Treaties and Public Goods, TDM 7 (2010) 1, p. 18; Alvarez/Khamsi, The Argentinean Crisis and Foreign Investors: A Glimpse into the Heart of the Investment Regime, in: Sauvant (ed.), *Yearbook on International Investment Law & Policy 2008-2009*, 2009, pp. 379 et seq. (478): "BIT parties can change the treaties they ratify (...) to incorporate more sovereignty-protective provisions. (...) Demanding that arbitrators recalibrate BITs by rewriting them for the state parties is not the best route to legitimize the investment regime."

by host states is prevented by provisions that bear resemblance to the existing nondiscrimination and fair and equitable treatment standards in IIAs. An additional possibility for balancing interests should follow from a "proportionality of compensation" that balances the investors' interests in their investments against the importance of the public interest at issue. Naturally, these ideas need to be further developed. However, they form a starting point for an incorporation of the right to regulate in future IIAs – and should also be of interest for possible future IIA negotiations in accordance with the Common Commercial Policy of the EU.

EUROPEAN COMMISSION

Brussels, 7.7.2010
COM(2010)343 final

COMMUNICATION FROM THE COMMISSION TO THE COUNCIL, THE EUROPEAN PARLIAMENT, THE EUROPEAN ECONOMIC AND SOCIAL COMMITTEE AND THE COMMITTEE OF THE REGIONS

Towards a comprehensive European international investment policy

EN EN

COMMUNICATION FROM THE COMMISSION TO THE COUNCIL, THE EUROPEAN PARLIAMENT, THE EUROPEAN ECONOMIC AND SOCIAL COMMITTEE AND THE COMMITTEE OF THE REGIONS

Towards a comprehensive European international investment policy

Investment presents itself as a new frontier for the common commercial policy. The Lisbon Treaty provides for the Union to contribute to the progressive abolition of restrictions on foreign direct investment. The Treaty grants the Union exclusive competence to that effect.[1] This Communication explores how the Union may develop an international investment policy that increases EU competitiveness and thus contributes to the objectives of smart, sustainable and inclusive growth, as set out in the Europe 2020 Strategy.[2] It looks at the main orientations of an EU investment policy for the future, as well as the main parameters for immediate action in this area.

In parallel to this Communication, the Commission has adopted a proposal for a Regulation that would establish transitional arrangements relating to investment agreements between Member States and third countries.[3] Its objective is to provide legal certainty to both EU and foreign investors operating under the terms of these agreements. The proposed Regulation and this Communication are only first steps in the development of a European international investment policy, which will be gradual and targeted and will also take into account responses to this Communication.

1. DEFINITION, IMPACT AND RECENT TRENDS

Foreign direct investment (FDI) is generally considered to include any foreign investment which serves to establish lasting and direct links with the undertaking to which capital is made available in order to carry out an economic activity.[4] When investments take the form of a shareholding this objective presupposes that the shares enable the shareholder to participate

---

1 Article 206 of the Treaty on the Functioning of the European Union (TFEU) provides that by establishing a customs union in accordance with Articles 28 to 32, the Union shall contribute, in the common interest, to the progressive abolition of restrictions on international trade and foreign direct investment, and the lowering of customs and other barriers. Article 207 includes foreign direct investment as one of the areas covered by the common commercial policy of the Union. The common commercial policy is an area of exclusive competence pursuant to Article 3(1) of the TFEU.

2 Commission Communication "Europe 2020: a strategy for smart, sustainable and inclusive growth" – COM(2010) 2020, 3.3.2010.

3 Commission Proposal for a Regulation of the European Parliament and of the Council establishing transitional arrangements for bilateral investment agreements between Member States and third countries.

4 The terms "direct investment" appeared in the Chapter on capital movements and payments of the EC Treaty and now in Articles 63-66 TFEU. In that context, they have been interpreted by the Court of Justice in light of the Nomenclature annexed to Directive 88/361/EEC of 24 June 1988 for the implementation of Article 67 of the Treaty (OJ L 178, 8.7.1988, p. 5-18), which in turn is largely based on widely accepted definitions of the IMF and the OECD. See e.g. Judgment of 12 December 2006, *Test Claimants in the FII Group Litigation*, Case C-446/04, ECR p. I-11753, para. 181. See also e.g. the Judgments of 24 May 2007, *Holböck*, C-157/05, ECR. p. I-4051, para. 34; 23 October 2007, *Commission/Germany*, C-112/05, ECR p. I-8995, para. 18; 18 December 2007, *Skatterverket v A*, C-101/05, para. 46; 20 May 2008, *Orange European Smallcap Fund*, C-194/06, para. 100; 14 February 2008, *Commission/Spain*, C-274/06, para. 18; and 26 March 2009, *Commission/Italy*, C-326/07, para. 35.

effectively in the management of that company or in its control.[5] This contrasts with foreign investments where there is no intention to influence the management and control of an undertaking. Such investments, which are often of a more short-term and sometimes speculative nature, are commonly referred to as "portfolio investments".[6]

Globalisation has seen a dramatic increase of capital movements, including notably of FDI. Both a cause and an effect of globalisation, FDI flows were, in 2007, the year before investment was affected by the global economic and financial turbulence, at a record high of almost EUR 1.500 billion.[7]

FDI represents an important source of productivity gains and plays a crucial role in establishing and organising businesses and jobs at home and abroad. Through FDI, companies build the global supply chains that are part of the modern international economy. Innovation in transportation and information technologies has in turn facilitated trade and the globalisation of business enterprise beyond the confines of large corporations. Investment and trade are today inter-dependent and complementary. Around half of world trade today takes place between affiliates of multinational enterprises, which trade intermediate goods and services.

While the relationship between FDI and economic growth and welfare is a complex one, on balance, both inward and outward investment have a positive impact on growth and employment in and outside the EU, including in developing countries. In the EU, outward investment makes a positive and significant contribution to the competitiveness of European enterprises, notably in the form of higher productivity. Contrary to a view that is sometimes voiced, a review of the current state of research on FDI and employment shows that no measurable negative impact on aggregate employment has so far been identified in relation to outward investment.[8] However, while the aggregate balance is positive, negative effects may of course arise on a sector-specific, geographical and/or individual basis. Conversely, the overall benefits of inward FDI into the EU are well-established, notably in relation to the role of foreign investment in creating jobs, optimising resource allocation, transferring technology and skills, increasing competition and boosting trade. This explains why our Member States, like other nations around the world, make significant efforts to attract foreign investment.

Today, the EU is both the world's leading host and source of FDI. As a "market leader", the EU benefits from its openness to the rest of the world, including in the area of investment.

While FDI stocks and flows are today still heavily concentrated among industrialised countries, emerging market economies have become increasingly active both as investors and recipients of investment, including through state-sponsored investment like Sovereign Wealth

---

[5] See e.g. Judgments of 12 December 2006, *Test Claimants in the FII Group Litigation*, Case C-446/04, ECR p. I-11753, para. 182; of 24 May 2007, *Holböck*, C-157/05, ECR p. I-4051, para. 35; 23 October 2007, *Commission/Germany*, C-112/05, ECR p. I-8995, para. 18; 20 May 2008, *Orange European Smallcap Fund*, C-194/06, para. 101; and 26 March 2009, *Commission/Italy*, C-326/07, para. 35.

[6] The Court of Justice of the European Union has described the notion of "portfolio investment" as "the acquisition of shares on the capital market solely with the intention of making a financial investment without any intention to influence the management and control of the undertaking". See Judgment of 26 September 2008, *Commission/Netherlands*, Joined Cases C-282/4 and C-283/04, ECR p. I-9141, para. 19.

[7] 2009 World Investment Report of the United Nations Conference on Trade and Development (UNCTAD).

[8] 2010 Impact of EU outward FDI, Copenhagen Economics.

Funds, which hold not only more assets but have also more diversified investment policies than before.[9] This trend has become more visible during the current period of turbulence in the world economy when investments to and from emerging economies have either surged or dropped less dramatically than flows between industrialised countries. Overall, this has translated in an increase of the relative share of emerging economies in global FDI flows, both for inward and outward flows. Therefore, the EU cannot afford to take a backseat in the global competition to attract and promote investment from and to all parts of the world.

2. INVESTMENT AS A NEW FRONTIER FOR THE COMMON COMMERCIAL POLICY

Investment decisions are driven primarily by market considerations, i.e. expected gains from investments. Yet, these decisions are deeply affected by the economic, political and legal environment of any given economy. Investors thrive in a stable, sound and predictable environment. A common international investment policy is not the only determinant of inward and outward FDI flows. However, it serves the fundamental purpose of assuring investors that they are able to operate in an open, properly and fairly regulated business environment, both within and across a host country's borders. In this respect, openness to investment should continue to serve as a touchstone to set our policies. The EU will continue to be an open investment environment, welcoming foreign investors and their contribution to the European economy and society at large. At the same time, the Union should ensure that EU investors abroad enjoy a level playing field, which assures both uniform and optimal conditions for investment through the progressive abolition of restrictions on investment. A more activist approach to ensuring that EU investment relations with third partners constitute a "two-way street" is therefore warranted. A number of important building blocks and background studies are already available, including through the extensive analytical work performed by international organisations such as OECD and UNCTAD. These lay the basis for a common international investment policy.

(a) The "BITs and pieces" of investment policy

The most visible manifestation of Member States' policies on investment over the last 50 years is the number of so-called Bilateral Investment Treaties (BITs) that they have concluded with third countries. Germany was the first nation in the world to conclude a BIT, in 1959, and many countries around the world, including all but one Member State, have followed suit.[10] With a total of almost 1200 agreements that cover all forms of investment, Member States together account today for almost half of the investment agreements currently in force around the world.[11] An overview of the BITs entered into by the Member States is set out in the annex to this Communication.

Through BITs, Member States have sought, and obtained, from third countries specific guarantees on the treatment of their investors and investments by those third countries, for

---

9 The Commission has set out its approach towards Sovereign Wealth Funds in 2008. See: COM(2008) 115, 27.02.2008.

10 Bilateral Investment Treaty between Germany and the Islamic Republic of Pakistan, 1959. Ireland is the only EU Member State that does not maintain any Bilateral Investment Treaty with a third country.

11 2009 World Investment Report of the United Nations Conference on Trade and Development (UNCTAD), p. 32. The UNCTAD reports a total of 2676 BITs, but this figure includes intra-EU BITs, which are BITs among EU Member States. The latter category of agreements is not covered by this Communication.

example commitments against unfair or discriminatory treatment or a guarantee of prompt, adequate and effective compensation in case of expropriation. These investment protection guarantees constitute one important element of building confidence in the legal security required for taking sound investment decisions. Hence, such investment protection agreements are considered an effective manner to promote and attract investment, in particular in countries where domestic institutions and domestic economic policies in and of themselves are not considered sufficient to confer such guarantees.

However, not all Member States have concluded such agreements, and not all agreements provide for the same high standards. This leads to an uneven playing field for EU companies investing abroad, depending on whether they are covered as a "national" under a certain Member State BIT or not.

Another feature of the agreements of Member States is that they relate to the treatment of investors "post-entry" or "post-admission" only. This implies that Member States' BITs provide no specific binding commitments regarding the conditions of entry, neither from third countries regarding outward investment by companies of our Member States, nor vice versa. Gradually, the European Union has started filling the gap of "entry" or "admission" through both multilateral and bilateral agreements at EU level covering investment market access and investment liberalisation. These have improved the conditions of market access for all EU investors, notably by ensuring the non-discriminatory treatment of investors upon entry to a third country market.[12]

(b) Towards a common international investment policy

A comprehensive common international investment policy needs to better address investor needs from the planning to the profit stage or from the pre- to the post-admission stage. Thus, our trade policy will seek to integrate investment liberalisation and investment protection. Research confirms that substantive investment provisions in broad trade agreements impact trade and FDI flows more profoundly, or that the combination of substantive investment rules and provisions liberalising other parts of the economy jointly impact trade and investment more significantly.[13]

An international investment policy geared towards supporting the competitiveness of European enterprises will be best served by cooperation and by negotiations at the level of the Union.[14] In order to be effective, guarantees from third countries on the conditions of investment should come in the form of binding commitments under international law. Hence, investment negotiations with third countries, for which we can build on the body and substance of the more than 1100 BITs which currently exist, will enable the EU to enlarge, better define and protect the competitive space that is available to all EU investors. In the long

---

12 At the multilateral level, the General Agreement on Trade in Services (GATS) provides for a framework for undertaking commitments on the supply of services through a commercial presence (defined as "mode 3" by GATS Article I). At the bilateral level, the Union has concluded negotiations with Korea on a Free Trade Agreement, which includes provisions on market access for investors and establishments.

13 OECD (2006), Analysis of the economic impact of investment provision in regional trade agreements, OECD Trade Policy Working Paper No. 36, 11.07.2006.

14 Note that, under Article 207(2) TFEU, the Union has exclusive competence to autonomously legislate on FDI, as in the other areas of the common commercial policy, such as the import and export regulation.

run, we should achieve a situation where investors from the EU and from third countries will not need to rely on BITs entered into by one or the other Member State for an effective protection of its investments.

Investment policy is often complemented by investment promotion efforts by Member States and sub-national levels of government. Authorities engage competitively in promoting both inward and outward investment to and from their jurisdictions, just like in the area of trade or export promotion. Their efforts commonly rely on a variety of instruments, ranging from investment incentives to assistance and support schemes. While it is the Union's responsibility to promote the European model and the single market as a destination for foreign investors[15], it seems neither feasible nor desirable to replace the investment promotion efforts of Member States, as long as they fit with the common commercial policy and remain consistent with EU law.

3. AN AGENDA FOR EU INVESTMENT NEGOTIATIONS

As in all areas of European policy-making, the thrust of the Union's action should be to deliver better results as a Union than the results that have been or could have been obtained by Member States individually. Thus, the Union's future action in this field should be inspired and guided by the best available standards, so as to offer a level playing field of a high quality to all EU investors.

However, a one-size-fits-all model for investment agreements with 3rd countries would necessarily be neither feasible nor desirable. The Union will have to take into account each specific negotiating context. The interests of our stakeholders as well as the level of development of our partners should guide inter alia the standards the Union sets in a specific investment negotiation. In the same way, the nature of the existing agreements of Member States with any given third country need to be taken into account. While BITs recently concluded by Member States have largely a similar structure and content, there are some variations. These might equally determine the objectives to be pursued in a specific negotiating context.

The Commission submits the following broad principles and parameters for future investment agreements. These are to be developed and fleshed out in country-specific negotiating recommendations which the Commission will submit subsequent to this Communication.

(a) Criteria for the selection of partner countries

FDI is at present heavily concentrated among developed economies. While this reflects these countries' economic importance in terms of GDP, it also underscores the generally favourable conditions for foreign investors prevailing in some of these markets. Actual trade and investment flows are in and of themselves important determinants for defining the priorities for EU investment negotiations. The Union should go where its investors would like to go, just like it should pave their way abroad, through the liberalisation of investment flows. Markets with significant economic growth or growth prospects present a particular opportunity in the current increasingly competitive environment. It is important that EU investors have access to these markets and that amid the changes that these economies might

15 Commission Communication "A single market for 21st century Europe" - COM(2007) 725

be undergoing, benefit from the availability of sufficient guarantees for fair and predictable treatment. The EU's interests in investment negotiations would also be determined inter alia by the political, institutional and economic climate of our partner countries. The 'robustness' of investor protection through either host country or international arbitration would be important determinants in defining priority countries for EU investment negotiations. In particular, the capacity and the practice of our partners in upholding the rule of law, in a manner that provides a certain and sound environment to investors, are key determinants for assessing the value of investment protection negotiations.

In the **short term**, the prospects for realising the integration of investment into the common commercial policy arise in ongoing trade negotiations, where the Union has so far only focused on market access for investors.[16] The latest generation of competitiveness-driven Free Trade Agreements (FTAs) is precisely inspired by the objective of unleashing the economic potential of the world's important growth markets to EU trade and investment. The Union has an interest in broadening the scope of negotiations to the complete investment area. In some cases, we could also respond to a request from our negotiating partners themselves. In the EU-**Canada** negotiations towards a Comprehensive Economic and Trade Agreement, our partner has expressed an interest in an agreement that would cover investment protection. Other ongoing negotiations in which investment protection should be considered include the EU-**India** negotiations towards a Broad-based Trade and Investment Agreement, the EU-**Singapore** negotiations towards a Free Trade Agreement, and the EU-**Mercosur** trade negotiations.

In the **short to medium term**, the Union should also consider under which circumstances it may be desirable to pursue stand-alone investment agreements. **China**, which is characterised by a high proportion of greenfield investments, including from the EU, may be one candidate for a stand-alone investment agreement, in which the protection of all kinds of assets including intellectual property rights should be covered. The Commission will explore the desirability and feasibility of such an investment agreement with China, and report to the Council and the European Parliament. **Russia** also presents particular opportunities and challenges to European investors. The negotiation with Russia of investment including investment protection should be further considered and discussed, for example in the context of a comprehensive agreement, such as the agreement that would replace the Partnership and Cooperation Agreement.

Should a comprehensive, across-the-board, investment agreement with a country, or a set of countries, prove impossible or inadvisable in the foreseeable future, sectoral agreements may be an option whose desirability, feasibility and possible impact would be further assessed. These sectoral negotiations should be based on the principles set out in this Communication and remain in line with further developments of the common investment policy. In the same vein, the feasibility of a multilateral initiative could be further considered in the long term.

---

16 A further legal argument for incorporating investment commitments into trade agreements relates to the fact that trade agreements, when they comply with relevant WTO rules on economic integration, are sheltered from the WTO obligation of most-favoured nation treatment, which requires WTO members to immediately and unconditionally extend the most favourable treatment to the rest of the membership. In other words, only if offered inside a trade agreement, preferential treatment, for example on investment market access, can remain preferential. This is most relevant for FDI in services sectors, given that the General Agreement on Trade in Services (GATS) addresses the supply of services through a commercial presence, which is essentially FDI.

(b) Looking beyond foreign direct investment

While investors have a key interest in establishing and controlling their assets abroad, such direct investments will always give rise to additional transfers, like for example the repatriation of profits. It is important that a common international investment policy not only enables the execution of a direct investment itself – the acquisition of a foreign enterprise or the establishment of one - but also that it enables and protects all the operations that accompany that investment and make it possible in practice: payments, the protection of intangible assets such as Intellectual Property Rights, etc.

In this respect, the articulation of investment policy should be consistent with the Treaty's Chapter on capital and payments (Articles 63-66 TFEU), which provides that, in principle, all restrictions on payments and capital movements, including those involving direct as well as portfolio investments, both between Member States and between Member States and third countries, are prohibited. That chapter does not expressly provide for the possibility to conclude international agreements on investment, including portfolio investment. However, to the extent that international agreements on investment affect the scope of the common rules set by the Treaty's Chapter on capitals and payments, the exclusive Union competence to conclude agreements in this area would be implied.[17]

(c) Setting standards of investment protection

A key question relates to the substantive rules the Union would seek to introduce in trade and investment agreements. Currently in investment negotiations, the Union relies mostly on the principle of non-discrimination, which is the cornerstone of the global trading system. Non-discrimination is usually implemented through two basic standards, 'most-favoured-nation treatment' and 'national treatment', which are both relative standards, because they involve making a comparison between the treatment provided based on origin, rather than defining an absolute standard of treatment. Consequently, their content is determined on the basis of the treatment that a country grants to its foreign investors and investments and to its own investors and investments

While non-discrimination should continue to be a key ingredient of EU investment negotiations, BITs employ other standards as well, such as "fair and equitable treatment" after admission and "full security and protection" treatment. These standards do not imply a comparison to the manner in which comparable investments are treated. Moreover, a number of Member State BITs provide for the protection of contractual rights granted by a host government to an investor ("umbrella clause"). They have been traditionally used in Member States BITs and are an important element among others that should inspire the negotiation of investment agreements at the EU level.

An important cornerstone of Member State best practices are clauses which place certain conditions upon the exercise of the host country's right to expropriate. While it follows from Article 345 TFEU that the Treaty does not affect a Member State's right to decide whether a given asset should be in public or private ownership, the Court's case law shows that this does

---

17 Article 3.2 of the Treaty on the Functioning of the European Union provides that "the Union shall also have exclusive competence for the conclusion of an international agreement when its conclusion is provided for in a legislative act of the Union or is necessary to enable the Union to exercise its internal competence, or in so far as its conclusion may affect common rules or alter their scope."

not have the effect of exempting expropriation measures from the fundamental rules of the Treaty, including those on freedom of establishment and free movement of capital.[18] Accordingly, expropriation measures in the EU should be non discriminatory[19] and proportionate to attain their legitimate objective (e.g. by providing for adequate compensation)[20]. Hence, the Union should include precise clauses covering this issue into its own future investment or trade agreements. A clear formulation of the balance between the different interests at stake, such as the protection of investors against unlawful expropriation or the right of each Party to regulate in the public interest, needs to be ensured. Likewise, EU clauses ensuring the free transfer of funds of capital and payments by investors should be included.

Finally, it should be recalled that the Union's trade and investment policy has to fit with the way the EU and its Member States regulate economic activity within the Union and across our borders. Investment agreements should be consistent with the other policies of the Union and its Member States, including policies on the protection of the environment, decent work, health and safety at work, consumer protection, cultural diversity, development policy and competition policy. Investment policy will continue to allow the Union, and the Member States to adopt and enforce measures necessary to pursue public policy objectives.

A common investment policy should also be guided by the principles and objectives of the Union's external action more generally, including the promotion of the rule of law, human rights and sustainable development (Article 205 TFEU and Article 21 TEU). In this respect, the OECD Guidelines for Multinational Enterprises, which are currently being updated, are an important instrument to help balance the rights and responsibilities of investors.

(d) Enforcing investment commitments

Ensuring the effective enforceability of investment provisions is a key objective of the Union. The Union has increased its focus in recent years on ensuring that agreements negotiated in the field of the common commercial policy can be, and are, effectively enforced, if necessary through binding dispute settlement. The Union has included in all of its recent FTAs, an effective and expedient state-to-state dispute settlement system. This dispute settlement system will, in the future, cover the investment provisions of EU trade and investment agreements.

In order to ensure effective enforcement, investment agreements also feature investor-to-state dispute settlement, which permits an investor to take a claim against a government directly to binding international arbitration.[21] Investor-state dispute settlement, which forms a key part of the inheritance that the Union receives from Member State BITs, is important as an investment involves the establishment of a long-term relationship with the host state which cannot be easily diverted to another market in the event of a problem with the investment.

---

18 See e.g. Judgments of 23 February 2003, C-452/01, *Ospelt* [2003] ECR I-9743, para. 24; 1 June 1999, C-302/97, *Konle* [1999] ECR I-3099, para. 38; and of 6 November 1984, *Fearon*, C-182/83, ECR [1984] p. 3677, para. 7.

19 ECJ, Judgment of 6 November 1984, Fearon, C-182/83, ECR [1984] p. 3677.

20 EFTA Court, Judgment of 26 June 2007,Case E-2/06, EFTA Surveillance Authority/Norway, para. 79; Article 17 (1)of the EU Charter of Fundamental Rights.

21 The Energy Charter Treaty, to which the EU is a party, equally contains investor-state dispute settlement.

Investor-state is such an established feature of investment agreements that its absence would in fact discourage investors and make a host economy less attractive than others.

For these reasons, future EU agreements including investment protection should include investor-state dispute settlement. This raises challenges relating, in part, to the uniqueness of investor-state dispute settlement in international economic law and in part to the fact that the Union has not historically been a significant actor in this field. Current structures are to some extent ill-adapted to the advent of the Union. To take one example, the Convention on the Settlement of Investment Disputes between States and Nationals of Other States (the ICSID Convention), is open to signature and ratification by states members of the World Bank or party to the Statute of the International Court of Justice. The European Union qualifies under neither.

In approaching investor-state dispute settlement mechanisms, the Union should build on Member State practices to arrive at state-of-the art investor state dispute settlement mechanisms. Among the main challenges are:

- The **transparency** of investor-state dispute settlement. In line with the EU's approach in the WTO, the EU should ensure that investor-state dispute settlement is conducted in a transparent manner (including requests for arbitration, submissions, open hearings, amicus curiae briefs and publication of awards);

- The **atomisation of disputes and interpretations**. Consistency and predictability are key issues and the use of quasi-permanent arbitrators (as in the EU's FTA practice) and/or appellate mechanisms, where there is a likelihood of many claims under a particular agreement, should be considered;

- **Rules for the conduct of arbitration**. The Commission will explore with interested parties the possibility that the European Union seek to accede to the ICSID Convention (noting that this would require amendment of the ICSID Convention).[22]

(e) International responsibility

In line with the Commission's aim to develop an international investment policy at EU level, the issue of the international responsibility between the EU and the Member States in EU investment agreements needs to be addressed. The European Union, represented by the Commission, will defend all actions of EU institutions. Given the exclusive external competence, the Commission takes the view that the European Union will also be the sole defendant regarding any measure taken by a Member State which affects investments by third country nationals or companies falling within the scope of the agreement concerned. In developing its new international investment policy, the Commission will address this issue, and in particular that of financial compensation, relying on available instruments, including, possibly, new legislation.

---

22 The European Communities successfully negotiated the amendment of, and subsequent accession to a number of international agreements/organisations. A recent example is the World Customs Organisation.

4. CONCLUSION

The Lisbon Treaty's attribution of EU exclusive competence on FDI integrates FDI into the common commercial policy. It also allows the EU to affirm its own commitment to the open investment environment which has been so fundamental to its prosperity and to continue promoting investment, both direct investment and portfolio investment, also as a tool of economic development.

Until now, the Union and the Member States have separately built around the common objective of providing investors with legal certainty and a stable, predictable, fair and properly regulated environment in which to conduct their business. While Member States have focused on the promotion and protection of all forms of investment, the Commission elaborated a liberalisation agenda focused on market access for direct investment. In this respect, a clear and complementary division of labour in the field of investment has resulted in a rather large and atomised universe of investment agreements.

With a view to ensuring external competitiveness, uniform treatment for all EU investors and maximum leverage in negotiations, a common international investment policy should address all investment types and notably assimilate the area of investment protection. The Union should follow the available best practices to ensure that no EU investor would be worse off than they would be under Member States' BITs.

While investment protection and liberalisation become key instruments of a common international investment policy, there will remain significant scope for Member States to pursue and implement investment promotion policies that complement and fit well alongside the common international investment policy. In general, a common policy will require more, rather than less, cooperation and coordination among the Union and the Member States.

Through investment negotiations, which in principle would be conducted as part of broader trade negotiations, the EU should seek to obtain binding commitments from its partners that guarantee and protect the free flow of all forms of investment. Stand-alone investment negotiations would also remain an option. In the short term, the Commission will seek the adaptation of negotiating directives to enlarge the scope of negotiations for a number of countries with whom trade negotiations are ongoing, where strong interests exist and where requests have been formulated. While the principles and parameters for such negotiations will be inspired by 'best practices' that Member States have developed, this Communication already submits some broad contours of the scope and standards the Union should be setting through international investment negotiations.

As set out above, the proposed Regulation regarding transitional arrangements relating to investment agreements between the Member States and third countries and this Communication are only first steps in the development of a European international investment policy, which will be gradual and targeted and will also take into account responses to this Communication.

Annex:Overview of the number of Bilateral Investment Treaties concluded by Member States

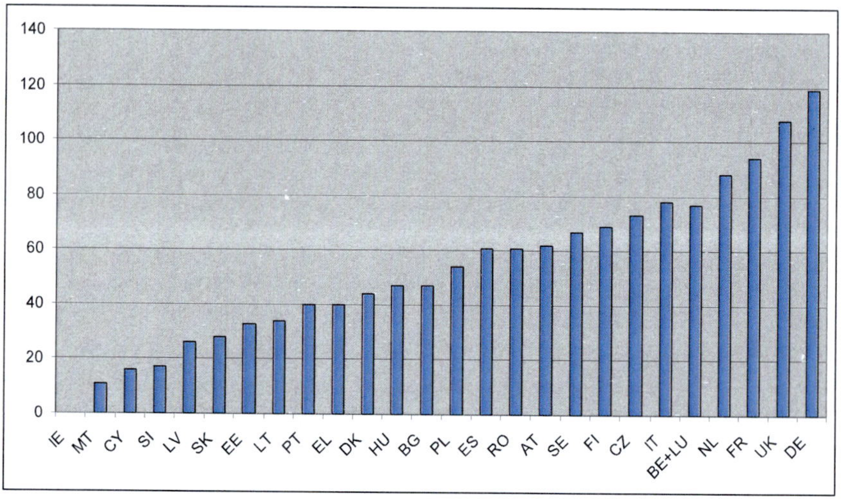

Note: Information as known to the Commission services on 15 June 2010

EUROPEAN COMMISSION

Brussels, 7.7.2010
COM(2010)344 final

2010/0197 (COD)

Proposal for a

REGULATION OF THE EUROPEAN PARLIAMENT AND OF THE COUNCIL

establishing transitional arrangements for bilateral investment agreements between Member States and third countries

EXPLANATORY MEMORANDUM

1. CONTEXT OF THE PROPOSAL

The Treaty on the Functioning of the European Union (hereafter: "the TFEU") establishes the European Union's exclusive competence on foreign direct investment, as part of the common commercial policy (Article 207(1) and Article 3(1)(e). In accordance with Article 2(1) of the TFEU, only the Union may legislate and adopt legally binding acts in an area where exclusive competence is conferred upon the Union.

Prior to the entry into force of the TFEU, Member States concluded more than 1000 bilateral agreements relating to investment with third countries, which relate in part or in full to foreign direct investment. Such agreements include Bilateral Investment Treaties (BITs) which provide *inter alia* guarantees on the conditions of investment in Member States and in third countries, in the form of specific commitments that are binding under international law.

Although agreements remain binding on the Member States as a matter of public international law, in the light of the entry into force of the TFEU the existence of Member States' agreements relating to investment and the commitments undertaken therein should be addressed from the perspective of the EU's exclusive competence on foreign direct investment.

In the absence of an explicit transitional regime in the TFEU clarifying the status of Member States' agreements, the present proposal for a Council and Parliament Regulation will authorise the continued existence of all investment agreements currently in force between Member States and third countries. As such, this proposal provides for an explicit guarantee of legal certainty as regards the conditions under which investors operate.

This approach, which reflects an evolutionary handling of the entry into force of the TFEU, much like the introduction of the common commercial policy in the 1960s,[1] allows for the gradual formulation and elaboration of an EU investment policy, which is to serve all investors and investments equally.

In recognition of the fact that Member States may be required or may find it necessary to amend or modify investment agreements, in particular to bring them in compliance with Treaty obligations, this proposal also establishes a framework and conditions to empower Member States to enter into negotiations with a third country with a view to modifying an existing bilateral agreement relating to investment. This framework is equally available to allow Member States to negotiate and conclude, under certain conditions set out by this proposal, a new bilateral agreement with third countries relating to investment. Given that the Union is exclusively competent for foreign direct investment, and that an EU investment policy will be gradually developed, the procedure established by this proposal must be regarded as an exceptional transitional measure.

---

[1] Council Decision of 9 October 1961 on the standardisation of the duration of trade agreements with third countries and Council Decision of 16 December 1969 on the progressive standardisation of agreements concerning commercial relations between Member States and third countries and on the negotiation of Community agreements.

This Regulation only addresses the transitional aspects of the management of the new EU competence on investment. The objectives, criteria and content of the new EU investment policy, to be developed on the basis of the newly-gained exclusive competence on foreign direct investment, is not addressed by this Regulation and is addressed in a separate Communication from the Commission to the European Parliament and the Council, adopted simultaneously with this proposal for a Regulation.

2. POLICY OPTIONS AND CONSULTATIONS WITH INTERESTED PARTIES

Taking into account the particular nature of the subject, the Commission evaluated a number of options to achieve the objective described above, although without carrying out a formal impact assessment. A meeting with experts from the Member States was held in Brussels on 25 January 2010 to discuss the status of bilateral agreements concluded between Member States and third countries relating to investment.

The extent to which investment agreements of Member States are incompatible with EU law can be the subject of discussions. The Commission is of the view that *any* legal uncertainty on the status and validity of these agreements, which could be detrimental for the activities of EU investments and investors abroad or foreign investments and investors in Member States, is to be avoided. Indeed, such uncertainty goes against the core rationale of investment protection, i.e. to provide legal certainty on the behaviour of host countries. In view of the situation that has arisen since the entry into force of the TFEU, swift and decisive action is therefore to be preferred over inaction or a delayed re-action.

Soft-law instruments, such as a declaration or statement by the Commission services or by the College on the status and validity of bilateral investment agreements, would not establish the legal certainty that is required to guarantee the agreements concerned. This is why a legal instrument is the preferred option.

This proposal maintains the status quo and offers a transitory solution by authorising the continued existence of bilateral agreements relating to investment concluded between Member States and third countries. The main impact of this proposal is to avoid a very negative result, i.e. the potential erosion of rights and benefits available to investors and investments under international investment agreements. In this respect, the impact of inaction is considered to be much higher than the impact of this action, which is neutral given that it preserves the status quo.

The authorisation provided in this proposal neither prejudges the contours of a future EU investment policy, nor allows the agreements covered to undermine the exercise of Union competence. In this respect, the authorisation granted pursuant to this proposal may be withdrawn, in accordance with the procedures specified therein. This procedure also takes account of the obligation of Member States to eliminate any incompatibilities with the TFEU that may exist in their existing agreements, as identified by the Court of Justice of the European Union.

3. LEGAL ELEMENTS OF THE PROPOSAL

The objective of this proposal is to authorise the continuation in force of international agreements relating to investment concluded between Member States and third countries and to establish conditions and a procedural framework for the negotiation and conclusion by Member States of such agreements.

Chapter I sets out the subject matter and scope of the Regulation. Article 1 provides that the Regulation covers agreements between Member States and third countries relating to investment.

Chapter II provides for authorisation for existing bilateral agreements that Member States have concluded with third countries to remain in force.

Article 2 requires Member States to notify to the Commission of all agreements that they wish to maintain under the terms and conditions of the Regulation. Agreements which have been concluded but not entered into force would equally fall under Article 2.

Article 3 authorises the maintenance in force of all existing agreements between Member States and third countries relating to investment that have been notified by Member States, starting upon the entry into force of this Regulation. This authorisation is without prejudice to the obligations of Member States under the law of the Union.[2]

Article 4 provides for the annual publication of all notified agreements in the Official Journal, to ensure that the exact scope of the legal coverage provided by the Regulation is known by all stakeholders.

Article 5 provides for the review of agreements which have been notified. The review will identify quantitative and qualitative aspects of the agreements in place, as well as the possible obstacles the agreements could present to the implementation of the common commercial policy. In particular, the Commission will assess whether the agreements or provisions thereof conflict with the law of the Union, undermine negotiations or agreements relating to investment between the Union and third countries, or undermine the Union's policies relating to investment, including in particular the common commercial policy. No later than five years after the entry into force of this Regulation, the Commission will present a report based on the review of the agreements and any possible recommendations to discontinue the application of the provisions of Chapter II or to modify these provisions.

Article 6 details the possible withdrawal of the authorisation granted under this Chapter. A withdrawal of authorisation may be necessary for one or more agreements with a given third country when these agreements conflict with the law of the Union. Secondly, authorisation could be withdrawn where an agreement overlaps, in part or in full, with an agreement of the Union in force with that third country and this specific overlap is not addressed in the latter agreement. For example, reference is made to a scenario where the Union concludes a free trade agreement with a third country with provisions concerning investment and six Member States have an agreement in place with similar provisions concerning investment. If the agreement concluded by the EU with the third country does not provide for the replacement of the six agreements of the Member States with the third country, then Article 6 would be

[2] For recent case law, see judgments *C-205/06 and C-249/06* of 3 March 2009 and judgement *C-118/07* of 19 November 2009, in which the Court of Justice of the European Union found that specific provisions of Bilateral Investment Treaties concluded by Austria, Sweden and Finland were incompatible with the EC Treaty and that the Member States concerned had not taken the appropriate steps to eliminate those incompatibilities. The same or similar clauses exist in other BITs concluded either before or after accession to the Union. In its judgements, the Court has called upon the Commission to engage in the role of facilitator on these matters.

applicable. The Commission has set out in a Communication adopted in parallel with this proposal its views on the international investment policy that it intends to pursue, including the countries with which it contemplates, in an initial phase, to negotiate agreements concerning investment. Finally, the authorisation of one or more agreements could be withdrawn where an agreement undermines the Union's policies relating to investment, including in particular the common commercial policy (e.g. where the existence of agreements undermines the willingness of a third country to negotiate with the Union), or where the Council has not taken a decision on the authorisation to open negotiations concerning investment within one year of the submission of a recommendation by the Commission pursuant to Article 218(3) of the Treaty. Article 6 provides for consultation between the Commission and Member State(s) concerned through which the concerns giving rise to a possible withdrawal of authorisation are to be addressed.

Chapter III provides for the modification of existing agreements and the conclusion of new agreements. The procedural framework proposed is inspired by the empowerment mechanism set by *Regulation No 662/2009 of 13 July 2009 establishing a procedure for the negotiation and conclusion of agreements between Member States and third countries on particular matters concerning the law applicable to contractual and non- contractual obligations* and *Regulation No 664/2009 of 7 July 2009 establishing a procedure for the negotiation and conclusion of agreements between Member States and third countries concerning jurisdiction, recognition and enforcement of judgments and decisions in matrimonial matters, matters of parental responsibility and matters relating to maintenance obligations, and the law applicable to matters relating to maintenance obligations.*[3]

Article 7 provides for the general framework under which Member States may conclude or modify bilateral agreements relating to investment.

Article 8 requires the notification to the Commission of a Member States' intent to modify an existing or to conclude a new bilateral agreement with a third country. Member States are requested to provide all relevant documentation relating to the re-negotiation or negotiation of an agreement, which can be made available to other Member States and the European Parliament subject to the requirements of confidentiality.

Article 9 details the substantive grounds on the basis of which the Commission would not authorise the opening of formal negotiations by Member States, which include notably the ground that a Member State initiative could undermine the objectives of EU negotiations or EU policy. The Commission may require a Member State to include in a negotiation appropriate clauses, for example with respect to (a) the termination of the agreement in the event of the conclusion of a subsequent agreement between the Union, or the Union and its Member States, on the one hand, with the same third country on the other hand (see for example the denunciation or replacement clauses set forth in Regulation 662/2009, Article 5), (b) transfer provisions or (c) most-favored nation treatment with a view to ensuring equal treatment of all EU investors in the relevant third country.

Article 10 requires that Member States keep the Commission informed of (re-)negotiations that have been authorised. In addition, the Commission may request to participate as an observer in the negotiations concerning investment between the Member State and the third country, to ensure full transparency and consistency with the Union's investment policy.

---

3 OJ L 200/52 of 31 July 2009, p. 25 and p. 46.

Article 11 deals with the end of the negotiating process and provides for the procedure and conditions under which Member States can be authorised to sign and conclude an agreement. Further to the notification of the agreement, which is to be submitted to the Commission before it is signed, the Commission assesses whether the agreement does not undermine imminent or ongoing EU investment negotiations or conflict with the obligations of EU law, including those under Part Three, Chapter 4 of Title V of the TFEU.

Article 12 provides for the review of authorisations that would be made pursuant to Chapter III of this Regulation. By reviewing the quantitative and qualitative aspects of the negotiations and agreements authorised, the Commission will assess the appropriateness of continuing the application of the provisions of Chapter III. The report and any possible recommendation to discontinue the application of the provisions of this Chapter or to modify these provisions will be presented no later than five years after the entry into force of the Regulation.

Chapter IV sets out certain requirements regarding the conduct of Member States with regard to agreements covered by this Regulation.

Article 13 requests Member States to provide information with respect to meetings which take place under the auspices of covered agreements. Furthermore, Member States are requested to inform the Commission of any request for dispute settlement lodged against themselves under the auspices of their agreements as soon as they become aware of such request and to co-operate with the Commission as regards the activation of dispute – which they would be allowed to lodge against another third country party to such agreement – or consultation mechanisms under an agreement.

Article 14 provides that Member States may indicate whether any of the information they provide in accordance with Articles 8 and 11 is to be considered confidential and whether it can be shared with other Member States.

Article 15 creates a new committee which shall assist the Commission in the management of the Regulation and stipulates the procedures under which this committee shall operate. This provision can be revised to bring it in line with the future regulation adopted pursuant to Article 291 TFEU on the control of the Commission's exercise of implementing powers.[4] In the event that the present proposal is adopted before the regulation on the control of the Commission's exercise of implementing powers enters into force the Commission envisages that it will be automatically updated to refer to the regulation adopted pursuant to Article 291 by operation of that proposal.[5]

Article 16 provides that this Regulation enters into force 20 days following the day of its publication, which means that Chapter II applies to agreements in force before that date.

4. BUDGETARY IMPLICATION

The proposal has no implication for the EU Budget.

---

4 See Proposal for a regulation of the European Parliament and of the Council laying down the rules and general principles concerning mechanism for control by Member States of the Commission's exercise of implementing powers, COM(2010) 83 final of 9 March 2010.

5 See Article 10 of the abovementioned Commission proposal.

2010/0197 (COD)

Proposal for a

REGULATION OF THE EUROPEAN PARLIAMENT AND OF THE COUNCIL

establishing transitional arrangements for bilateral investment agreements between Member States and third countries

THE EUROPEAN PARLIAMENT AND THE COUNCIL OF THE EUROPEAN UNION,

Having regard to the Treaty on the Functioning of the European Union, and in particular Article 207(2) thereof,

Having regard to the proposal from the European Commission,

After transmission of the draft legislative act to the national Parliaments,

Acting in accordance with the ordinary legislative procedure,

Whereas:

(1) Following the entry into force of the Treaty of Lisbon, foreign direct investment is included in the list of matters falling under the common commercial policy. In accordance with Article 3(1) (e) of the Treaty on the Functioning of the European Union (hereinafter "the Treaty"), the Union has exclusive competence with respect to the common commercial policy. Accordingly, only the Union may legislate and adopt legally binding acts within that area. The Member States are able to do so only if empowered by the Union, in accordance with Article 2(1) of the Treaty.

(2) In addition, Part Three, Chapter 4 of Title IV of the Treaty lays down common rules on the movement of capital between Member States and third countries, including in respect of capital movements involving investments. Those rules can be affected by international agreements relating to foreign investment concluded by Member States.

(3) At the time of the entry into force of the Treaty of Lisbon, Member States of the Union maintained a significant number of bilateral agreements with third countries relating to investment. The Treaty does not contain any explicit transitional provisions for such agreements which have now come under exclusive Union competence. Furthermore, some of those agreements may include provisions affecting the common rules on capital movements laid down in Part Three Chapter 4 of Title IV of the Treaty.

(4) Although bilateral agreements remain binding on the Member States under public international law and will be progressively replaced by future agreements of the Union relating to the same subject matter, the conditions for their continuing existence and their relationship with the Union's policies relating to investment, including in particular the common commercial policy, require appropriate management. That relationship will develop further as the Union exercises its competence.

(5) In the interest of EU investors and their investments in third countries, and of Member States hosting foreign investors and investments, bilateral agreements that specify and guarantee the conditions of investment should be maintained in force.

(6) This Regulation lays down the conditions under which Member States should be authorised to maintain in force or to permit to enter into force international agreements relating to investment.

(7) This Regulation lays down the conditions under which Member States are empowered to amend or conclude international agreements relating to investment.

(8) As the authorisation to maintain, amend or conclude agreements covered by this Regulation is granted in an area of exclusive Union competence, it must be regarded as an exceptional measure. The authorisation is without prejudice to the application of Article 258 of the Treaty with respect to failures of Member States to fulfil obligations under the Treaties other than those concerning incompatibilities arising from the allocation of competences between the Union and its Member States.

(9) Member States are required[6] to take the necessary measures to eliminate incompatibilities, where they exist, with the law of the Union contained in Bilateral Investment Treaties concluded between them and third countries.

(10) The Commission should be able to withdraw the authorisation if an agreement conflicts with the law of the Union other than the incompatibilities arising from the allocation of competence between the Union and its Member States. The authorisation may also be withdrawn if an agreement of the Union in force with a third country contains investment provisions similar to those of a Member State agreement. In order to ensure that agreements of Member States do not undermine the development and implementation of the Union's policies relating to investment, including in particular of autonomous measures of common commercial policy, authorisation may be withdrawn. Finally, should the Council not take a decision on the authorisation to open negotiations concerning investment within one year of the submission of a recommendation by the Commission pursuant to Article 218(3) of the Treaty, the possibility would exist to withdraw the authorisation.

(11) The authorisation to amend or conclude agreements provided for by this Regulation notably allows Member States to address any incompatibilities between their international agreements relating to investment and the law of the Union, other than incompatibilities arising from the allocation of competences between the Union and its Member States, which are addressed in this Regulation.

(12) No later than five years after the entry into force of this Regulation, the Commission should present to the European Parliament and the Council a report on the application of Chapters II and III of this Regulation. This report should, inter alia, review the need for the continued application of these chapters. Where the report recommends to discontinue the application of the provisions of these Chapters or where it would propose to modify these provisions, it should be accompanied by an appropriate legislative proposal. Unless replaced by an agreement of the Union concerning

---

6 For recent case law see judgments of the Court of Justice of the European Union in cases C-205/06, *Commission* v. *Austria*, C-249/06, *Commission* v. *Sweden*, and C-118/07, *Commission* v. *Finland*.

investment, or otherwise terminated, bilateral agreements concluded by Member States with third countries remain binding on the parties under public international law.

(13) Agreements authorised under this Regulation or authorisations to open negotiations to amend an existing or to conclude a new bilateral agreement with a third country should not in any case be allowed to constitute an obstacle to the implementation of the Union's policies relating to investment, in particular common commercial policy.

(14) The European Parliament, the Council and the Commission should ensure that any information identified as confidential is treated in accordance with Regulation (EC) No 1049/2001 of the European Parliament and of the Council of 30 May 2001 regarding public access to European Parliament, Council and Commission documents.[7]

(15) Agreements between Member States relating to investment should not be covered by this Regulation.

(16) It is necessary to provide certain arrangements to ensure that agreements maintained pursuant to this Regulation remain operational, including as regards dispute settlement, while at the same time respecting the Union's exclusive competence.

(17) The measures necessary for the implementation of this Regulation should be adopted in accordance with Council Decision 1999/468/EC of 28 June 1999 laying down the procedures for the exercise of implementing powers conferred on the Commission[8],

HAVE ADOPTED THIS REGULATION:

CHAPTER I

Scope

Article 1

Subject matter and scope

This Regulation establishes the terms, conditions and the procedure under which Member States are authorised to maintain in force, amend or conclude bilateral agreements with third countries relating to investment.

CHAPTER II

Authorisation to maintain agreements in force

Article 2

Notification to the Commission

Within thirty days from the entry into force of this Regulation, the Member States shall notify the Commission of all bilateral agreements with third countries relating to investment

---

7 OJ L 145, 31.5.2001, p. 43.
8 OJ L 184, 17.7.1999, p. 23.

concluded before the entry into force of this Regulation that they either wish to maintain in force or permit to enter into force under this Chapter. The notification shall include a copy of those bilateral agreements.

Article 3

Authorisation to maintain agreements in force

Notwithstanding the Union's competences relating to investment and without prejudice to other obligations of Member States under the law of the Union, Member States are authorised in accordance with Article 2(1) of the Treaty to maintain in force bilateral agreements relating to investment that have been notified in accordance with Article 2 of this Regulation.

Article 4

Publication

1. Every twelve months the Commission shall publish in the *Official Journal of the European Union* a list of the agreements notified pursuant to Article 2 or Article 11(7).

2. The first publication of the list of agreements referred to in paragraph 1 shall take place no later than three months after the deadline for notifications pursuant to Article 2.

Article 5

Review

1. The Commission shall review the agreements notified pursuant to Article 2, including by assessing, in particular, whether the agreements:

   (a) conflict with the law of the Union other than the incompatibilities arising from the allocation of competences between the Union and its Member States, or

   (b) overlap, in part or in full, with an agreement of the Union in force with that third country and this specific overlap is not addressed in the latter agreement, or

   (c) constitute an obstacle to the development and the implementation of the Union's policies relating to investment, including in particular the common commercial policy.

2. Consultation may take place between the Commission and the notifying Member State, either at the request of the Member State or on the initiative of the Commission, to facilitate the review referred to in paragraph 1.

3. No later than five years after the entry into force of this Regulation, the Commission shall present to the European Parliament and the Council a report on the application of this Chapter which shall review the need for the continued application of this chapter, based on the review referred to in paragraph 1.

4. Where the report referred to in paragraph 3 recommends to discontinue the application of the provisions of this Chapter or to modify these provisions, it shall be accompanied by an appropriate legislative proposal.

Article 6

Withdrawal of authorisation

1. The authorisation provided for in Article 3 may be withdrawn where:

   (a) an agreement conflicts with the law of the Union other than the incompatibilities arising from the allocation of competence between the Union and its Member States, or

   (b) an agreement overlaps, in part or in full, with an agreement of the Union in force with that third country and this specific overlap is not addressed in the latter agreement, or

(c) an agreement constitutes an obstacle to the development and the implementation of the Union's policies relating to investment, including in particular the common commercial policy, or

   (d) the Council has not taken a decision on the authorisation to open negotiations on an agreement which overlaps, in part or in full, with an agreement notified under Article 2, within one year of the submission of a recommendation by the Commission pursuant to Article 218(3) of the Treaty.

2. When the Commission considers that there are grounds to withdraw the authorisation provided for in Article 3, it shall deliver a reasoned opinion to the Member State concerned on the necessary steps to be taken to comply with the requirements referred to in paragraph 1. Consultations shall take place between the Commission and the Member State concerned.

3. Where the consultations referred to in paragraph 2 fail to resolve the matter, the Commission shall withdraw the authorisation for the agreement concerned. The Commission shall take a decision on the withdrawal of the authorisation in accordance with the procedure referred to in Article 15(2). It shall include a requirement that the Member State takes appropriate action, and where necessary terminate the relevant agreement.

4. Where an authorisation is withdrawn, the Commission shall remove the agreement from the list referred to in Article 4.

CHAPTER III

Authorisation to amend or conclude agreements

Article 7

Authorisation to amend or conclude agreements

Subject to the conditions laid down in Articles 8 to12, a Member State shall be authorised to enter into negotiations to amend an existing or to conclude a new agreement relating to investment with a third country.

Article 8

Notification to the Commission

1. Where a Member State intends to enter into negotiations in order to amend an existing or to conclude a new agreement with a third country relating to investment, it shall notify the Commission of its intentions in writing.

2. The notification shall include relevant documentation and an indication of the provisions to be addressed in the negotiations, the objectives of the negotiations and any other relevant information. In the case of amendments to an existing agreement, the notification shall indicate the provisions that are to be renegotiated.

3. The Commission shall make the notification and, on request, the accompanying documentation, available to other Member States subject to the requirements of confidentiality laid down in Article 14.

4. The notification referred to in paragraph 1 shall be transmitted at least five calendar months before formal negotiations are to commence with the third country concerned.

5. Where the information transmitted by the Member State is not sufficient for the purposes of authorising the opening of formal negotiations in accordance with Article 9, the Commission may request additional information.

Article 9

Authorisation to open formal negotiations

1. The Commission shall authorise the opening of formal negotiations unless it concludes that the opening of negotiations would:

   (a) be in conflict with the law of the Union other than the incompatibilities arising from the allocation of competence between the Union and its Member States, or

   (b) undermine the objectives of negotiations underway or imminent between the Union and the third country concerned, or

   (c) constitute an obstacle to the development and the implementation of the Union's policies relating to investment, including in particular the common commercial policy.

2. As part of the authorisation referred to in paragraph 1, the Commission may require the Member State to include in such negotiation any appropriate clauses.

3. Decisions on the authorisation referred to in paragraph 1 shall be taken in accordance with the procedure referred to in Article 15(2). The Commission shall take its

decision within 90 days of receipt of the notification referred to in Article 8. Where additional information is needed to take a decision, the 90 days shall run from the date of receipt of the additional information.

Article 10

Participation of the Commission in negotiations

The Commission shall be kept informed of the progress and results throughout the different stages of negotiations and may request to participate in the negotiations between the Member State and the third country concerning investment.

Article 11

Authorisation to sign and conclude an agreement

1. Before signing an agreement, the Member State concerned shall notify the Commission of the outcome of negotiations and shall transmit the text of the agreement to the Commission.

2. The notification duty provided for in paragraph 1 shall include agreements which were negotiated prior to the entry into force of this Regulation but not concluded and therefore not subject to the notification duty provided for in Article 2.

3. Upon notification the Commission shall make an assessment as to whether the negotiated agreement does not:

   (a) conflict with the law of the Union other than the incompatibilities arising from the allocation of competences between the Union and its Member States, or

   (b) undermine the objectives of negotiations underway or imminent between the Union and the third country concerned, or

   (c) constitute an obstacle to the development and the implementation of the Union's policies relating to investment, including in particular the common commercial policy, or

   (d) conflict with the requirement of Article 9(2), where applicable.

4. Where the Commission finds that the negotiations have resulted in an agreement which does not fulfil the requirements referred to in paragraphs 3, the Member State shall not be authorised to sign and conclude the agreement.

5. Where the Commission finds that the negotiations have resulted in an agreement which fulfils the requirements referred to in paragraphs 3, the Member State shall be authorised to sign and conclude the agreement.

6. Decisions pursuant to paragraphs 4 and 5 shall be taken in accordance with the procedure referred to in Article 15(2). The Commission shall take the decision within 90 days of receipt of the notifications referred to in paragraphs 1 and 2. Where additional information is needed to take the decision, the 90 days shall run from the date of receipt of the additional information.

7. Where an authorisation has been granted in accordance with paragraph 5, the Member State concerned shall notify the Commission of the conclusion and entry into force of the agreement.

Article 12

Review

1. No later than five years after the entry into force of this Regulation, the Commission shall present to the European Parliament and the Council a report on the application of this Chapter which shall review the need for a continued application of the Chapter.

2. The report referred to in paragraph 1 shall include an overview of authorisations requested and granted under this Chapter.

3. Where the report referred to in paragraph 1 recommends to discontinue the application of this Chapter or to modify the provisions of this Chapter, it shall be accompanied by an appropriate legislative proposal.

CHAPTER IV

Final provisions

Article 13

Conduct of Member States with regard to agreements with a third country

1. For all agreements falling within the scope of this Regulation, the Member State concerned shall inform the Commission without undue delay of all meetings which take place under the provisions of the agreement. The Commission shall be provided with the agenda and all relevant information permitting an understanding of the topics to be discussed. The Commission may request further information from the Member State concerned. Where an issue to be discussed might affect the implementation of the Union's policies relating to investment, including in particular the common commercial policy, the Commission can require the Member State concerned to take a particular position.

2. For all agreements falling within the scope of this Regulation, the Member State concerned shall inform the Commission without undue delay of any representations made to it that a particular measure is inconsistent with the agreement. The Member State shall also immediately inform the Commission of any request for dispute settlement lodged under the auspices of the agreement as soon as the Member State becomes aware of the request. The Member State and the Commission shall fully cooperate and take all necessary measures to ensure an effective defence which may include, where appropriate, that the Commission participates in the procedure.

3. For all agreements falling within the scope of this Regulation, the Member State concerned shall seek the agreement of the Commission before activating any relevant mechanisms for dispute settlement included in the agreement and shall, where requested by the Commission, activate such mechanisms. Such mechanisms shall include consultations with the other party to the agreement and dispute settlement

where provided for in the agreement. The Member State and the Commission shall fully cooperate in the conduct of procedures within the relevant mechanisms, which may include, where appropriate, that the Commission participates in the relevant procedures.

Article 14

Confidentiality

In notifying the Commission of negotiations and their outcome in accordance with Articles 8 and 11, Member States may indicate whether any of the information provided is to be considered confidential and whether it can be shared with other Member States.

Article 15

Committee

1. The Commission shall be assisted by the Advisory Committee for the Management of Transitional Arrangements on International Investment Agreements.

2. Where reference is made to this paragraph, Articles 3 and 7 of Decision 1999/468/EC shall apply.

Article 16

Entry into force

This Regulation shall enter into force on the twentieth day following that of its publication in the *Official Journal of the European Union*.

This Regulation shall be binding in its entirety and directly applicable in all Member States.

Done at Brussels, [...]

For the European Parliament
The President

For the Council
The President